IRISH LAW TEXTS

BUSINESS LAW

by

LIAM O'MALLEY, LL.B., M.A., M.B.A.

Lecturer in Business Law
University College, Galway

LONDON
SWEET & MAXWELL
1982

Published in 1982 by
Sweet & Maxwell Ltd. of
11 New Fetter Lane, London
Photoset by Promenade Graphics Ltd., Cheltenham
Printed in Scotland

British Library Cataloguing in Publication Data

O'Malley, Liam
  Business law.—(Irish law texts)
  1. Corporation law—Ireland.
  I. Title II. Series
  344.1706'65   KDK 502

  ISBN 0-421-28500-1

Introduction

Both Irish jurisdictions have long suffered from the problems associated with the lack of a developed local legal literature. This lack of development has been particularly acute in the Republic of Ireland, where it is only in the last few years that any works at all have appeared in the main fields of law and where many gaps still remain. The combination of the small market for law books in the Republic and a considerable lag between the achievement of political independence and the emergence of a corpus of indigenous law deterred the production of legal literature. For many years law students and the legal profession made do with the older editions of English textbooks or else did without. In Northern Ireland, the problems were never so acute since the local law generally kept pace with changes in Britain. Nevertheless, there are also significant differences between the available works on English law and procedure and the law taught and practised in that jurisdiction.

Over the last two decades a variety of factors has brought about change. In the first place there is a much greater output of local law both in legislation and through court decisions. The number of students in the universities and other third level colleges who are studying law has increased enormously. There has also been a proportionate increase in the numbers engaged in the full-time teaching of law with correspondingly a greater number of academic lawyers available to undertake research and writing. The size of the legal profession has doubled in both jurisdictions in the last decade.

One happy result of the new circumstances has been the coincidence of acute concern about the dearth of works devoted to Irish law and sufficient local demands to encourage authors to write and publishers to publish. It was in these circumstances that *Irish Law Texts* was conceived. Modelled on Sweet & Maxwell's *Concise College Texts*, it is the first series devoted exclusively to Irish law. The series aims to produce reasonably priced short works on the main fields of Irish law to meet the needs of the broadest student population. The first two titles, *Contract* and *Business Law*, have been written therefore not only with university students in mind, but also students of law, business and related subjects in the regional technical colleges, the National Institutes of Higher Education, and the professional schools. Since these two titles are the first books to be written on these areas of Irish law, the practising lawyer and other professions will also find them of considerable value.

   Books in the series will be concerned primarily with the law of the
Republic of Ireland, which is the larger Irish jurisdiction and the
one which has seen the greatest changes in legal principles and
statute law from Britain. However, wherever possible, reference will
be made to the law of Northern Ireland, particularly the decisions of
the courts. *Irish Law Texts* therefore hopes to make a contribution to
the needs of students and the professions in both parts of the island.
   Other titles in the series are planned, including a book on Irish
Company Law.

Kevin Boyle
University College Galway

Preface

Law has always played an important role in resolving disputes over business transactions. In recent years the law affecting business has expanded enormously to include, among other things, consumer protection and the regulation of employment and competition. It has, as a result, become increasingly difficult to work in business without some knowledge of the underlying law which regulates business enterprise.

This book attempts to bring together and explain in a factual way the principal laws governing the many aspects of business activity. It is hoped that it will be useful to businessmen, legal practitioners and to students who intend to make a career in the business world.

It is increasingly recognised that students of commerce or business require a sufficient legal knowledge and analytical skill to enable them to cope with, and to make decisions regarding, the routine legal problems which they will encounter in their future employment. While this book is not intended to transform business students into lawyers, it is hoped that it will provide them with as much law as they need to know for the purposes of their future work. A study of its contents should help the reader feel comfortable rather than threatened by the legal dimensions of business, should help him to avoid legal pitfalls and to know when expert legal advice is needed.

In a concise text of this nature it was necessary to be selective in the topics covered and in the depth of coverage. I have tried to cover what I believe are the most relevant business law issues. As regards what has been included, every effort has been made to state the law as at January 1, 1982.

I have received help and advice from a number of people in writing this book. I wish to thank in particular my family for their help and encouragement; Professor K. Boyle, without whose assistance and enthusiasm the book would not have been written; and the library staff at the University College Galway, who helped me in my research. I acknowledge with gratitude the help given to me by Professor J. M. G. Sweeney, Mr. Maurice Curran, and Mr. Jim Nestor for their valuable suggestions on parts of the text.

January 1982   Liam O'Malley

Contents

Table of Cases

Table of Statutes

Irish Statutes

Other Jurisdictions

United Kingdom

Table of References to the Irish Constitution

Table of Abbreviations

Irish Reports and Journals

Alc. & Nap.	Alcock and Napier, King's Bench reports, 1831–33
Alc. Reg. Cas.	Alcock, Registry Cases, 1832–41
Arm. Mac. & Og.	Armstrong, Macartney and Ogle, **Nisi Prius** Reports, 1840–42
Ba. & B.	Ball and Beatty, Chancery Reports, 1802–9
Batty	Batty, King's Bench Reports, 1825–26
Beat.	Beaty, Chancery Reports, 1813–30
Con. & L.	Connor and Lawson, Chancery Reports, 1841–43
Cr. & Dix.	Crawford and Dix, Cases on the Circuits, 1839–46
Cr. & Dix, Abr. Cas.	Crawford and Dix, bridged Notes on Cases, 1837–46
Dru. *emp*. Nap.	Drury, Select Cases during the time of Lord Napier, 1858–59
Dru. *temp* Sug.	Drury, Report of Cases during the time of Chancellor Sugden, 1843–44
Dr. & Wal.	Drury and Walsh, Chancery Reports during the time of Lord Plunket, 1837–40
Dr. & War.	Drury and Warren, Chancery Reports during the time of Lord Sugden, 1841–43
D.U.L.J.	Dublin University Law Journal 1966– (current)
Fl. & K.	Flanagan and Kelly, Chancery (Rolls) eports, 1840–42
Hayes	Hayes, Exchequer Reports, 1830–32
Ir.Ch.R.	Irish Chancery Reports, 1850–66
Ir.Cir.Rep.	Irish Circuit reports (Cases on the Six Circuits), 1841–43
I.C.L.R.	Irish Common Law Reports, 1849¾466
Ir.Eq.R.	Irish Equity Reports, 1838–51
Ir.Jur.	Irish Jurist 1935–65
Ir.Jur.(N.S.)	Irish Jurist (N.S.) 1966– (current)
Ir.Jur.(OS.)	Irish Jurist Reports (Old Series), 1849–55
Ir.Jur.(N.S.)	Irish Jurist Reports (New Series), 1855–66
Ir.Jur.Rep.	Irish Jurist Reports, 1935–65
Ir.L.R.	Irish Law Reports, Common Law, 1838–50
I.L.R.M.	Irish Law Reports Monthly 1981– (current)
I.L.T.R.	Irish Law Times Reports, 1867–(1980). (*Note*: notes or digests only of cases in the Irish law Times and Solicitors Journal are signified by the reference "I.L.T. or "I.L.T.S.J.".).
I.R.	Irish Reports, 1894–(current)
I.R.C.L.	Irish Reports, Common Law, 1867–77
I.R.Eq.	Irish reports, Equity, 1866–77
Ir. Term Rep.	Irish term Reports (Ridgeway, lapp and Schoales), 1793–95
Jebb & B.	Jebb and Bourke, Queen's Bench reports, 1842–42
Jebb & Sym.	Jebb and Symes, Queen's Bench Reports, 1838–41
Jo. & Lat.	Jones and Latouche, Chancery Reports, 1844–46
Jon.	Jones, Exchequer Reports, 1834–38
L.R.(Ir.)	Law Reports, (Ireland), 1878–93

Moll.	Molley, Chancery Reports, 1827–31
N.I.J.R.	New Irish Jurist Reports, 1900–5
N.I.	Northern Ireland Law Reports, 1925–(current)
N.I.L.Q. (N.S.)	Northern Ireland Legal Quarterly (New Series) Vol. 1960– (current)
Ridgw.P.C.	Ridgeway, Parliamentary Reports, 1784–96
Sch. & Lef.	Schoales and Lefroy, Chancery Reports, 1802–6
Sm. & Bat.	Smith and Batty, King's Bench Reports, 1824–25
Vern & Scriv.	Vernon and Scriven, Irish Reports, 1786–88

Court References

C.A.N.I.	Court of Appeal Northern Ireland
C.C.	Circuit Court
Ch.D.N.I.	Chancery Division Northern Ireland
Co. Ct.	County Court
E.A.T.(Eng.)	Employment Appeals Tribunal, England
E.A.T.(Irl.)	Employment Appeals Tribunal, Ireland
E.C.A.	English Court of Appeal
E.Ch.D.	English Chancery Division
E.C.P.	English Common Places
E.Ex.	English Exchequer
E.Ex.Ch.	English Exchequer Chambers
E.K.B.	English King's Bench
E.Q.B.	English Queen's Bench
E. Rolls C.	English Rolls Court
H.C.	High Court
H.L.	House of Lords
Ir.C.A.	Irish Court of Appeal
Ir.Ch.D.	Irish Chancery Division
Ir.C. of Ch.	Irish Court of Chancery
Ir.C.P.	Irish Common Pleas
Ir.Ex.	Irish Court of Exchequer
Ir.Ex.Ch.	Irish Exchequer Chamber
Ir.K.B.	Irish King's Bench
Ir.Q.B.	Irish Queen's Bench
Ir. Rolls C.	Irish Rolls Court
K.B.N.I.	King's Bench Northern Ireland
N.P.	Nisi Privs
P.C.	Privy Council
S.C.	Supreme Court

1 Introduction to Irish Law

WHAT IS LAW?

The word "law" can be defined in many ways. In an office, for example, one employee might say to another who is about to embezzle funds or steal company property "you must not do that, it is against the law, you will be gaoled." He is implying that there are rules of law which forbid this behaviour and if a person disobeys those rules he will be punished. Used in this sense "law" means a body of rules, principles and standards, applied by the courts. If such rules are not obeyed by persons subject to them fines, imprisonment or some other undesirable legal consequence will result.

In a dispute over a contract one businessman may threaten another in words such as "I intend to take you to law over this." When used in this way "law" refers to the totality of legal machinery by which a grievance may be remedied. It is a part of what is called "legal process," *i.e.* the process by which laws are made and adjudicated by judges.

In yet another context we talk of "law and order" or "rule of law" and by such phrases we are considering law as a system maintaining order in society.

The subject-matter of this book is primarily concerned with law as the body of principles, standards and rules which Irish courts apply in reaching decisions on disputes brought before them. More specifically it will examine such law as it relates to business.

THE CLASSIFICATION OF LAW

The law is strictly speaking indivisible but for convenience it is sub-divided into a number of coherent topics. It is traditional to distinguish substantive law from its adjectival or administrative rules. The substantive law deals with actual rights and obligations enforced by the courts. Adjectival law determines the procedures and forms of action which may be taken by litigants involved in legal action. It comprises the law governing evidence, practice and procedure, and the court system.

Substantive law is divided into public and private law. Public law consists of those legal issues in which one of the parties involved is usually the state or a state body. Such issues may involve criminal law, revenue law, administrative law, social welfare law, or the law of the constitution.

Private law normally concerns rights and obligations of a private nature between individuals. It encompasses the law of property, inheritance, torts, contract, trusts, labour law and family law.

COMMON LAW

Irish law is a common law system derived from, and similar to, English law. The English common law is to be found today as the basis of the legal systems of Ireland, the United States, Australia, New Zealand, Canada, India, and parts of Africa.

Until the foundation of the Irish Free State in 1922, Irish common law remained substantially the same as the law in England. Since 1922 Irish law has gradually taken on a character of its own, partly due to enactment of different statutes and partly to the influence of a written Irish Constitution (Bunreacht an hEireann) which came into force on December 29, 1937. However, the legal systems of Ireland and England remain similar, having, in most areas of the law, a common base.

FROM WHERE DOES OUR LAW COME?

1. Legislation or Statute Law

Previous legislatures

The body of law which governs our lives today has been created mainly by legislators and by the judiciary.

Statutes are laws made by an institution, called a legislature, which is recognised as having the right to make law for the community. Some of our oldest statutes were simply ordinances made by English Kings before parliaments existed, and which were applied to Ireland. Statutes were also made for this country by the Parliament of Ireland which disappeared following the Act of Union, 1800, joining Ireland and Great Britain in the United Kingdom of Great Britain and Ireland. Between 1800 and 1922 statutes applying to Ireland were made by the United Kingdom Parliament at Westminster, which had Irish members to represent the Irish people. Legislative independence was restored to the country upon establishment of the Irish Free State in 1922, and statutes have been made by a solely Irish legislature since that time. Legislation prior to 1922 continues in force, by virtue of article 50 of the Constitution, to the extent that it is not inconsistent with the Constitution's provisions.

The Oireachtas or National Parliament

Our current legislative body is the Oireachtas which is empowered to legislate for the country by our Constitution which states under article 15.2.1:

> "The sole and exclusive power of making laws for the State is hereby vested in the Oireachtas: no other legislative authority has power to make laws for the State."

Before a statute becomes law it is known as a Bill and it must go through five stages in the Oireachtas, be agreed to by the Dail and Senate, and be signed by the President. It is then promulgated by the President who publishes a notice in Iris Oifigiuil (the Official Gazette) stating that the Bill has become law. A statute, like all law, is subject to the superior law of the Constitution. Any statute or part of a statute which is contrary to the Constitution may be declared void by the courts.

2. Subordinate Legislation

A relatively modern form of law

Subordinate legislation has developed to help legislators make laws for our modern, complex, industrialised state. It would be impossible for the Oireachtas on its own to consider all the regulations required to carry out its extensive programmes. For this reason it has delegated power to Government Ministers, local authorities and other bodies to "legislate" in specified areas. The result is subordinate or "delegated" legislation consisting of statutory instruments, orders, regulations and bye-laws which have the same force of law as statutes passed by the Oireachtas.

The validity of subordinate legislation

Persons making subordinate legislation must have authority to do so. Thus persons who make or apply subordinate legislation are required by law to act *intra vires, i.e.* within the confines of powers delegated under statute. If they act outside those powers their acts are illegal and void. Bodies or persons acting in an *ultra vires* manner, *i.e.* outside the scope of their authority, can be checked by the courts.

A close watch is also kept on subordinate legislation by the Seanad Select Committee on Statutory Instruments.

3. The Irish Constitution 1937

The legal rules which "govern the government"
The Constitution is the basis of our constitutional law. It deals with such topics as the nation and national territory, the state, the office and function of the President, the nature, powers and functions of the Oireachtas, the Executive Government and the courts. It also concerns itself with the offices of the Attorney-General, the Comptroller and Auditor General, and the Council of State. A most important section of the Constitution guarantees certain fundamental rights to every citizen. These include Personal Rights (Article 40), rights in relation to the Family (Article 41), Education (Article 42), Private Property (Article 43) and Religion (Article 44).

The Constitution as a source of law
The Constitution is an important source of law in at least two ways. It provides a body of rules which must be followed by our governmental institutions because it is from the Constitution that they receive their legitimacy and authority to act. The Government is subject to the law in the same way that citizens are subject to it. The law of the constitution, therefore, regulates the structure and function of the principal organs of Government and regulates the relationship of these organs to each other and to the citizen. The principal organs of Government in this context are the legislature, *i.e.* the Oireachtas, the Executive Government consisting of the Taoiseach and his ministers, and the judiciary.

The Constitution is also a source of law precisely because it is fundamental law. The law of the constitution has a higher status than other law in that it can only be changed by referendum and in that any legislation which is held to be repugnant to the Constitution is invalid. Even before a Bill becomes law the President has power, after consulting the Council of State, to refer it to the Supreme Court for a decision as to its constitutionality. Where a party has an actionable interest he may himself initiate a constitutional action in the High Court and such actions, which have become commonplace in recent years, have led to significant changes in important areas of our law.

In *Murphy v. The Attorney-General* (S.C. 1980) provisions in the Income Tax Act 1967 were held to discriminate against married working couples in violation of article 40.1 and so were unconstitu-

tional. The government was forced to modify its tax laws by mean
of the Finance Act 1980. There have been numerous significant
decisions in other areas of the law, *e.g.* concerning the right of
freedom of association. In *The Educational Company of Ireland* v.
Fitzpatrick (No. 2) (1961) the Supreme Court held that picketing for
the purpose of forcing persons to join a union against their wishes
was inconsistent with the right to freedom of association guaranteed
in article 40.6.1 of the Constitution. The law, therefore, continues to
change as a result of judicial interpretation of the Constitution.

4. European Community Law

Although the Constitution represents our fundamental law it has
not been supreme in all respects since Ireland joined the European
Economic Community in January 1973. EEC membership requires
that Community law should become part of the internal law of the
Member States and be applied in the national courts. This
stipulation required a modification of the Constitution, carried out
by the third amendment to the Constitution in 1972, and by special
statutes, namely, the European Communities Act 1972 and the
European Communities (Amendment) Act 1973. The primary law
of the Community, which is contained in the principal treaties, takes
precedence over domestic law. The secondary law of the Community, made by the Council of Ministers or the Commission, consists of
regulations which apply to Ireland directly and automatically, and
of directives which are made obligatory by special Irish statutes,
statutory instruments, or other political action. The result is that we
now have an additional source of written or enacted law arising from
EEC membership. This law must be applied by Irish courts. EEC
law was relevant, *e.g.*, in a claim made by the Pigs and Bacon
Commission for levies due on pig carcasses. The issue arose as to
whether the levies were contrary to Community law and Mr. Justice
Costello in the High Court had to refer the matter to the European
Court. The court ruled that part of the Board's activities were
unlawful (*Pigs and Bacon Commission* v. *McCarren and Company Ltd.*,
H.C. 1980).

5. Judge-Made Law

Our laws come, therefore, from a number of written or enacted
sources comprising statutes, subordinate legislation, the Constitution, and European Community law, but our law has been, and is,
created in other ways too. We have seen how statute law relating to
income tax and freedom of association was changed in the *Murphy*

and *Educational Company* cases above. The court, in these cases, changed the law, or, to put it more strongly, the decisions of the judges made new law.

Judge-made law is called the "common law" in order to distinguish it from written or enacted law. The common law consists of law made or applied in two sets of courts which developed historically, the common law courts (originally the King's Bench, Common Pleas, and Exchequer), and the law made or applied in the Court of Chancery, which law is often referred to separately as "equity" and which developed to fill in the gaps and deficiencies of the common law.

Common law and equity

In earlier times written or enacted law was the exception and judges had to create rules of law with nothing to guide them except custom, previous decisions, and good sense. As the law became more sophisticated, decisions of judges were recorded and reports were made of law cases. It became possible to follow previous decisions ensuring a measure of certainty and progressive development in judge-made law. By the nineteenth century it had become the rule for judges in the common law courts and the Court of Chancery to respect and follow previous decisions or precedents. By this time it was evident that two sets of courts applying two systems of law was most unsatisfactory. It was decided to merge the administration of equity and the common law. Reforms were introduced in England and Ireland by means of the Supreme Court of Judicature Act, 1873 and 1875, and the Supreme Court of Judicature (Ireland) Act 1877. These Acts established a logical court structure, simplified procedures and fused the administration of common law and equity.

The doctrine of precedent. The reforms introduced by the Judicature Acts led to the modern doctrine of binding precedent. A precedent or previous decision may be persuasive or binding. A persuasive precedent is one which does not have to be followed by a court but which may influence its decision because it is worthy of the court's respect. A binding precedent is a decision which the court must follow. Not all of the decision is binding on a later court, but only its authoritative element which is called the *ratio decidendi* (reason for the decision). The *ratio decidendi* is not a precise statement of law like a statute but is a rule, concept, or principle of law which can be formulated in a number of ways and which must be extracted from the case or cases in question by the court in relation to the matter at issue. The court may decide that the *ratio decidendi* of the previous cases is not relevant to the current action because of factual differences which justify it in not following the earlier case or cases although it still accepts the earlier case as good law in its proper sphere. This is called distinguishing the case. Thus, while the doctrine of binding precedent gives "certainty" and uniformity to judicial decisions, it still allows the judge sufficient discretion to adapt the law to changing needs.

A court is not, of course, bound by the previous decisions of all other courts. Lower courts are bound by higher ones and decisions of courts of equal seniority act as persuasive authority only. Within the limits discussed above the present day district court is bound by the decisions of the circuit court, the circuit court by the decisions of the High Court, and the High Court is bound by the Supreme Court.

The stare decisis rule. Another aspect of binding precedent is the rule that the highest court of authority, the Irish Supreme Court, is bound by its own previous decisions. This is called the rule of *stare decisis* (let the decision stand), and it was eventually modified in the 1960s. In *Attorney-General* v. *Ryan's Car Hire Ltd.* (S.C. 1964) Kingsmill Moore J. accepted the need to follow precedents in order to avoid uncertainty in the law but was of opinion that "The rigid rule of *stare decisis* must in a court of ultimate resort give place to a more elastic formula. Where such a Court is clearly of opinion that an earlier decision was erroneous it should be at liberty to refuse to follow it, at all events in exceptional cases."

HOW DOES THE LAW WORK?

The Legal Profession and the Courts

We have briefly examined what law is and how it is created and we must now consider how it is enforced. The law is made effective via the courts and the legal profession, supported by the state. The purpose of the courts is to conduct a fair trial or investigation into the guilt or innocence of the accused in a criminal case, or an investigation into the liability or non-liability of the defendant in a civil action, and to pass judgment in accordance with their findings. This specialised work is conducted almost exclusively by the legal profession. The courts do not make a full investigation into the facts in dispute and then draw appropriate conclusions. This would be too wasteful and time-consuming. They depend on the parties in dispute to do most of the work for them. In a criminal action the prosecution (usually the State) prepares its case precisely against the accused and the accused attempts to counter it. In civil litigation the plaintiff makes a precise claim or claims against the defendant and the latter defends the action. It is an adversary procedure in which the courts are only concerned to investigate and to rule on the relevant issues brought to them for settlement and decision. Both sides in the dispute will usually employ lawyers to give them specialised help to make the best of their case but the judge or judges, who must resolve the dispute, must do so fairly and objectively in accordance with law.

The legal profession

If a person has a legal problem or if he needs legal advice he normally consults a solicitor. When a person is conducting important or complex litigation, however, he will be represented in court by a barrister who is also referred to as counsel.

The solicitor's profession is regulated by the Incorporated Law Society of Ireland which controls entry to the profession and exercises disciplinary power over its members. The solicitor does routine legal work for the public, gives legal advice, and prepares cases for trial. He is the approachable lawyer who occupies an office in the city or town and acts as a medium to interpret the mysteries of the law to the layman. It is through him that the public normally gains access to the courts. In addition the solicitor provides legal services of a routine business nature in relation to the forming of companies, drafting of wills and contracts, and the conveyancing of property. The solicitor often represents his clients in the lower courts but he will not do so where the special talents of the barrister are required.

Barristers are specialists in the art of advocacy, *i.e.* in the logical and effective presentation of a case in court. Because legal dispute is resolved by an adversary procedure, the barrister can be essential to success in some legal actions, and he is extremely useful to the lay client in any action. The barrister's profession is regulated by the Honourable Society of the King's Inns. Experienced and successful members of the profession may be called to the Inner Bar and if so they are called Senior Counsel. Barristers work on their own account and tend to specialise in a particular area of law. A lay client cannot consult a barrister directly but must go through a solicitor. When the solicitor and his client are in doubt about the law they may seek counsel's opinion on the problem. If an important court action is contemplated the solicitor will gather the evidence but he will instruct a barrister to draft the pleadings, to advise on the evidence, and to present the case in court. The solicitor prepares a brief for the barrister which contains all the information and documents required to enable the barrister to present the case.

The Judges. The judges of all courts are chosen by the government in power when a vacancy occurs and are formally appointed by the President. Appointments to the district court are open to solicitors and barristers who have 10 years' experience. Judicial positions in the other courts are open to barristers with 10 years' experience, or 12 years' experience in the case of the High or Supreme Courts. The function of the judge is to hear and determine the issues and to do justice according to law based on his findings. It is not the function of the judge to present the case for either party or to investigate or examine the total circumstances of the dispute. He is a neutral and independent decision-maker who hears the facts and arguments presented by both sides, judges their merits, and applies the law accordingly.

The law courts

The present Irish courts structure was first established by the Courts of Justice Act 1924. It now derives its authority from article 34 of the Constitution, which declares that "Justice shall be administered in courts established by law by judges appointed in the manner provided by this Constitution, and, save in such special and limited cases as may be prescribed by law, shall be administered in public."

The court structure is organised on a hierarchical basis with the district courts, which have the narrowest jurisdiction, at the bottom of the hierarchy and the Supreme Court, which is the final Court of Appeal, at the top. In between are the circuit and High Courts and the Court of Criminal Appeal. The cases heard by these courts divide into two types, civil cases and criminal cases. The jurisdiction of the courts depends on a number of factors – where the defendant resides, the type of legal problem involved, the gravity of an offence, the amount of the claim or the nature of the remedy sought. As a rule the more serious the offence or the greater the claim the higher up in the hierarchy the court will be which hears the case.

The district court. The district court is a unified court which consists of a president and up to 39 justices. The country is divided into over 200 district court areas for the exercise of summary criminal jurisdiction and about the same number of similar areas for the exercise of civil jurisdiction. In civil actions the jurisdiction of the district court is limited in relation to the nature and amount of the claim. In most actions, such as in contract and tort, it has jurisdiction where the claim does not exceed £250 but this will be increased to £2,500 when the Courts Act 1981 comes into force.

The circuit court. The circuit court is an integrated court which
has a president and 12 ordinary judges. The country is divided into
eight circuits and five judges are permanently assigned to the Dublin
circuit with one judge for each of the other circuits. The judges
travel within their circuits and hold court in the designated circuit
court towns. The circuit court can try almost all indictable offences
except the most serious ones and it will have civil jurisdiction in
contract and tort under the Courts Act 1981 for claims up to
£15,000. An accused has a right to trial by jury in a criminal case but
civil juries have been abolished in the circuit court since the passing
of the Courts Act 1971.

The High Court. The High Court, under the Constitution, is
invested with "full original jurisdiction in and power to determine
all matters and questions whether of law or fact, civil or criminal"
(Article 34). A president and up to 12 ordinary judges make up the
High Court. (The Courts Bill 1981 proposes to increase the number
of High Court judges by two.) The president of the circuit court is
also by virtue of his office a judge of the High Court but rarely acts
as such. Normally the High Court hears cases with the judges sitting
alone but for some cases three judges sit together. The High Court
has unlimited jurisdiction. When the High Court is exercising
criminal jurisdiction it is known as the *Central Criminal Court.* It
mainly hears the most serious crimes reserved to it such as murder
or cases which have been transferred from the circuit court to avoid
trial before a local jury. The Central Criminal Court is usually based
in Dublin with a resident High Court judge assigned to it by the
President of the High Court.

A jury may be used by the High Court in civil cases and must be
used in criminal cases where the accused pleads "not guilty." In
civil cases a vote of 9 out of 12 jurors is sufficient to award a
judgment but in criminal cases the verdict must be unanimous.

The Supreme Court. At the top of the hierarchy of courts is the
Supreme Court which is the court of final resort. It consists of the
Chief Justice and four ordinary judges. The judges sit together for all
cases and it takes three judges to form a quorum. The Supreme
Court is mainly an appeal court and its appellate jurisdiction
includes cases begun in the High Court as well as those cases which
have made their way upwards to the High Court or which were
directly appealed to the Supreme Court on a point of law. Appeals
from the Court of Criminal Appeal can also be made to the Supreme
Court on important points of law. The record of the trial court is
used so that there is no rehearing of the case in the Supreme Court.

Additional courts. An additional court may be brought into existence to deal with criminal cases when the government believes that the ordinary courts are not able to provide for the proper administration of justice or where such a court is necessary to provide for public peace and order. This is the Special Criminal Court which may be set up under Part V of the Offences Against the State Act 1939. It is usually established to deal with subversive crimes and has been in continuous operation since 1972.

Criminal appeals from this court, from the circuit court, and from the Central Criminal Court are heard by the Court of Criminal Appeal which consists of a judge from the Supreme Court and two High Court judges.

Although these are the normal courts of justice in Ireland there are other courts and tribunals which affect our lives. We have already mentioned the European Court of Justice which is the court which interprets Community (EEC) law. There are also the European Commission and Court of Human Rights which rule on matters arising under the European Convention of Human Rights. It was to these bodies that Mrs. Airey took her case in which Ireland was found in breach of two articles of the Convention and as a result of which Ireland has had to introduce Civil Legal Aid (*Airey* v. *Ireland* 1979).

There are other administrative tribunals in Ireland itself which, in their special spheres, act as courts in relation to planning, land commission activities, social welfare benefits, trademarks, tax, censorship, discrimination in employment and other administrative issues. The Employment Appeals Tribunal, for example, plays an important role in dealing with disputes arising under the Unfair Dismissals Act 1977.

THE LAW IN ACTION

Arbitration

When a legal problem arises in business it may sometimes be settled privately, "out of court," or by arbitration. Arbitration is a procedure whereby the parties agree to refer their dispute to an independent person called an arbitrator who decides the issues between them by making an award. Arbitration is often preferred to a court action on the grounds that it is usually faster, cheaper and private. An arbitration agreement is governed by the principles of contract and the Arbitration Act 1954.

LEGAL ACTION

Where an issue cannot be resolved privately or by arbitration, or where arbitration fails, the aggrieved party or parties will usually resort to the law courts. As the court process is fairly technical the parties normally put the matter in the hands of a solicitor who will first wish to examine the circumstances of the dispute in detail. The solicitor will obtain detailed statements, names and addresses of witnesses, copies of contracts or other relevant documents and, having considered the case, will advise his client on his best course of action. If the aggrieved person's solicitor believes he has a good case he will normally try to persuade the other side to settle and, failing this, will initiate court proceedings, *e.g.* by issuing a summons.

The Pleadings

The procedures to be adopted in the conduct of the action are governed by the rules of the court. A High Court action for example is mainly regulated by the Rules of the Superior Courts 1962 which determine the conduct of the pleadings. The pleadings consist of written statements delivered alternately by the parties to one another. The purpose of the pleadings is to ascertain and clarify the issues of fact and law which are in dispute and which are to be decided in the court action. The pleadings are also intended to inform both parties of the allegations they will have to meet in court so that they can prepare their case properly. In a High Court action the plaintiff files a statement of claim which sets out in detail his allegations against the defendant. It is then the turn of the defendant, who may file a reply in the form of a defence which sets out the grounds on which he resists the plaintiff's claim. In some cases the defendant may wish to make a claim of his own and this can be added to his defence as a counterclaim. The plaintiff may be obliged to serve a defence to the counterclaim.

High Court pleadings are under the control of the Master of the High Court. When the pleadings have closed there may be a discovery and inspection of documents in which the parties exchange a list of all documents relevant to the case which are or have been in their possession and they allow the opposing side to inspect all documents which are not privileged. During the course of the pleadings there may be any number of attempts to settle out of court especially when the inspection of documents reveals the strengths and weaknesses of the cases. If the defendant's offer to settle is rejected he may make a payment into court. If the plaintiff refuses to take it and recovers that amount or less from the court he must pay his own costs and all the defendant's costs subsequent to the offer of settlement.

The Trial

If no settlement is reached the issues go forward for trial. In the High Court the Master, in consultation with the litigants, ensures that the case is ready for hearing and that the place, mode and period of trial are set down. The trial begins with the opening address by counsel for the plaintiff in which he ensures that the judge is made familiar with the facts of the case. Counsel for the plaintiff calls his evidence, and the evidence for the defence is presented in the same manner. The witnesses are examined by counsel for the party calling the witnesses, they may be cross-examined by counsel for the opposing party and then be re-examined again if necessary. The defendant's counsel gives his closing address followed by that of the plaintiff's counsel. If there is a jury, the judge will review the evidence and instruct the jurors on the questions they must answer in reaching a verdict on the facts. The judge applies the law to the facts as found by the jury. If there is no jury the judge must reach a verdict, pass judgment, and make an order as to damages, if any, and costs. In this way the issue between the parties has been examined and the matter resolved by court order, and justice has hopefully been done.

2 The Legal Structure of Business Enterprise

There are a number of legal forms or structures which can be adopted for the purpose of conducting business activity. The structures normally used are those of the "sole trader," the partnership, and the incorporated company. There are other legal structures in use but these are applied to specialised types of enterprise and are not suitable for the generality of manufacturing or commercial business. These include Building Societies, Trustee Savings Banks and cooperatives. There are also some companies which are special in that they are regulated by the Government or are in a unique line of business such as banking and insurance. Most persons, however, who are involved in business of a general nature, use the sole trader, partnership, or company structure. In this chapter we are going to examine the legal characteristics of these three types of business undertaking, and we will also examine briefly the legal nature of the cooperative, which plays an important role in the Irish economy.

The Sole Trader

Any human person who is engaged in business for himself only and who is not associated with others in his enterprise is referred to as a "sole trader" or "single trader." This is the one-man or one-woman business run by the proprietor, usually in his own name and with his own money. This is typically the structure adopted by the local grocer, newsagent, farmer, workshop or small manufacturing unit. Few legal restrictions are placed on a person who wishes to conduct business in this manner. It is a general principle of our law that any person is free to engage in any kind of business activity he wishes. The law makes no distinction between such a person as private house-owner and business proprietor, and does not distinguish his business from his private assets. If his business prospers his profits after tax are his own and if he incurs losses he is liable for his

14

debts to the extent of his business and private assets. There is nobody with an obligation to save him from personal bankruptcy. He is a sole trader, of course, only in that he alone runs the business and he may take on as many employees as he wishes, without changing that status.

Registration of business names

There are essentially no legal restrictions on the person who wishes to commence business as a sole trader. If, however, the proprietor carries on business under any name other than his own, he must register certain particulars concerning the business as required by the Registration of Business Names Act 1963. These particulars include the business name, the date it was adopted, the nature and principal place of the business as well as the residence, the name, the former names, and nationality of the proprietor. Business letters, circulars and catalogues used in trading, and in which the business name appears, must also give the name and any former names of the proprietor, and his nationality if not Irish. The certificate of registration must be exhibited in a conspicuous position at the principal place of business and any changes must likewise be registered. The Act provides penalties for failure to comply with its provisions. Similar provisions apply to partnerships, companies, and the publishers of newspapers.

Prohibited business names

Under the Registration of Business Names Act 1963 the Minister for Trade, Commerce and Tourism may refuse to pemit the registration of any name which in his opinion is undesirable but an appeal may be made to the High Court against such a refusal. Indeed the person or partners using the name are liable on summary conviction to a fine up to £100. There is a similar provision in section 21 of the Companies Act 1963 which states that no company shall be registered by a name which is undesirable in the opinion of the Minister.

But even where the registration of a name is allowed the use of the name may still be unlawful. Section 14(3) of the Registration of Business Names Act 1963 states that the registration of a name under the Act "shall not be construed as authorising the use of that name if apart from such registration the use thereof could be prohibited." Under the law of torts or civil wrongs a businessman cannot take unfair advantage of the reputation of another business by adopting a similar name or by using a similar description or trade mark for his goods. A successful business gains goodwill by activities which are associated with its name or with the distinctive way in which it provides or markets its goods. This goodwill is protected by the law from unfair competition. Persons who attempt to mislead the public into believing that they are associated with another business so as to take advantage of its reputation will be liable in tort for passing off. In *Dockrell (Thomas) Sons and Co. Ltd.* v. *Dockrell (William H.) and Co. Ltd.* (H.C. 1941) the plaintiffs were well known builders' merchants who carried on business in Dublin for many years. The defendant company was incorporated in 1939 to carry on the business of money-lending. There was nobody with the surname Dockrell connected with the defendant company or no explanation for the use of the name. The court held that it must be presumed that the name was adopted to benefit from the reputation of the plaintiff firm and it granted an injunction to prohibit its use. Similar principles may be seen in operation in *C & A Modes* v. *C & A (Waterford) Ltd.* (1976). The plaintiff company was registered in England in 1953 and operated one of its retail clothing outlets in Belfast. Although it had no outlet in the Republic of Ireland at this time it did advertise extensively here using the identifying trade mark "C & A." The defendant company, C & A (Waterford) Ltd., was registered in Ireland in 1972 and was also involved in the retail clothing business. The Supreme Court held that this involved a passing off which violated the English company's proprietary right to goodwill. As there was a continuing completed tort the plaintiffs were entitled to an injunction to prevent the Irish company using a name so like their own that the public might be deceived by it. The same principles apply to marketing a business so as to "cash in" on the reputation of another venture. Thus an injunction was granted against the "Vogue" restaurant in Dublin so as to prevent it from representing that it had any connection with the international fashion magazine of that name (*Condé Nast Publications Ltd.* v. *Reuters Restaurant Ltd.* H.C. 1980).

Other restrictions on sole traders

Where a particular type of business requires special qualifications or safeguards a person cannot set up such a business without complying with the appropriate regulations. Certain qualifications are imposed, for example, on pharmacists, lawyers and auctioneers among others. Similarly a licence is required to sell intoxicating liquor, to operate a dance hall, a bookmaker's shop, or an amusement hall involving gaming or lottery. A person must also hold a licence to act as a moneylender, pawnbroker, to slaughter animals or to store petrol. The purpose of these restrictions is to protect the public from danger or abuse at the hands of "shady" or unqualified operators, to ensure public safety and to prevent indiscriminate drinking.

The position of the sole trader

Except for these restrictions which apply to all types of business, the sole trader is in the happy position of being able to operate as a businessman without recourse to lawyers or other formality. He is in full control of his business and does not have to disclose his profits except for income tax purposes. He can sell his business or transmit his interest to his heir on his death in the same way as he might sell or will his house.

These advantages, however, are offset by severe limitations. If the sole trader wishes to expand his business to take advantage of a market opportunity he is limited to his personal wealth and the sum he can borrow which is strictly tied to his ability to repay and the security he can offer. If the market opportunity is a risky one his problems are increased. He will find it more difficult to borrow and he will be putting his family property in danger if the venture fails. The sole trader has unlimited liability for his business debts which are not distinguished in law from his private debts and so he has no protection against bankruptcy. The outstanding disadvantages of this form of business, therefore, are that it cannot readily acquire capital for expansion and the trader must be wary of risk. Business expansion must depend on the trader's assets and capacity to borrow, and he must be cautious because he is liable for all the debts of his business to the extent of the whole of his personal assets.

Partnership

One way in which a sole trader can expand his business and share its liabilities is by taking into the business with him a person or a number of persons. These business partners may contribute capital of their own and the enterprise will be able to borrow larger amounts of money, especially if the new business associates are independently wealthy. The problem of liability remains, however, because the law will continue to treat the individual proprietors of the business as being personally liable for all the debts of the business. Once a person brings others into his business in this way he ceases to be a sole trader. His business, regardless of his wishes, becomes a partnership by operation of law, and will be treated as such by the courts on the basis of an implied contract between them to that effect. Alternatively two or more persons may consciously decide to set up a partnership business and enter a contract to achieve this. Their contract may be in any form but quite often it is put in writing as an agreement or is drawn up by a solicitor in the form of a partnership deed which regulates all aspects of their business association. Regardless of the form in which the agreement is made, however, it can be changed by the subsequent decision of the partners, or maybe held to have been changed, by the implied agreement of the members, when a new practice has been adopted by them.

Contract and agency as the basis of partnership

The practice of two or more people cooperating together in a joint business effort is as old as civilisation and most developed codes of law have had to develop rules to regulate their mutual rights and their relationship with outsiders. Under common law their mutual rights were deemed to be regulated by an express or implied contract and their liability to third parties was held to be based on agency. Each partner made the others his agents for the purpose of making contracts as agreed among themselves. In addition, under the principle of apparent authority, each partner was bound by the contracts and other acts of his co-partners made in the ordinary course of the partnership business regardless of any mutual limitation of authority agreed among themselves. Partnership is therefore a form of business association in which all the members are entitled to be its managers unless they otherwise agree.

Codification of partnership law

The rules governing partnership had been developed to more or less their present state by the mid-nineteenth century but were contained in numerous cases which were difficult to find. It was a period in which there was a great interest in codifying the law and eventually the law relating to partnership was codified in the Partnership Act 1890, a statute which had been drafted by an eminent English jurist, Sir Frederick Pollock. There was also considerable interest in changing the law to allow some form of limited liability for partners similar to what was available in continental Europe in a special type of partnership called the Société en Commandite. This was accomplished, but without much success, by passing the Limited Partnerships Act 1907.

In spite of the adoption of these statutes, however, the case law developed by the courts remains of fundamental importance. The Partnership Act 1890 is mostly a codification of the legal rules developed by the courts and in the event of doubt about its provisions, or in regard to issues not covered by the Act, one must follow the case law, if any. It must be remembered also that in many instances the statutes will only affect a partnership to the extent to which the partners have not made their own contract. Their rights among themselves are governed primarily by their express or implied agreement and not by the statutes. These rights and duties may also be altered by mutual consent. Under section 19 of the 1890 Act the rights and duties of the partners, whether arising from their agreement or the Act itself, "may be varied by the consent of all the partners, and such consent may be either express or inferred from a course of dealing."

Partnership defined

Partnership is "the relation which subsists between persons carrying on business in common with a view to profit" excluding the situation where persons carry on business as an incorporated company (1890 Act, s.1). By this definition there will not be a partnership unless the parties are conducting a business with the intention of making profits. "Business" is defined as including "every trade, occupation, or profession" (s.45).

A partnership requires a minimum of two members and the maximum is limited by statute. The Limited Partnerships Act 1907 fixed the upper number of partners in a limited partnership to 20 for an ordinary business and 10 for a banking partnership. These restrictions were imposed on other partnerships, which were not limited, by the Companies Act 1963. (It is proposed to remove the restriction on the number of partners in firms of accountants and solicitors under the Companies (Amendment) Bill 1981).

For the purposes of the 1890 Act the partners are collectively called "a firm" and the name under which their business is carried on is called "the firm name" (s.4). If the firm name does not represent the real names of the partners then similar particulars concerning the business and the partners, as required of sole traders, must be registered under the Registration of Business Names Act 1963.

It is not always easy to determine whether or not a business is a partnership or whether a particular person is or is not a partner. The partnership issue is important for two reasons. It is important in determining the rights and duties of the parties among themselves and it is also important to third party creditors of the business who will only be able to sue a person for the debts of the business if that person is a partner. Some of the earliest reported cases concern these issues. In *Greenham* v. *Gray* (Ir. Ex. 1855) a dispute arose over an agreement between the plaintiff and defendant concerning the operation of the Drogheda Mill Company. A cotton spinning mill at Greenhills, Drogheda, was owned by Gray. Under the agreement the plaintiff Greenham was to have full control and manage the mill for five years. He was to be paid £150 per annum salary and one-fifth of the profits. Gray was to receive rent for the premises and interest on his capital. Accounts were to be taken and presented to both. After about eight months Gray "forcibly expelled" the plaintiff from the mill. Greenham claimed this was unlawful as he was a partner in the business while Gray alleged that he was merely his manager or servant. Although the word "partnership" was not used in the agreement and although the plaintiff's only contribution to the business was his expertise, the court held that the legal effect was to create a partnership. The agreement was a joint contract to carry on the trade of cotton spinning as partners and not as employer and employee.

The other type of problem relating to liability for business debts can be seen in *Shaw* v. *Galt* (Ir. Q.B. 1864). The plaintiff, Shaw, had drawn four bills of exchange on the firm of J. and W. Wallace who were described as Sewed Muslin Manufacturers in Glasgow. The bills were accepted but the Wallaces became bankrupt. Shaw alleged that Galt was also a partner with the firm and was liable on the bills of exchange. Under Galt's agreement with J. and W. Wallace he was to have control and management of their Manufacturing Department for three years and was to be paid a salary of £500 and "a sum equivalent to one-third of the free profits" for the three years. The Irish Court of Queen's Bench held that Galt was not a partner. O'Brien J., relying to a great extent on the House of Lords decision in *Cox* v. *Hickman* (1860), was of the opinion that participation in profits was not in itself a sufficient test. The agreement made with Galt indicated that he was to act under the control of the Wallaces. If a person is a partner he must be able to act as a principal and the business must be conducted on his behalf. In this case the defendant's right to participate in the profits was merely a method of paying him for his services.

Does a partnership exist?

A partnership comes into existence when the parties make an express or implied contract to operate a business in common with a view to profit. They may adopt formal partnership articles or the partnership may be held to have arisen from their conduct on the grounds that their actions can only be explained on the basis of an implied partnership agreement between them. No writing or other formality is required to create a partnership, but if there is a transfer of an interest in land involved, the transfer must be evidenced by writing. In practice a comprehensive deed of partnership is often preferred so as to avoid subsequent doubts and conflicts between the partners.

Where there is a written agreement there is usually little doubt regarding the nature and existence of a partnership. Where partnership is alleged to arise from conduct, however, difficulties may arise. The 1890 Act merely gives guidelines in determining the existence of a partnership. Thus, for example, section 2(3) states that "the receipt by a person of a share of the profits of a business is prima facie evidence that he is a partner in the business, but . . . does not of itself make him a partner."

The question as to the existence of a partnership is one for the court to decide from all the circumstances of the case before it. The approach taken by the court can be seen, for example, in *Macken* v. *The Revenue Commissioners* (H.C. 1960). In this case the court had to determine for tax purposes the date at which a partnership had been formed. It had been agreed, in or around September 1953, that a painting contractor, his son and daughter should form a partnership. This partnership was to be effective from January 1, 1954, but a partnership deed was not executed until April 30, 1954. Did the partnership exist from January 1, or April 30, 1954? The court examined all the relevant factors and the judge concluded that no partnership existed until the deed was executed. "All that issued," Teevan J. ruled, "from the conference in September, 1953, and existed from then until the solicitors had completed the matter was an intention, or decision, to form a future partnership to be effective (whenever it should be formed) from the 1st. January, 1954."

The partnership property

Legal difficulties may arise in determining the ownership or title to property used by the partnership for the purpose of its business. This should be provided for by express agreement, but if it is not then it is primarily a matter of intention as disclosed by the facts in a particular case. All property used by a partnership need not be partnership property to be used and disposed of as such. Some of the property used in the partnership business may remain in the private ownership of one of the partners and this may be as a result of express agreement or be indicated to be so by the facts of the particular arrangement adopted, from which such an intention can be inferred. If the partnership business pays an individual partner for the use of his property under a contractual licence then quite clearly the property remains in the ownership of the partner in his private capacity. Alternatively where a partner has the private use of partnership property, it still remains the property of the firm. In *Lee* v. *Crawford* (1912), for example, the representatives of a deceased partner were held not to have a tenancy in a house belonging to the partnership in which the partner had lived and for which he had been paying a "rent." Where a partnership agreement allows the surviving partner to purchase the interest of the deceased partner the assets remain partnership assets until this right is put into effect (*Re Fox, decd., Brunker* v. *Fox* (Ir. Ch. D. 1915).

Cash introduced into the firm when formed, or property brought in which is given a money value in the accounts, will probably be intended to be partnership property. On the other hand subsequent advances of cash to the firm on which the partner is paid interest may not be partnership property and may have to be paid back to the particular partner as he is, in this respect, merely a creditor of the firm, and the advance is not put immediately at risk. Any property bought with the firm's money is prima facie, partnership property. Section 20 of the Partnership Act 1890 states that:

> "all property and rights and interests in property originally brought into the partnership stock or acquired, whether by purchase or otherwise, on account of the firm or for the purposes and in the course of the partnership business, are called in this Act partnership property, and must be held and applied by the partners exclusively for the purpose of the partnership and in accordance with the partnership agreement."

In this way the law tries to delimit the pool of partnership property which is outside the private control of individual partners. The rights in this common property and the partners' rights to profits earned depend primarily on any agreement which they have made for this purpose. In the absence of express or implied agreement the 1890 Act entitles each partner to an equal share of the profits and an equal share in the capital on dissolution regardless of the amounts contributed or role played in earning profits. Where a partner contributes 80 per cent. of the capital, the court is free to find an implied right by agreement to 80 per cent. of the profits but will only do so if this is held to be what the partners intended. It is important that all such matters should be clearly set out in an express written agreement, and that the agreement be adhered to by all involved so that disputes may be avoided.

The management of a partnership

The internal management of a partnership is a matter to be regulated by agreement between the partners. In the absence of agreement every partner is entitled to take part in the management of the partnership business and irrespective of what the agreement says each partner can bind the firm under the principles of agency (see p. 116). It is stated as follows in section 5 of the 1890 Act:

> "Every partner is an agent of the firm and his other partners for the purpose of the business of the partnership; and the acts of every partner who does any act for carrying on in the usual way business of the kind carried on by the firm of which he is a member bind the firm and his partners, unless the partner so acting has in fact no authority to act for the firm in the particular matter, and the person with whom he is dealing either knows that he has no authority, or does not know or believe him to be a partner."

Thus whereas a partner's actual authority to bind the firm may be limited, his firm, that is his fellow partners, will still be liable and bound by acts done within the scope of his apparent or ostensible authority. In the English case of *Mercantile Credit Co. Ltd.* v. *Garrod* (E.Q.B. 1962), a partnership operated a garage business but it was not allowed to buy or sell cars under its partnership deed. In spite of this a partner sold a car to the plaintiffs who claimed the return of the money from the defendant Garrod, who was a co-partner. Although the sale was not authorised by the partnership deed, or by Garrod himself, he was nevertheless held liable under section 5 of the 1890 Act. In selling the car the partner was acting in the usual way in which garages conduct business. The plaintiffs knew they were dealing with a partner and they had no notice of his lack of authority so that the transaction was perfectly valid and binding on the firm.

The validity of a partner's acts or contracts depends not only on his actual authority, therefore, but also on whether such actions could be considered as normally practised in business of that nature. Any partner will have apparent authority to buy necessary goods, sell the firm's goods, hire staff and to accept payment of the firm's debts. If the firm is involved in trading he will have apparent authority to issue cheques, to borrow money, to pledge personal property, to create an equitable mortgage of land but not to bind the firm by deed or not usually to bind it as guarantor for a loan.

The liability of the partners

When a partner binds his firm a joint obligation is created on all the partners, irrespective of their wishes or involvement, provided the debt or obligation is incurred while they are in fact partners. Each partner must contribute equally to the losses of the partnership unless otherwise agreed, and, except to the extent allowed under the Limited Partnerships Act 1907, every partner is jointly liable for the debts or obligations of the firm to the full extent of his wealth. Each partner is individually liable for the whole amount due by the firm. The plaintiff can bring only one action but he may sue all the partners or simply one partner for the total amount.

The partner's fiduciary duties

Individual partners are so dependent on each other that there must be a high degree of trust and good faith between them in their mutual dealings. This has been recognised by the courts which have imposed a fiduciary duty on each partner to act with the utmost good faith towards his co-partners. As one judge put it:

> "If fiduciary relationship means anything I cannot conceive a stronger case of fiduciary relations than that which exists between partners. Their mutual confidence is the life blood of the concern. It is because they trust one another that they are partners in the first place; it is because they continue to trust one another that the business goes on."

Bacon V.-C in *Helmore* v. *Smith*, (E. Ch. D. 1886). Every partner is therefore entitled to full disclosure concerning all aspects of the business, he must account to his co-partners for any private gain made through a partnership transaction, or the use of the partnership property, name, or business connection, and will be liable to them for any profits made in direct competition with the firm without their consent (1890 Act, ss. 28–30). Because of this personal nature of the relationship no partner can assign his interest to an outsider without the consent of his co-partners. This consent can, however, be given in advance by means of the partnership articles and in this way a partner can sell his interest, or retire and hand it over to another person, without a dissolution of the partnership if this is part of their agreement. Unless the partners agree otherwise, a difference arising on ordinary matters of business may be decided by a majority, the nature of the business cannot be changed except by the consent of all, and there is no authority to expel a partner. If they agree to a procedure for expulsion, however, it must be used bona fide (in good faith) for the benefit of the partnership as a whole.

Ending the partnership

Subject to any contrary agreement a partnership may be dissolved after a fixed term, on the completion of a specified venture or, where there is no time limit, it can be dissolved at will by a partner giving notice to that effect. Unless some other arrangement is made the partnership is dissolved by the bankruptcy or death of a partner. It can also be dissolved by court order on the grounds of the insanity, incapacity, or misconduct of a partner, the hopeless state of the business or when the court is of opinion that it is just and equitable to do so (1890 Act, ss. 22, 33, 35). On dissolution the partnership property is usually sold, the accounts are finally made up, and unless otherwise agreed any losses are made good, and the assets distributed as set out in section 44 of the Partnership Act 1890.

Limited partnerships

It is also possible to form a limited partnership consisting of one or more general partners with full liability for the firm's debts and obligations, and one or more limited partners whose liability is limited to their initial capital contribution which, however, must be left in the firm during its existence (Limited Partnerships Act 1907, s.4). A limited partnership must be registered and the register is open to inspection by the public. A limited partner, which may be a body corporate, is prohibited from becoming involved in the management of the firm and has no power to bind it. If he does become involved in management (other than in inspecting the books or discovering the state of business) then he becomes fully liable for debts and obligations incurred at that time (1907 Act, ss. 5, 6). Although the Act allows a form of limited liability for partners it is not very satisfactory. A partnership still has to have at least one general partner with unlimited liability for the firm's debts and the limited partners are denied all active participation in the business.

Conclusions

Partnership overcomes some of the problems associated with the single trader form of conducting business. It allows the increased accumulation of capital and expertise which many types of business require. It shares the burden of risk and to some extent can confer limited liability. Partnership is a very personal and adaptable structure and can be created without formality although not without dangers. Unless carefully thought out articles of partnership are adopted, it may result in conflict and failure because of the trust and good faith required among the partners – any one of whom, by mismanagement, can render his co-partners bankrupt. The partner also has difficulty in transferring his interest in the firm, which may result in the dissolution of the business or the admission of an undesirable newcomer. The limited partnership was not in itself satisfactory and became virtually redundant as soon as it was introduced when it became possible to form a private company under the Companies Act 1907. The private company became relatively easy and cheap to create and had as much financial privacy as in the case of a partnership. Indeed partnership as a whole has ceased to be a popular method of doing business. Most partnerships nowadays are confined to the professions, such as accountants, solicitors, architects, which in some instances are prohibited from forming companies on the grounds that they must maintain individual professional accountability to clients. It must be remembered that partnership remains important in its own right in that it is always open to the court to hold that persons are in fact acting in partnership and to regulate their affairs accordingly. With the recent tendency to regulate the private company and deprive it of some of its advantages there may be a revival in the partnership mode of conducting business. Partnerships have also been recognised as a means of overcoming the reluctance of farmers to transfer some control of the farm to younger family members. Macra na Feirme operate a Farm Partnership Advisory Service to assist farm families in drawing up suitable farm partnerships so that the needs of both generations can be better fulfilled.

The Incorporated Company

The third and most important form which a business unit may adopt is that of the incorporated company. A company is an association of persons formed to carry on some business or undertaking in the name of the association. It may be incorporated or unincorporated. We are concerned here with the incorporated company which is an entity distinct from its members. The fundamental difference between the sole trader or partnership form of business and the company is that the company is a corporate body or corporation while the others are not. If a company is incorporated, that is, if it is a corporation, it is a thing in itself which is regarded in law as distinct from the persons to whom it belongs. From this quality all the benefits of a company come, including the privilege of limited liability for its members. Companies are regulated by the Companies Acts 1963–1977. The Companies (Amendment) Bill 1981 is, however, being considered by the Oireachtas and the Irish Government is obliged to implement EEC directives to further the harmonisation of company law within the European Community.

The origins of company law
The benefits of incorporation are not confined to business associations but have been granted for centuries to cities, universities, and other bodies. Prior to the nineteenth century incorporation

could only be had by means of a Royal Charter from the Crown or by means of an Act of Parliament.

Incorporation by registration

The need for reform was keenly felt with the upsurge of economic activity in the early nineteenth century. Following a report by a Parliamentary Committee on Joint Stock Companies in 1844 an Act was passed which provided for the incorporation of companies by registration and which drew a clear distinction between companies and partnerships. It was the heyday of the laissez-faire philosophy which held that the interests of the community could best be served by placing as few restrictions on people as possible. The Limited Liability Act 1855 was passed allowing limited liability to members of companies. The Joint Stock Companies Act 1856 simplified the process of company registration still further. The law relating to companies was consolidated in the Companies Act 1862 which was itself frequently amended. The Companies Act 1907 permitted the formation of private companies with a minimum of two members which made incorporation and limited liability available to the small family business. In the following year the law up to that date was consolidated in the Companies (Consolidation) Act 1908 which remained the principal Act governing Irish companies until repealed by the enactment of the present Companies Act 1963.

The meaning of incorporation

The benefits available to the businessman in forming a company arise from the creation thereby of corporate personality for his undertaking and limited liability for himself. When a business is transformed into a company it is said to have been "incorporated" which means it is now a body (corpus) recognised by law as having an existence and reality of its own which is separate from the persons who formed it. The company is a corporate body like Dublin Corporation, or Galway County Council, and in that capacity it has such powers as are set out in the Companies Acts and in its registered documents called the Memorandum of Association and the Articles of Association. These powers include the capacity to own property, sue in the courts, to make contracts, and all such other powers necessary to carry out the business objects set out in its Memorandum. Thus an incorporated company is, in the eyes of the law, a "person" which, like any human being, has legal rights and duties. It is sometimes called an artificial legal person.

A company, like all corporations, exists only because it is recognised by law. It is a legal creation and its powers are also regulated by law. Companies established by Royal Charter are regarded as having full legal capacity. They have the same powers as an adult to conduct business in any way they like. Companies formed by statute, however, are expected to confine themselves to the powers and objectives given to them by statute. If they act beyond their powers such actions could be declared *ultra vires* and void. The same principles are applied to companies formed by registration so that they must confine themselves to the powers given them in the Memorandum and Articles.

Thus in the leading case *Ashbury Rail, Carriage and Iron Co. Ltd.* v. *Riche* (1875) the House of Lords held that a contract made by a company beyond its powers was void and could not be subsequently ratified by the shareholders. Persons forming or operating a company, therefore, must ensure that they give the company sufficiently wide powers and that these powers are not exceeded. It should be noted also that the rule was modified so as to protect creditors dealing with the company. Contracts made by creditors with the company's directors or officers are enforceable against the company even if they are *ultra vires* provided they are made in good faith. The director who makes an *ultra vires* contract, however, is personally liable to the company for any loss it suffers thereby (see p. 104).

At one time, as we have seen, the privilege of incorporation could only be obtained by getting a charter from the Crown or by means of an Act of Parliament (statute). No new corporations can be created in Ireland by Royal Charter, but we still have corporations formed in this way such as the University of Dublin (Trinity College, Dublin) and the Bank of Ireland. Companies can still be incorporated by statute and some of our state-sponsored bodies have been created in this way. When the Government wishes to create a company to provide a nationwide service or utility it normally does so by statute, for example Coras Iompair Eireann (C.I.E.) and the Electricity Supply Board (E.S.B.).

How a company is formed

The normal method of incorporation nowadays is by registration under the Companies Acts, which is relatively cheap and simple. Using this method the following documents are sent to the Registrar of Companies for registration.

(1) A Memorandum of Association signed by at least two persons in the case of a private company and at least seven in the case of a public company. This Memorandum must contain the name of the company, the objects it was formed to pursue, its nominal capital

and, if the liability of the members is to be limited, there must be a statement to that effect.

(2) Articles of Association signed in the same way. A company limited by shares may adopt, or where it does not exclude or contradict them, may be held to have adopted, the model articles set out in Schedule 1, Table A, of the Companies Act 1963. The Articles set out the rules needed for the internal management of the company. They deal with such matters as the shares, the rights attaching to shares, share certificates, liens, calls, the transfer, transmission, and forfeiture of shares; notice of, proceedings at, and voting at, company meetings; the number, powers, duties, qualification, rotation, election and proceedings of directors; the managing director, if any; the company secretary; regulations concerning dividends, reserve, the accounts and the audit. If the company is to be a private one, which it will usually be in the case of a family business, then the company's Articles must put some restriction on the transfer of the shares, for example, by only allowing a transfer of shares subject to the directors' discretion. The maximum number of members must be limited to 50, and all invitations to the public to subscribe for any shares or debentures in the company must be prohibited (1963 Act, s.33)

(3) A statutory declaration by a solicitor or by a person named in the articles as a director or company secretary that all the requirements of the Companies Act 1963 relating to registration have been complied with.

(4) A statement relating to the company's capital.

(5) In the case of a public company certain returns must also be made in relation to directors. A list of persons who have consented to become directors must be sent to the registrar, or if they are named in the Articles, then, their written consent to act in that capacity must be sent instead. Where directors must hold shares in the company an undertaking to take and pay for those qualification shares must be signed by the directors named in the Articles unless they have already signed the Memorandum for them. These documents together with the prescribed fee are sent to the Registrar of Companies. If he is satisfied that everything is in order he registers the company and issues a certificate which certifies that the company is incorporated and, if it is a limited company, that it is limited. The effect of this is set out in section 18 (2) of the Companies Act 1963:

"From the date of incorporation mentioned in the certificate of incorporation, the subscribers of the Memorandum, together with such other persons as may from time to time become

members of the company, shall be a body corporate with the
name contained in the memorandum, capable forthwith of
exercising all the functions of an incorporated company, and
having perpetual succession and a common seal, with such
liability on the part of the members to contribute to the assets of
the company in the event of its being wound up as is mentioned
in this Act."

The resulting company may be a public or a private one, and one
in which the liability of the members for the debts of the company is
unlimited, limited by shares or limited by guarantee, depending on
the wishes of the subscribers who drafted the Memorandum and
Articles accordingly. It should be noted that the process of company
formation can be speeded up when the businessman contacts a
solicitor or other person who has already formed a number of
companies and can alter one to suit the client and transfer it to him
without delay.

Limited liability

The second significant quality of an incorporated company is that
it can confer the benefit of limited liability on its members. Liability
means the extent to which a person can be made accountable for his
actions at law. A member of a company will be fully liable for a
company's debts in an unlimited company but he will be liable only
to a limited extent for the debts of a limited company. Under the
Companies Act 1963 it is possible to set up an unlimited public or
private company in which the members will be fully liable to pay its
debts in the event of liquidation. It is also possible to set up a
company in which the liability of the members for the company's
debts is limited by shares or by guarantee. In a company limited by
guarantee each member undertakes to contribute a fixed sum of
money to meet the company's debts, if it is needed, on a winding up
of its activities. If the guarantee company issues shares (and a
private company must have a share capital) then the members may
have a liability on the shares also. In a company limited by shares
the liability of the members is limited to the amount, if any, unpaid
on their shares. Thus a person who owns 100 £1 shares which are
fully paid-up has no further liability to contribute to the company's
debts. If, however, he holds 100 £1 shares and only 50p has been
paid up on each share, he can be called upon to pay the outstanding
50p per share held, a total of £50, but this is the limit of his liability.

The company owns and operates the business

These two characteristics of the typical company, corporate status and limited liability, make it fundamentally different from a partnership. In law a partnership is no more than the sum of its members and as long as a partner is actively involved with his business he has unlimited liability for its debts. Once a company has been incorporated, however, it becomes an entity completely separate from its members and this is the case even when the new company consists of the former proprietor and one or more nominee or "dummy" shareholders. This was clearly established in the leading case *Salomon* v. *Salomon & Co. Ltd.* (1897). Salomon was a London leather merchant and wholesale boot manufacturer who formed a limited company to take over his business. The only shareholders were Salomon himself, his wife, and his five children. In exchange for his business the company gave Salomon 20,000 fully-paid £1 shares, and debentures to the value of £10,000 secured on the company's assets. Salomon was now the holder of almost all the company's issued shares and his wife and five children had merely one share each. Obviously Salomon himself had complete control of the business just as he had before incorporation. The new company very quickly got into financial difficulties and on liquidation its assets realised only slightly more than £6,000 whereas it owed £10,000 by way of secured debentures and £7,000 to unsecured creditors. The liquidator claimed that the company was a one-man affair and a sham and that Salomon and the company were really one and the same. He maintained that Salomon should not be paid on his secured debentures until the other creditors were paid first as he must be responsible for its debts because it acted as his agent. The House of Lords, however, rejected these arguments and found in favour of Salomon. The company had been properly formed and there was no fraud involved so it was held to be completely separate from Salomon who was entitled to have his loan repaid to him. As Lord McNaghten put it: "The Company is at law, a different person altogether from the subscribers to the memorandum; and, though it may be that after incorporation the business is precisely the same as it was before, and the same persons are managers, and the same hands receive the profits, the company is not in law the agent of the subscribers or trustee for them. Nor are the subscribers as members liable, in any shape or form, except to the extent and in the manner provided by the Act."

The debts of the company were held to be its own affair and were not those of Salomon who had no further liability for them because his shares were fully paid-up. The same applies to any limited liability company – its debts are the company's debts and the members have usually no further liability for them.

If Salomon and his family had operated their business as a

partnership the outcome in law would have been completely different. The debts of the business would have been held to be those of Salomon and he would be personally liable for those debts down to his last pound with bankruptcy resulting if necessary. One of the main attractions therefore of the company structure is that it allows a businessman to undertake even a risky venture with the security that he is only to lose at worst a fixed amount, usually only the share capital which he takes in the company.

The corporate identity of the company

In law the company and its members are completely separate. Incorporation has been compared to a veil which covers the company and the law will only rarely look behind that veil at the persons who in reality control its activities. This separation can be seen in the case of *The Roundabout Ltd.* v. *Beirne* (H.C. 1959). A limited company called the Marian Park Inn Ltd. operated a public-house in Dublin with non-union labour. In May 1958 all of the staff became unionised. The three directors closed the premises in November and dismissed the staff. The union picketed the premises on the grounds that the closure was to force the staff to leave the union or to reopen with non-union labour. The premises were reopened for business in December by a new company called The Roundabout Ltd. This new company had the same three persons as its permanent directors and had an accountant and three barmen as its other directors. The premises had been leased from the first company and the directors ran the business themselves. The new company claimed an injunction against the union to prevent them picketing the premises. It was argued that the business was being conducted by a new person in law and that there was no trade dispute with the new company. The judge agreed. "The new company," Dixon J. said, "is in law a distinct entity, as is the old company. Each company is what is known as a legal person. I have to regard the two companies as distinct in the same way as I would regard two distinct individuals. I must, therefore proceed on the basis that a new and different person is now in occupation of the premises and carrying on business there." For this and other reasons it was held that there was no trade dispute and an injunction was granted.

The extent to which the law is prepared to go in respecting the corporate identity of the company can also be seen in *J. L. Smallman Ltd.* v. *O'Moore and Newman* (H.C. 1957). The defendants, O'Moore and Newman, carried on the business of building contractors as a partnership. The plaintiff supplied the business with goods on credit. In July 1954 O'Moore and Newman converted their business into a limited company. Although notice of the conversion had been given, the supplier was unaware of it and continued to supply goods to the defendants as before. In August 1956 this action was brought against the defendants to recover the balance of the price of goods sold to them. O'Moore and Newman argued that they were not liable as the goods were supplied not to them but to the company. The court had to agree and the action was dismissed.

It is only on rare occasions that the law will disregard the corporate identity of a company. There are certain situations listed in the 1963 Act in which this will be done, as when membership falls below the legal minimum. It will also look at the realities when incorporation is a cloak for fraud or where a company is acting solely as the agent of another company.

The private company and the family business

Although private and public companies have many features in common such as corporate status, limited liability, shareholders and directors, they are often different from each other in practice. In many ways the small private family company has more in common with a partnership than with a public company, and the courts have to some extent recognised this. Most private companies are formed by family businesses or partnerships and in spite of the change in structure they usually continue to operate in much the same way as before. When the company is formed it acquires the business assets and capital from the persons who register it, who obtain shares in the company in return. Unlike the situation in a public company, however, the promoters will form the company, act as its directors, run it as its managers, and will often be its major creditors when they lend it money.

In these circumstances although the company's corporate status is never in doubt the private company does in fact tend to operate as a quasi-partnership or incorporated partnership but without some of the obvious inconveniences of the partnership structure. The private company by its nature tends to keep the business a family or personal one just as a partnership does. This is achieved by the statutory restriction on the private company which limits the number of members to 50, prohibits public issue of shares or debentures, and restricts the free transfer of shares. These factors, of course, make the private company structure more attractive to the small business. It will have the other advantages of incorporation too. Limited liability, ease in the transfer of shares and continuity, all make the company structure a desirable one. A further advantage of a company is that it can borrow money on the convenient security of a floating charge which increases its borrowing capacity. This is a charge on the general assets of the company which permits the company to deal with its assets in the normal course of business until the security is enforced by the lender, whereupon the charge crystallises and attaches to the actual assets then held, subject to any prior charge on such assets. There may be an additional inducement in forming a private company where variations between corporation tax and income tax give the company structure a tax advantage. It can also be a convenient method of giving younger family members a stake in the business without handing over complete control to them. In return for such benefits the private company must observe formalities and returns and follow procedures more appropriate to the large public company.

The public company

Whereas, technically speaking, a public company is a company which does not qualify to be a private company, a real public company is one which raises capital from the public. The obvious danger in such capital issues is that the investing public will be abused. To avoid this the law puts an obligation on company promoters to act in a fiduciary manner towards the company and not make a secret profit at its expense. It also protects the public by making the company publicise or disclose relevant facts about itself in a prospectus or statement in lieu of prospectus, by preventing the allotment of shares until a certain minimum capital has been subscribed, and by imposing criminal sanctions or allowing legal remedies against those who make false statements in prospectuses. In such companies there may be a large number of shareholders who will elect a board of directors to manage the company. The directors in turn will usually employ professional salaried managers to operate the business of the company. It is in the context of such a company that the many rules and formalities imposed by the law on companies make sense. These include disclosure of accounts, returns as to share issues, meetings, maintenance of capital, voting, shareholders' rights and the powers and duties of directors.

Operating a company

We have seen how problems may arise in a partnership over issues such as defining a partner, partnership property, and management. In a company, however, these issues are better defined, mainly due to the separate corporate nature of a company. A person becomes a member of a company when he signs the memorandum, consents to take qualification shares as a director, or when he agrees to become a member and is the registered holder of its shares. Capital acquired by the company in the form of cash or property becomes company property owned by the company in its own right as a legal person and it can sue to protect its interest in it.

Whereas every partner has a prima facie right to participate in management, the members of a company only have such residual rights as are specified by the share issue, the articles, and the general law. Their more important rights are exercised at general meetings and include the power to elect or remove the directors.

Power to manage the business of the company is usually vested in a board of directors who need not be shareholders unless the articles require a share qualification. In practice, of course, directors will be major shareholders or must command the respect of a substantial number of shareholders. Except for such powers as may be expressly reserved to the shareholders in general meeting the company is controlled by the board of directors which has considerable autonomy and independence in this respect. This separation of membership from management facilitates the member who wishes to transfer his interest – usually in the form of shares. When a shareholder contracts to sell shares, for example, the equitable title to them passes at once to the purchaser. When a share transfer is executed and the transfer is registered by the company the purchaser becomes a member, and the seller ceases to be a member, in respect of those shares. Because membership is not an entitlement to participate in management the transfer has no immediate effect on the operations of the business. Similarly the introduction of a new member or the death or retirement of an existing member does not effect a dissolution of the company which continues to exist in perpetuity until dissolved by a special process.

Ending the life of a company

The life of a company is ended by liquidation or winding up and its property is administered for the benefit of its creditors and members. An administrator, called a liquidator, is appointed who assumes the functions of the directors. He takes control of the company and, in accordance with the rules set out in the Companies Acts, he collects its assets, pays its debts, and distributes the surplus, if any, among the members according to their rights. When the winding up is complete the company is dissolved. The liquidation may be a compulsory one ordered by the court or it may be a voluntary one initiated by a resolution of the members.

A framework for capitalist enterprise

The company structure gives businessmen the important benefit of limited liability. But when we consider large public companies the advantages of the company structure are even more indispensable.

In such companies, the number of members is unlimited and this makes possible the vast accumulation of capital required to manufacture new products, provide capital-intensive services, undertake mineral exploration and extraction, and carry out the myriad activities associated with medium, large and multinational corporations. The structure allows the separation of management from ownership so that large companies can become self-sustaining and flexible business machines. It gives flexibility to the shareholder members who can sell or transfer their interest in the company without difficulty and without affecting the company's operations. It provides a stimulus to investment and enterprise. The company structure is the framework on which the capitalist system is based and it partly explains the successes and failures of modern national and international business. The company enjoys considerable stability and continuity because, as a corporation, it can exist for an indefinite number of lifetimes and is dissolved only by a legally controlled process called liquidation or winding up. In these respects the company is superior to the partnership. These advantages and others have made the incorporated company the dominant form of modern business.

Cooperatives

Introduction

There have been voluntary associations in operation in Ireland for centuries. These have been concerned with the provision of self-help of one form or another. The earlier associations were created mainly to provide mutual relief and maintenance for their members in times of sickness, infirmity or old age. Legislation to facilitate the development of those voluntary associations was introduced in the nineteenth century, and regulated "friendly societies" and "industrial and provident societies."

The principal Act governing cooperatives in force at present is the Industrial and Provident Societies Act 1893, although it has been amended in some particulars since that time.

The formation of a cooperative

A cooperative society, which is otherwise known as an industrial and provident society, can be formed and registered by any group of eight or more citizens who are over the age of 18 years. An application is made, on Form A, to the Registrar of Friendly Societies, 13 Hume St., Dublin 2. The application must be signed by seven members and the secretary, and must be accompanied by two copies of the draft rules of the society which are signed by the same eight persons (1893 Act, s.5). There is a £50 fee payable to the registrar. The name of the cooperative must not be identical to, or likely to be confused with, the name of another registered society, and the word "limited" must be the last word in its name.

A cooperative society may become affiliated to certain organisations which will supply it with model rules which can be used and modified with the organisation's consent. These include the Irish Cooperative Organisation Society Limited (I.C.O.S.), the National Association of Building Cooperatives Limited, the Cooperative Development Society Limited and the Civics Institute of Ireland Limited. A society may apply for registration through one of these bodies.

The rules of a cooperative society can be drawn up to suit the needs of the members provided they comply with the Industrial and Provident Societies Acts 1893–1978 and are approved by the registrar. The rules of a society are similar to the Articles of Association of a limited company and bind the members in the same way. The rules of a cooperative society typically deal with such things as the society's objectives and its registered office, rules governing membership, the share capital, the registration and transfer of shares, borrowing powers, the conduct of general and special meetings, the election and powers of the committee of management or directors, the keeping of accounts, the annual return and other provisions. Matters which must be covered by the rules are specified in Schedule 2 to the 1893 Act and include the making, altering, or rescinding of the rules themselves. Amendments to the rules are not valid until registered under section 10. An acknowledgment of registration of an amendment is conclusive of its validity even if the amendment was made by the committee of management and not by a special meeting as required by the rules (*Butler* v. *Springmount Co Op. Dairy Society*, Ir. C.A. 1906). If the rules are not registered they have no validity (*Re Londonderry Equitable Co-Operative Society* Ir.C.A. 1910).

A body corporate with limited liability

When the Registrar of Friendly Societies has examined the rules and approved them, the society is registered and a certificate of registration is issued. On registration the cooperative society becomes a corporation with limited liability. As section 21 of the 1893 Act puts it: "The registration of a society shall render it a body corporate by the name described in the acknowledgment of registry, by which it may sue and be sued, with perpetual succession and a common seal, and with limited liability . . . ." The society must submit its accounts for audit once in every year and must make an annual return to the registrar of its receipts, expenditures and funds, as audited. A copy of the last balance sheet, together with the auditor's report must be hung up in a conspicuous place at the society's registered office. A copy of the certificate of registration and rules when bound together form the rule book of the society and must be made available to members at a cost not exceeding 5p.

The nature of a cooperative

There are obvious similarities between an incorporated company and the industrial and provident society. Both usually enjoy corporate status and limited liability and both are normally involved in business. An industrial and provident society is defined by section 4 of the 1893 Act as "a Society for carrying on any industries, businesses, or trades specified in or authorised by its rules, whether wholesale or retail, and including dealings of any description with land." Provisions are contained in the 1893 Act for the conversion of a society into a company and the conversion of a company into a society although these provisions do not apply to credit unions.

One of the basic differences is in relation to shareholding. In a company there is no limit to the shareholding interest which a member may have in the company. In a registered society, however, no member can have an interest exceeding £3,000 in the shares of the society. except in the case of agricultural or fishing societies where the maximum permitted is £10,000 (1978 Act). This restriction tends to keep registered societies democratic in nature and to attract members because the society will help meet practical needs rather than produce a return on their capital. There is no limit to the interest which one society can have in another.

Any other differences in the registered society derive from the philosophy of the members as expressed in the rules adopted and not from legal restriction. Where a society describes itself as a cooperative it will be following, to a greater or lesser extent, internationally recognised principles of cooperation. The cooperative is seen as a voluntary movement open to all who can benefit from membership provided they are willing to accept the duties involved. The cooperative society is intended to be democratic in that it adopts the rule of one man one vote and the members elect the committee of management, or committee of directors, to direct the affairs of the society. The holders of share capital should receive a strictly limited rate of interest, if any, and any surplus should be distributed in such a way as to best promote the good of all the members. This may be achieved by expanding the society's activities, providing services needed by the members, or by making a return to members in proportion to their transactions with the society. The emphasis is on providing a service to members rather than providing a straightforward dividend on capital invested. It is also recommended that the cooperative society should be actively promoting the cooperation ideal so as to maximise the benefits of the society and to make the ideal work.

Cooperatives in Ireland

There are different types of cooperatives which pursue conflicting objectives depending on the type of membership operating them. The earliest British cooperatives were consumer-orientated societies in the big cities. They ran wholesale and retail grocery stores with the objective of providing cheap food to industrial workers. There are industrial cooperatives or worker cooperatives which exist to benefit the workers by giving them control of business assets and ownership of the profits. In Ireland cooperatives are mainly agricultural, for the benefit of their farmer members. The strongest societies are based on the sale and marketing of dairy produce. These primarily benefit the milk producers and the basic objective is to maximise the return on the milk supplied. Other activities are based on obtaining farm inputs such as seeds and fertilisers. The objective in relation to supplies is to acquire them at the cheapest price possible. Other societies are geared towards provision of services to members such as the use of agricultural machinery.

Cooperative societies exist therefore for the good of their members. Whereas companies are organised to benefit the owners of capital, these societies are more concerned with the members as suppliers, consumers or workers.

In other respects the operation of a cooperative is similar to the operation of a company. Many Irish cooperatives have amalgamated into large corporations in order to remain competitive by producing and marketing their products more efficiently. The result has been that the organisation has often become remote from the original farm members. Professional managers tend to operate such organisations in the way in which all corporate enterprise is run.

The Industrial and Provident Societies Acts 1893–1978 were not specifically designed to provide a legislative framework for cooperatives, although they do provide a structure within which the cooperative self-help ideal can be pursued. The legislation, however, has not kept pace with changing circumstances. The Irish Cooperative Organisation Society Limited, as the coordinating body of the movement, has called for a new Cooperative Societies Act to facilitate the management of what has become a £2,500 million business.

3 Business Premises and the Law of Property

Every business, regardless of its legal structure, requires a premises or location at which it will carry on its activities. For this reason a business must have or must acquire a legal interest in landed property which will adequately meet its needs. The commercial property market, therefore, provides factories, office space, warehouses and retail shops to meet this demand. The rights which the business can exercise over such property depends on the legal interest offered and acquired. Typical interests include "99 year leases" of factories, commercial properties held on "freehold tenure" or held in "fee simple," or short term leases with rent reviews. Terms such as tenure, freehold, lease, fee simple, and the legal problems associated with business premises can only be understood from an examination of some aspects of property law.

What the Law Means by "Property"

In everyday language we use the word property to designate things that are owned by legal persons. "John," we say, "owns a lot of property." In this sense "property" is a synonym for physical or tangible objects over which a person has exclusive control. The law, however, is more concerned with what gives him control over such objects. Quite clearly his control comes from the fact that the law recognises John has rights to the property which it will enforce if necessary. In law, therefore, to have property or ownership is to hold a certain aggregate of rights recognised by the law which are guaranteed and protected by the state and the Constitution through the courts.

Real Property and Personal Property

Traditionally the law of property has been sub-divided into real property and personal property. The most important property in earlier times was land, to include the air-space above it, anything below it, including minerals, and anything attached to the land such as crops and buildings. The law distinguished such immovable and permanent property from movable property such as animals, merchandise and goods. In the early days of the law a person with a freehold estate or interest in land could, if necessary, bring a special court action to recover it. It was an action for the "Thing," that is the land, in dispute. The Latin for "Thing" is *Res* and the action was called a real action. The freehold property protected by such an action became known as real property. Movable goods, however, were only protected by a personal action. The owner could pursue his claim against an individual who stole his cattle but, if he succeeded, he might only recover their value and so such goods became known as personal property. There was one type of interest in land, however, which was anomalous in early law. This was a grant of land for a period of years, or a letting, which was regarded as being a personal contractual interest only. Such interests were regarded as a special type of personal property and were called chattels real to distinguish them from other types of movables which were called chattels personal.

Tenures and Estates

English land law, which was adopted in Ireland with subsequent modifications, had its origin in the medieval feudal system. The feudal lord not only determined the services due from his tenant, *i.e.* the tenure, he could also specify the rights the tenant had over the land – what he could do, how long his interest would last, etc. The tenant's rights or interest in the land became known as his estate.

In time the services due to the lord under various tenures were changed to money payments and, when the value of money declined, the dues became worthless and were not collected. Feudal tenure lost its significance and the Tenures Abolition Act (Ireland) 1662 converted most free tenures into Common Socage or simply "freehold" tenures. There are rarely any "services" attached nowadays to freehold tenure and any that might exist would be in the form of money payments similar to a rent. Estates, however, remain fundamental to an understanding of land law. A person with land was in theory not the full "owner" of it but had a certain interest which was defined by the rights he could exercise over it. Could he dispose of it during his lifetime and dictate who was to receive it after he died? Could he fully exploit the land? The answers depended on the interest, or estate, which he owned.

There are three types of estate: fee simple, estate tail, life estate.

The Fee Simple Estate in Freehold Land

Closest to absolute ownership

The most extensive ownership interest recognised by the law is that which may be exercised by a person who has a fee simple estate in land (including buildings) held on freehold tenure; the person with a fee simple estate has the widest powers of enjoyment of the land and the greatest rights over its disposal or 'alienation' as it is called in law. He has rights not only to the land surface, crops, and buildings, but also to the air-space above and the minerals under the land. A fee simple owner may even have property rights in clouds over his land if decisions in other common law jurisdictions are followed. The Texas Appeal Court, held that cloud seeding to modify the weather represents an infringement of the owner's property rights (*Southwest Weather Research* v. *Rounsaville,* 1958). The landowner is entitled to other benefits of nature. He is entitled to enjoy whatever flow of air there is over his property in an unpolluted state. If a stream runs through his land he has a right to the accustomed flow of unpolluted water and to use a reasonable quantity of the water for normal purposes such as watering stock. He has hunting and fishing rights and the right to have his land supported, in its natural state, by the land of his neighbours.

Restrictions in the interests of the public

These rights have been modified to some extent by common law and statute. For example, aircraft have a right to overfly property in a reasonable way and, by virtue of the Air Navigation and Transport Act 1936, this will not give rise to an action in tort for trespass or nuisance. The property owner would not be entitled to create an obstruction to aircraft near an air-strip. A householder who erected a 52 foot T.V. aerial said to interfere with the flightpath of aircraft landing at Casement Aerodrome, Baldonnell was ordered by the High Court in August 1979 to lower it to 19 feet 9 inches.

Although the fee simple owner of land was entitled to all minerals under the land this right has been modified by statute. The Minerals Development Act 1979, with some exceptions, gives the Minister with responsibility for industry the exclusive right to work all the mineral resources in the state. The rights of the fee simple owner of land have also been seriously modified to provide for common needs of the community. State agencies such as the Board of Works, County Councils, Urban Corporations, the E.S.B., P. and T., Health Boards and the Land Commission have been given considerable power to enter, use, or acquire landed property to fulfil their statutory functions. The uses to which land and buildings can be put have been cut back by the need to obtain planning permission under the Local Government (Planning and Development) Acts 1963 and 1976.

The common law, too, does not allow an owner to make use of his land in a way which interferes with the rights of others. Under the tort of nuisance, he may be held liable for noise, smells and fumes which result from the use of his land and which substantially interfere with his neighbour's enjoyment of their properties.

Modified fee simple interests. A holder's fee simple interest in land need not give him all the rights to enjoyment ideally associated with such an estate. He may have a modified fee simple and not a fee simple absolute. A determinable fee simple is one which can come to an end on the happening of some event which may never occur, such as a grant to a daughter until she marries. Within certain limits rights may be given to, or acquired by, other properties or persons which reduce the fee simple or other owner's right of enjoyment. These are called incorporeal hereditaments or servitudes and are of various kinds. A fee simple or other owner may have his land subjected to easements in which case the owner of the other property may have rights over his land such as a right of way, right to water, light, support, or a right to have fencing maintained. Similarly a neighbouring property holder or other persons may have profits (or profits à prendre) in the land which might allow them fishing or shooting rights, a right to take turf (turbary) or wood (estover). The land may also be the subject of a restrictive covenant or contract under which the owner may be obliged to restrict the use of his land for the benefit of a neighbouring landholder. These covenants are very often intended to prevent undesirable development to maintain the value of amenities of the benefiting land.

The transfer of a fee simple estate

One of the characteristics of a fee simple estate was that it allowed the holder to dispose of his interest, in whole or in part. The holder could make a transfer *inter vivos*, *i.e.* during his lifetime, or on his death by will. Dispositions during life have normally been made by a deed of conveyance since the passing of the Real Property Act 1845. Because the person transferring property may pass his full interest or a lesser one, the law requires the use of distinguishing words, called words of limitation, to define the extent of the interest granted. At common law the words "and his heirs" had to be used to pass a fee simple estate but since the Conveyancing Act 1881 the words "in fee simple" are normally used. If the grant was made in a will any words which showed an intention to give a fee simple estate sufficed. Under the Wills Act 1837 the testator's full interest passed unless there was evidence of a different intention. Similarly, under section 94 of the Succession Act 1965 any disposition without words of limitation will pass the testator's whole estate unless a contrary intention appears from the will. Under this Act, however, the fee simple owner is no longer completely free to dispose of his interest because he must consider the rights of his surviving spouse. It should be noted in relation to acquisition of property by a business that a disposition to a company in its own name and without words of limitation is sufficient to pass a fee simple estate when the company is incorporated.

The Fee Tail Estate

Keeping the land in the family
The fee tail estate emerged as a means of keeping land in the family by preventing descendants from alienating it. The word "fee" meant that the interest was inheritable and capable of lasting for as long as there were heirs. The word "tail" is from the Norman word "taillé" meaning cut down or reduced in value. The fee tail estate was "cut down" in the sense that the holder could not dispose of the full interest as he wished because the estate passed automatically to the general or specified descendants of the original grantee. When there were no more eligible descendants the estate tail ended and the land reverted to the grantor or to those entitled to the interest he had retained when making the grant, namely, a fee simple in reversion.

The common law required special words of limitation which had to include the word "heirs" to give an inheritable estate, and additional words indicating an interest to go to the descendants, *e.g.* "to A and the heirs of his body." The law was not as particular about the words used to grant an estate in fee tail in a will, and under the Conveyancing Act 1881 the words "to A in tail" were permitted. The estate created could be a general entail to all descendants but giving preference to males, or a special entail usually confined to male descendants only. The rights of the tenant in tail to enjoyment and use of the land are much the same as those of the fee simple owner.

The Life Estate

An interest for the life of the holder
The third freehold interest in land is the life estate which is an interest lasting for the life of the holder or some other named person. On the death of the person in question the life estate ends. There is

no interest which the former owner can dispose of to his heirs and the land passes to anybody who holds a remainder interest, or reverts back to the grantor or his estate. A life estate is created when a fee simple owner grants an interest by deed or in a will for life using such words as "to A for life." Obviously this grant does not exhaust the grantor's estate so that he continues to hold a fee simple estate in reversion which will take effect after A's life estate ends on A's death. If the grantor is still alive the land will return to him in fee simple or else go to his successors in title.

The grantor could also have given a grant "to A for life, with remainder to B for life," thus creating successive interests. B has a life estate in remainder, *i.e.* after A's death, and the grantor still retains a fee simple in reversion. If a life tenant transfers his estate to another during his lifetime, the new holder cannot have a greater interest than the life tenant himself had. The new holder has an interest which will only last as long as it would have done had it not been transferred. He holds a life estate for the life of another also called an estate *"pur autre vie."* Such an estate for the life of another could be created directly by a grant "To A for the life of B with remainder to B's son C in fee simple" which would give an interest to A while B lived.

Leasehold estates

The three basic estates or interests in land held in freehold tenure (freehold estates) did not meet fully the needs of commerce. Land owners began to make contracts which would give others the use of the land for a fixed period in return for money payments. A new type of estate in land became recognised by the law and was variously called a term of years, a lease, a demise, or a tenancy; all names for the same kind of interest.

The main difference in an estate created by lease is that it is of fixed or definite duration whereas freehold estates are of indefinite duration.

Legal and Equitable Estates

In earlier times, the law could not cope with complex arrangements concerning property. An owner might wish to set property aside for the benefit of some members of his family, or for charity, but there was no way of doing this other than by granting a fee tail estate which was of limited usefulness. The practice emerged of the property owner making a grant to a named person or persons (let us say to Murphy) but which was stated to be "to the use of" another

(Clarke). The common law courts could not take into account the wishes of the grantor. In common law Murphy owned the property and could do as he wished with it. He had a legal interest which was a legal fee simple or life estate or some other such interest depending on the grant made by the grantor. The Court of Chancery or Equity, however, developed rules based on justice and fair dealing and would not allow a person who was given property for the benefit of another to convert it to his own use. In equity, therefore, Clarke was the "real" owner of the property as it was intended for his benefit. He had an equitable estate which was an equitable fee simple or equitable life estate or some such other equitable interest depending on the grant made by the grantor.

Eventually these "uses" developed into the modern trust under which property is given to one person called the trustee, to hold for the benefit of another person called the beneficiary. The trustee has a legal estate and the beneficiary has an equitable estate or interest. Equitable estates may arise therefore because they are expressly created by a trust. They may also arise because equity implies from the circumstances that one person is obliged in conscience to hold the property in trust for another. Thus where a grant is made but the grantee gets no legal estate due to a failure to fulfil some formality, the grantee will nevertheless have an equitable estate. Equitable interests may be implied in other situations also. A purchaser who has an enforceable contract to buy a legal estate has an equitable interest implied from the contract. Where a husband or wife contributes to the purchase of a house held in one of their names the other has an equitable interest in proportion to the contribution made to the purchase (*C.* v. *C.*, H.C. 1976; *Heavey* v. *Heavey*, H.C. 1977). The same principle probably applies to a business (*K.* v. *K.*, H.C. 1978).

Settlements

To make provision for the family

The earliest method of doing this was by means of the fee tail estate which, as we have seen, was rather crude. The development of the trust and the associated recognition of beneficial interests resulted in a more sophisticated method of providing for the family by means of the strict settlement or the trust for sale.

A settlement is a disposition of property for the purpose of creating beneficial or equitable interests, usually in favour of a number of family members. A slightly different type of settlement may be used when the landowner is not concerned with keeping the land in the family. In a trust for sale settlement, the land is conveyed to trustees for the purpose of sale and reinvestment and the proceeds are held on trust for the beneficiaries of the settlement.

The Settled Land Acts

Settlements of land were useful in providing for the settlor's family but left the person in possession in a handicapped position. The estate was burdened with charges for the benefit of family members and the life tenant was merely a manager with limited powers to work the land. Incumbered Estates Courts, and later Landed Estates Courts, were established to facilitate the sale of such properties. The powers of the life tenant to manage the land were increased at first by the Settled Estates Acts and later by the Settled Land Acts 1882–90. These latter Acts in particular allowed the tenant for life to deal with the land almost as if he was the fee simple owner but made him responsible for the protection of the interests of other beneficiaries. The tenant for life has power of leasing the settled land or he may sell it. If he sells it, however, the purchase money must be paid to the trustees for reinvestment in other land or suitable securities which devolve in turn as if they were settled land.

Co-Ownership

Just as the law recognises that legal and equitable interests can exist in land simultaneously, so also it accepts that two or more individuals may be co-owners and have concurrent interests in the same property. The most usual kinds of co-ownership are called joint tenancy and tenancy in common.

Joint tenancy arises under a deed or a will when land is conveyed or devised to two or more persons without any intention of giving such persons distinct shares. In a joint tenancy the holders make up one owner in law. The interest is characterised by what are called "The Four Unities" and the right of survivorship. The co-owners are entitled to possession of the whole land; they have the same estate in the land; they have the same title; and the interest of each started at the same time. Survivorship or the *jus accrescendi* is a rule that on the death of one joint tenant his share passes to the surviving joint tenants.

Where there is a tenancy in common, the co-owners hold undivided, although not necessarily equal, shares in the same property but either one of the unities is missing or it was intended that they should hold distinct shares. Co-owners holding a tenancy in common are each entitled to possession of the whole of the land but there is no right of survivorship.

Joint tenancy will cease when one of the unities is broken and both joint tenancy and tenancy in common may be terminated by partition or by one co-owner acquiring the shares of the other co-owners by survivorship or otherwise.

Fee Farm Grants in Ireland

A fee farm grant is the conveyance of a fee simple estate subject to the payment of a perpetual rent to the grantor or to his successors in title.

Fee Farm Grants by Statutory Conversion

Certain more unusual fee farm grants arose as a result of statute. Some derived from the conversion of tenancies held by members of the Church of Ireland, Trinity College, and College Authorities into fee farm grants by statutory authority in the last century. Others arose from the conversion of leases for lives renewable forever into fee farm grants under the Renewable Leasehold Conversion Act 1849. Under such a grant a lease was given, usually for three lives, with a covenant to renew for another life in return for payment of a fine when any life died. This arrangement created a leasehold tenure under which the landlord had the usual remedies but it gave the tenant a freehold estate *pur autre vie*. The 1849 Act gave such lessees a right to obtain a fee farm grant and stipulated that any such lease created in the future would operate as a fee farm grant also. Section 74 of the Landlord and Tenant (Amendment) Act 1980 has converted all surviving leases for lives renewable forever into fee simple estates.

Statutory Conversion of Agricultural Tenancies

The "Irish land problem"

The large landholder could not, of course, work all the land himself so, regardless of whether he held his land in fee simple, fee farm grant, or an estate for lives renewable forever, he leased most of it to tenants in return for rent. As a result much of the land came to be let on yearly tenancies to the peasantry under the most onerous terms. The condition of the small farmers was progressively worsened by laws prohibiting agricultural exports, rack-renting, absentee landlords and the growth of population.

Tenants helped to purchase the land

Early attempts at solving the Irish land problem were a failure. The Incumbered Estates Act 1849 was enacted to facilitate the sale of the burdened estates of insolvent landlords and Deasy's Act of 1860 put the landlord and tenant relationship on a negotiated contractual basis. Such measures were of little use to the tenants. Under pressure from the Land League, statutes were passed to give positive protection to the agricultural tenant. These were the Landlord and Tenant (Ireland) Act 1870 and the Land Law (Ireland) Act 1881.

A more radical solution was required and this was found in schemes, funded by the Government, which enabled tenants to buy land from the landlord by paying a purchase annuity over a lengthy period. The first successful land purchase scheme was introduced by the Land Act 1885 (the Ashbourne Act) and was followed by similar schemes in 1891, 1903, and 1909 under which 65 per cent. of the land (about 11 million acres) was purchased by tenants. The process was completed after the formation of the Irish Free State by the compulsory transfer of tenanted land from the landlords to tenants for a standard price based on the judicially determined fair rent. This policy was initiated by the Land Act 1923 which entrusted the work to a reconstituted Land Commission, whose powers were extended by later statutes, particularly the Land Acts of 1933 and 1965. As a result almost 90 per cent. of Irish land has passed through the hands of the Land Commission, resulting in the elimination of the old landlord system. Most farms are now held by resident owners who have a fee simple estate in their land subject to any purchase annuity or other charge.

The Reform of Urban and Commercial Tenancies

Most urban land was also owned by large landowners and leased to tenants in much the same way as agricultural holdings. Until the Landlord and Tenant Act 1870 the same law applied to the urban as to the agricultural tenant. From that date on, however, agricultural tenants received special protection and their holdings were rapidly converted under the land purchase schemes. The first attempt to help the urban tenant was by means of the Town Tenants (Ireland) Act 1906 which was not a success. Rent restriction on a limited scale was introduced in 1915 to offset wartime housing shortages. The system was retained after the war and was reformed by means of the Rent Restrictions Act 1946, and again under the Rent Restrictions Act 1960 as amended by the Rent Restrictions Act 1967, and by the Landlord and Tenant (Amendment) Act 1971. Certain provisions of the 1960 Act have, however, been held to be unconstitutional (*Blake* v. *The Attorney-General*, S.C. 1981).

A major reforming statute, called the Landlord and Tenant Act, was enacted in 1931. Under this Act tenants who held under relatively long-term building or proprietary leases were given the right to claim a reversionary lease on the ending of their existing leases. This right was amended and extended by the Landlord and Tenant (Amendment) Act 1943 and the Landlord and Tenant (Reversionary Leases) Act 1958. These Acts have been repealed and the right to a reversionary lease is now governed by Part III of the Landlord and Tenant (Amendment) Act 1980. The second set of reforms, introduced by the Landlord and Tenant Act 1931, was designed to protect other uncontrolled non-agricultural tenants. These reforms covered a tenant's right to obtain compensation for improvements made to the holding, a right of an occupying tenant in certain circumstances to seek a new tenancy at a fair rent or to obtain compensation for disturbance. The 1931 Act was eventually repealed and most of its provisions were re-enacted in the Landlord and Tenant (Amendment) Act 1980.

The Typical Business Lease

Under section 4 of the Landlord and Tenant (Amendment) Act 1860 (Deasy's Act) the relationship of landlord and tenant arises "in all cases in which there shall be an agreement by one party to hold land from or under another in consideration of any rent." All tenancies are therefore based on an express or implied contract whether verbal or contained in a lease. Practically all modern business tenancies will be created by lease which is defined in the 1860 Act as "any instrument in writing, whether under seal or not, containing a contract of tenancy in respect of any lands, in consideration of a rent or return." "Rent" includes any "sum or return" so that it may be in the form of money or services and goods. In either case the rent is the consideration or return which the tenant gives to the landlord in exchange for possession and use of the property. There is unlikely to be any contract unless the parties agree on the material terms essential to any letting, namely, the extent of the property leased, the parties to the agreement, the commencement (*White* v. *McMahon*, Ir.C.P. 1886, *Kearns* v. *Manning*, S.C. 1935) and duration of the tenancy, and the rent (*McQuaid* v. *Lynam*, H.C. 1965). In practice other terms will also be included dealing with such important matters as the use which can be made of the property by the tenant, liability for outgoings such as rates and electricity, and liability for repair and insurance.

The rent

In a time of inflation a fixed rent may be a grave disadvantage to a landlord in a long letting. A rent review clause is often used, therefore, to allow the landlord to periodically increase the rent provided the premises is not subject to rent control. Such increases may be pre-determined, may be based on an escalator clause, or be subject to agreement or arbitration.

Use of the premises

The letting agreement may specify the use which the tenant can make of the premises, otherwise he has the same rights of enjoyment of the premises as his landlord. The tenant is always, of course, subject to the Planning Acts and the law of nuisance. His general liability for acts of waste, which are injurious to the landlord's interest, is set out in the 1860 Act. To protect his own business interests, a landlord may include a restrictive covenant which prohibits the use of the premises for a particular business, or for any business other than one specified, without the lessor's consent. Thus in *Green Property Co. Ltd.* v. *Shalaine Modes Ltd.,* (H.C. 1978) an injunction was granted to the lessor where a sub-tenant was selling toys on the premises contrary to such a covenant. General covenants are also frequently included which prohibit "offensive, noxious, and dangerous trades." Whether or not a trade is offensive depends on how appropriate it is to the locality in which the premises is situated.

Where, however, a leased premises is a "tenement" under the Landlord and Tenant (Amendment) Act 1980 and this usually includes business premises, the tenant has certain rights relating to the use of, and improvements to, the premises. Covenants in a lease absolutely prohibiting a change of use or improvement to the premises are to be construed as covenants prohibiting such changes or improvements "without the licence or consent of the lessor." It is also provided that such covenants, notwithstanding any express provision to the contrary, are subject to a proviso "that the licence or consent shall not be unreasonably withheld." In these lettings the landlord's rights are, therefore, restricted. The Act does allow him to be reimbursed for expenses, including any increase in rates or taxes, caused by the alteration in the use of the premises. He cannot charge any fine or increase the rent for giving consent to a change in use unless it will involve structural alterations which will change the identity of the premises (ss.67, 68).

Assignment and sub-letting

Lettings often include a term which prohibits or restricts the tenant from assigning or sub-letting his interest to others. The tenant may be required, for example, to obtain the landlord's consent. In the absence of such a restriction the tenant can assign his interest in any of the ways mentioned in section 9 of the 1860 Act, he can sub-let by making a letting agreement in the ordinary way. It is provided by the 1860 Act (ss. 12 and 13) that all agreements contained, or implied, in tenancies are enforceable by or against successors in title of both the landlord and tenant.

If, however, the leased premises is a tenement under the 1980 Act any bar on the alienation of the tenement will be construed "as if it were a covenant prohibiting or restricting such alienation without the licence or consent of the lessor" (s.66). As in the case of improvements or change of use (above) the licence or consent of the landlord cannot be "unreasonably withheld." In *White* v. *Carlisle Trust Ltd.* (H.C. 1977) consent to change the use of the premises from a tailoring and outfitting business to a confectionery business was deemed to be unreasonably withheld as the only ground for refusal was possible prejudice to other tenants. If the lease is for a term over 40 years and involves the tenant in erecting or doing substantial work to buildings, then, if there are more than seven years of the term to run, the tenant can alienate his interest by merely notifying the landlord within one month of the transaction and there is no need to get his consent.

Usual covenants by the landlord and the tenant

There is usually a covenant or promise by the landlord that he will not interfere with the quiet possession or enjoyment of the leased property by the tenant provided the tenant abides by the agreement. In the absence of an express provision to the contrary such a covenant, and a covenant by the landlord that he has a good title to make the lease, are implied into the agreement by section 41 of the 1860 Act.

The tenant is usually bound by a number of covenants such as to pay the rent, pay specified expenses such as rates and electricity, to undertake routine repairs, to allow the landlord to examine the premises and to allow him to re-enter if the rent is not paid. The tenant may be restricted, as already noted, in relation to alterations, improvements, use, assignment and sub-letting of the leased property. In some cases the tenant may be obliged to effect adequate insurance on the property for the benefit and protection of both himself and the landlord. It is important that such an insuring clause be carefully studied and implemented so as to avoid loss through damage to the tenant's own interest or arising from his contractual liability for damage to the landlord's interest. In *Taylor* v. *Moremiles Tyre Service* (H.C. 1978), for example, the plaintiff lessor was awarded £19,000 damages against the defendant lessee who had covenanted to insure and reinstate the premises which were destroyed by fire. In the absence of express provision to the contrary it is implied in every lease that the tenant shall pay the rent and other outgoings for which he is responsible, and that he shall maintain the premises "in good and substantial repair and condition" and give peaceable possession to the landlord on the termination of the lease (1860 Act, s.42). These obligations are altered in relation to rent controlled dwellings and "tenements" where the tenant may have a right to a new tenancy among other things. In any event the tenant will be entitled to remove his fixtures if they can be removed without substantial damage to the freehold or to the fixture itself, if he is not forbidden by agreement to do so, and provided he was not obliged to provide the fixtures and provided he did not erect them in violation of his agreement. The landlord is entitled to reasonable compensation for any damage caused to the premises by the removal of the fixtures (1860 Act, s.17).

The determination or ending of the tenancy

If the tenancy is for a fixed term or period it will end when the period agreed on has expired. A periodic tenancy is usually ended by the landlord giving the tenant a valid notice to quit. If no period of notice has been agreed the amount of notice required is regulated by common law. A week is required to terminate a weekly tenancy, a month for a monthly tenancy, and six months in the case of a yearly tenancy. A tenancy may also end by merger when the tenant acquires the landlord's interest or some third party acquires both interests.

The tenancy agreement may allow the landlord or the tenant to end the tenancy at an earlier date and they may always agree to do so. The landlord may also be entitled to re-enter, or to forfeit the lease and re-enter for breach of covenant by the tenant. The landlord can re-enter peacefully but not forcibly even if agreed to in the lease. If re-entry is resisted the landlord must bring an action of ejectment for recovery of possession.

Statutory Protection for Business Tenants

Protected tenements

The most important protection given to the business tenant is provided by the Landlord and Tenant (Amendment) Act 1980. We have already seen how it extends the tenant's right to alienate, improve, or change the use of the leased premises. It also gives the tenant, in certain circumstances, a right to a new tenancy and rights to compensation for disturbance and improvements.

The rights given apply to "tenements," an artificial concept defined by section 5 of the Act. A tenement is defined to exclude agricultural lettings and means any premises consisting of a defined portion of a building, or of land covered wholly or partly by buildings where the land not covered by buildings is subsidiary and ancillary to the buildings. Such premises must be held by the occupier on a tenancy and the letting must not have been made either for the temporary convenience of either party or be dependent on the continuance in any office, or employment, or appointment of the tenant.

Compensation for improvements

Under Part IV of the 1980 Act a tenant who quits his tenement, otherwise than by surrender or because of non-payment of rent, is entitled to be paid compensation by the landlord for every improvement made which adds to the letting value of the tenement on the termination date, and which is suitable to the character of the tenement. The amount of compensation may be agreed on by the landlord and tenant or in the absence of agreement it will be an amount determined by the court as "the capitalised value of such addition to the letting value of the tenement at the termination of the tenancy as the Court determines to be attributable to the improvements" (s.47.(1)). The court may consider all relevant circumstances but cannot, in any event, allow a capitalised value exceeding 15 times the annual amount of addition to letting value. Thus if improvements by the tenant are estimated to add £156 to the annual letting value of the tenement then the maximum compensation will be £156 × 15 or £2,340.

There are some restrictions on the right to compensation as where the improvements were made before the passing of the Landlord and Tenant Act 1931 and were in contravention of the tenancy contract. No compensation is available where the improvements were made without notice after the passing of the 1931 Act and the landlord satisfies the court either that he was prejudiced by the lack of notice, or the improvement was in contravention of any covenant in the contract or that the improvement injures the amenity or convenience of the neighbourhood.

Improvement notices

Detailed procedures are set out in the Act concerning improvement notices. The tenant may serve a notice concerning the proposed improvement on his landlord together with details of the work involved and an estimate of cost, and a copy of planning permission, if required. The landlord may within a month serve the tenant with an improvement consent, or an improvement undertaking (where he intends to have the work done himself) or an improvement objection. Where the landlord undertakes to make the improvements he may increase the rent upon the completion of the improvements, but if the tenant disagrees with the increase he may withdraw the improvement notice, or the increase in rent may be determined by the court. The landlord has only limited grounds on which he may object to the improvement. Where he does object the tenant may withdraw the improvement notice or apply to the court for an order authorising him to carry out the improvements. In some circumstances (such as when there is less than five years of the lease to run and the landlord plans to rebuild or develop the property) the court will reject the application. In other cases it may allow the improvement with or without modification. The 1980 Act includes a procedure whereby the landlord can also notify any superior landlord of proposed improvements so that he himself can also qualify for compensation.

Right to a new tenancy

The tenant of a "tenement," subject to certain exceptions, has a right to a new tenancy under Part Two of the 1980 Act in the following situations:

(a) Where the tenement was for three years continuously occupied by the tenant or his predecessors in title and bona fide used wholly or partly for the purpose of carrying on a business. The court may disregard a temporary break in the use of the tenement if it considers it reasonable to do so. "Business" is widely defined by the Act to include trade, profession or business, whether or not carried on for gain or reward, and any activity for providing cultural, charitable, educational, social or sporting services, for the public service, or for carrying out the functions of Local Authorities, Health Boards and Harbour Authorities.

(b) Where the tenement was for the previous 20 years continuously in the occupation of the tenant or of his predecessors in title; or

(c) Where such substantial improvements have been made on the tenement that they account for not less than half of the letting value of the tenement.

The right to a new tenancy also applies to dwellings decontrolled by the Rent Restrictions (Amendment) Act 1967 and to business premises decontrolled by the Rent Restrictions Act 1960.

Perhaps the most important of the above from the business viewpoint is the first, which is sometimes called the business equity, which gives the business tenant of three years' standing a right to renewal. Efforts have been made to frustrate the acquisition of this right, especially by the oil companies, by granting the tenancy to a dummy company rather than the filling station operator or by insisting that the operator enters a caretakers' agreement. In *Gatien Motor Co. Ltd.* v. *The Continental Oil Co. of Ireland* (S.C. 1979) the court refused an application for a new tenancy where the plaintiff was made to enter a caretakers' agreement to prevent him from acquiring a business equity of renewal. Although the 1980 Act states that any attempt to contract out of its provisions is void, the use of the caretaker agreement was upheld because the tenant had not been allowed to acquire rights and could not contract out of what he never had. In *Irish Shell* v. *John Costello Ltd.* (S.C. 1981), however, the court held that three agreements made between November 1971 and February 1974 created the relationship of landlord and tenant between the parties and gave the defendant a right to a new lease.

The terms of the new tenancy

Such persons are entitled to a new tenancy in the "tenement" on such terms as may be agreed on by them and their landlords or, where they fail to agree, on such terms as shall be fixed by the court. Normally the court applies the same provisions as in the existing tenancy. The 1980 Act empowers the court to fix the duration of the tenancy "at thirty-five years or such less term as the tenant may nominate" (s.23). The rent will be the "gross rent" which in the opinion of the court "a willing lessee not already in occupation would give and a willing lessor would take for the tenement" less any allowance for improvements made by the tenant or his predecessors in title. The courts have recognised that some allowance may be needed to account for the effects of inflation on rent (*Byrne* v. *Loftus*, S.C. 1978) and this is partly provided for in the 1980 Act by allowing the landlord or tenant to apply to the court for a rent review at five-yearly intervals (s.24).

A tenant will not, however, be entitled to a new tenancy, and neither will he be eligible for compensation for disturbance, in the following circumstances (s.17):

(a) If the tenancy has been terminated because of non-payment of rent;

(b) Where it was terminated because of a breach by the tenant of a covenant of the tenancy;

(c) The tenant terminated the tenancy by notice of surrender or otherwise;

(d) The tenancy was terminated by notice to quit given by the landlord "for good and sufficient reason," or if terminated in some other way and the landlord refused to renew it for good and sufficient reason or, if he had been asked to renew it, would have good and sufficient reason for refusing. It must be a good and sufficient reason arising from the action or conduct of the tenant.

Compensation for disturbance

There are some other situations also in which the tenant will not be entitled to a new tenancy but in which he will, if he has a business equity of renewal, have a right to compensation for disturbance. The tenant will have no right to a new tenancy where the landlord is to pull down and rebuild or reconstruct the property or where he requires vacant possession to carry out a scheme of development for which he has planning permission. A new tenancy may be refused when the landlord is a development authority and the tenement is in an "obsolete area" as defined by the Planning Act 1963, or where the landlord is a local authority and possession will be required within five years of a tenement which it can compulsorily acquire. A new tenancy may also be refused where it would be inconsistent with good estate management.

In these situations, however, a tenant with a business equity of renewal is entitled instead to be paid compensation for disturbance by the landlord. The amount of the compensation will usually be "pecuniary loss, damage or expense which the tenant sustains or incurs or will sustain or incur by reason of his quitting the tenement and which is the direct consequence of that quitting" (s.58). The compensation is payable on the delivery of possession to the landlord or one month after the amount due is settled, whichever is later. If the money is not paid the tenant is entitled to apply for a new tenancy instead.

Acquiring a Premises

A legal interest in business premises is normally acquired by the purchase of a suitable freehold or leasehold interest. The transactions are similar but there are some important differences. In both cases negotiations between the vendor and purchaser result in a contract of sale. A contract for the sale of land must usually be in writing or be evidenced by a note or memorandum in writing to be enforceable. As we shall see when discussing contract law, however, a contract without writing may still be enforceable if there was a sufficient act of part performance to establish its existence. Once the purchaser has an enforceable contract he has an equitable interest or equitable lease as the case may be.

Transferring a freehold estate

In most cases there will be no enforceable agreement until a contract is signed by both parties or until an "exchange of contracts" has taken place. In the latter case the vendor's solicitor sends a draft contract to the purchaser's solicitor and if it is approved it is signed by the purchaser and returned. The vendor signs a counterpart document and sends it to the purchaser. There is now a binding contract as both parties have a written copy signed by the opposite party.

The legal freehold estate, however, must be transferred by deed and a number of important steps must be taken to protect the purchaser before the price is fully paid and the deed executed. The vendor's title to the property must be examined to find out if it is good. The purchaser's solicitor is sent copies of the documents of title. He investigates the title and if further information is required he will submit "requisitions on title" which are queries on title which must be answered satisfactorily by the vendors. If satisfied as to title, the purchasers will submit a draft deed of conveyance which must be agreed to by both sides. Immediately before completion date the purchasers make a search in the Registry of Deeds to see if any incumbrances such as mortgages or charges have been registered against the property. If everything is in order the transfer is completed. The purchasers pay the money outstanding and the vendors deliver the signed and sealed deed of conveyance and usually hand over the title deeds. The purchaser now has the legal estate that the vendor previously had. He can take over possession of the premises and has such rights as the holder cf such an estate is entitled to in law.

Transferring a leasehold interest

A leasehold interest in business premises may be obtained under a new lease or by the assignment of an existing lease or tenancy. Where a person has a long-term lease at a low rent he has a substantial interest in the land which he may wish to sell. In such a case the transfer to a purchaser will be similar to the transfer of a freehold estate. The parties will normally enter a written contract and the purchasers will demand that the vendor shows a good title. A search is made to check for incumbrances of the land before the completion date. In this case, however, the completion takes the form of an assignment and not a conveyance. An assignment of a leasehold interest is the transfer or disposition by the vending lessee to the purchaser. The vendor is the assignor and the purchaser is the assignee. The old lease continues as formerly save that the assignee-purchaser takes the place of the former lessee. An assignment of a leasehold interest may be made by any instrument in writing signed by the assignor, or his agent lawfully authorised in writing, but is usually made by a deed of assignment (1860 Act, s.9).

Creating a new leasehold interest

At one time a leasehold was a type of tenure but since the Landlord and Tenant Amendment Act Ireland 1860 (Deasy's Act) all lettings are based on contract. A leasehold interest in property is created therefore by a contract under which the lessor or landlord grants the interest specified in the agreement to the lessee or tenant, in return for a rent. The person who grants a tenancy will usually own some freehold interest in the land, such as a fee simple estate. Sometimes, however, the grantor will hold the property as the tenant of another landlord. In the latter case the grantor cannot give a greater interest than he himself holds and can only assign his interest (as above) or sub-let all or part of his interest if the terms of his own lease do not prohibit assignment and sub-letting. A sub-lease, or under-lease as it sometimes is called, granted by a tenant, makes that tenant a landlord as regards the person holding from him. A business, for example, which leases a floor in an office block may not need the space and can sub-let part or all of it, if permitted to do so by the lease or by the 1980 Act.

If the tenancy is to last for less than a year or if it is a periodic tenancy not greater than from year to year, no writing is required and an oral or spoken contract is sufficient. Where the tenancy to be granted is greater than one from year to year the contract is required to be in writing or by a deed, signed by the landlord or his authorised agent (1860 Act, s.4). Where a business proposes to enter a substantial lease agreement the usual precautions are taken to enter a substantial lease agreement the usual precautions are taken to check the lessor's title and the terms of the tenancy offered.

Planning permission problems

Although the right of private property is protected by the

Constitution nobody has a right to do what they please with the land they own. Even the fee simple owner had obligations to other property owners at common law. The Constitution itself recognises that the natural right to private property must be regulated by social justice and reconciled with the common good. The common good demands that haphazard and destructive development must be prevented. For this reason the Oireachtas has enacted the Local Government (Planning and Development) Acts of 1963 and 1976 which have replaced and adopted many of the provisions of two earlier statutes called the Town and Regional Planning Acts 1934 and 1939.

Under the Planning Acts the local planning authority is obliged to make a development plan for its area. A person with land in that area cannot carry out any development on his land without permission from the local planning authority unless it was begun before October 1, 1964, or unless it is classified as an exempted development. Permission or refusal for a development is based on the local development plan and the applicant can appeal if necessary to the Planning Board (an Bord Pleanála) which was created on January 1, 1977.

A business, therefore, which is interested in acquiring a premises, whether freehold or leasehold, must consider whether planning permission for the conduct of the business in the premises is, or is likely to be, available. Without such permission the premises may not be of any immediate use. Development includes not only construction and repair work but also a use of the premises substantially different from the previous use made of it. In *Dublin Co. Council* v. *Carey* (1980), for example, the Supreme Court upheld an injunction against the defendant prohibiting him from using land in Clondalkin, Co. Dublin, for the parking of vehicles and storage of hardcore, blocks and other materials. The land had previously been used for agricultural and horticultural purposes and the defendant, who had no permission to change the use of the land, was ordered to clear it. Similarly in *Mayo Co. Council* v. *Byrne* (1979) the Supreme Court ordered the defendants to remove 15 foot advertising signs erected without planning permission at Knock, Co. Mayo, prior to the visit of the Pope.

Mortgages of land as security for debts

Businesses of all types require finance for the carrying on of their activities and may need credit or loans. Most lenders are not prepared to make loans unless the borrower can provide such security to ensure the repayment of the loan. The borrower may be able to provide personal security whereby some other third party agrees to guarantee the repayment of the loan or agrees to indemnify the lender against any loss suffered. The borrower may alternatively provide real security by giving the lender rights to goods or land which he owns. One of the most attractive types of security for most lenders is the mortgage of real property and a bank is often willing to lend a substantial portion of the purchase price of a premises secured by a mortgage on the premises.

A mortgage is any transaction in which a legal or equitable estate is granted by the mortgagor (borrower) to the mortgagee (lender), but the mortgagor remains in possession, and the transfer of ownership is treated merely as security for the money lent. A mortgage may be a legal mortgage or an equitable mortgage and may apply to freehold or leasehold land. A legal mortgage is granted by the borrower executing a deed of conveyance of his freehold, or an assignment or letting of his leasehold estate, to the lender subject to a proviso that the lender must convey it back to him again on the repayment of the debt. An equitable mortgage arises where the lender has a right to compel the borrower to grant a legal mortgage. An equitable mortgage is normally created when the parties agree to create a legal mortgage or by the borrower depositing the title deeds or land certificate with the lender with the intention of treating the land as security. The legal mortgagee (lender) has a number of remedies which he can exercise if the mortgagor fails to repay the money borrowed. He can, under certain circumstances, sell the property, or apply to the court for an order for sale; he can take possession of the property or appoint a receiver to collect the rents or profits from it; or he may sue the mortgagor on his personal promise to repay the money lent. The mortgagor too is protected in law from being exploited by the lender. In addition to having possession of the property he retains an equitable interest called the "equity of redemption" which is in effect a bundle of equitable rights including the right to redeem. The borrower redeems by repaying the loan and having the property reconveyed to him. This equity of redemption can be a very valuable property interest which can be bought and sold and transferred like any other property interest.

Registration

There are two distinct and mutually exclusive systems for registering interests in Irish land. The older is the registry of deeds system which was established under the Registration of Deeds Act (Ireland) 1707. This Act and the amendments made to it, allow for the voluntary registration of memorials or synopses of deeds and other documents dealing with interests in land in the Registry Office. Failure to register might mean a loss of priority so that it became standard practice to register deeds of conveyance on sale, voluntary deeds of gift, mortgages and other such interests. Letters or any other memorandum concerning a deposit of title deeds may require to be registered otherwise the deposit may be held to rank lower in priority to subsequent registered mortgages as happened in *Fullerton* v. *Provincial Bank of Ireland* (1903). For this reason the bank may request a customer to sign a memorandum withdrawing and cancelling correspondence prior to the equitable mortgage. The mortgage then becomes a purely verbal one, not requiring registration, but which retains its priority as the absence of the title deeds puts the holders of charges registered thereafter on notice of the bank's interest.

The other system dates back to 1865 but was only firmly established under the Registration of Title Act 1891, which has been repealed and replaced by the Registration of Title Act 1964. The purpose of the system is to simplify transfers of land by registering the ownership or title to it. A central office in Dublin is responsible for registration of all land but duplicates of the registers are also kept in the various counties. Land bought out by tenants under the Land Purchase Acts had to be registered and under the 1964 Act registration can be made compulsory in counties to be specified. Registration is already compulsory in counties Carlow, Laois and Meath, and, unless registered, the transfer of land will be void. Registration is conclusive evidence of the owner's title and also of any "right, privilege, appurtenance or burden" appearing on the register. When the land is registered a land certificate is issued to the person registered as owner and must be produced whenever any later transaction relating to the land comes up for registration. The certificate is an exact copy of the register and indicates the owner's title. A deposit of the land certificate as security for a loan is similar to the deposit of title deeds in that it may create an equitable mortgage. A certified copy of the registry entry, however, is not the same as the land certificate as it is merely evidence of the title at the date of issue and does not suggest that no changes have been made since. The objective is to eventually have all land in Ireland registered and when that happens it is hoped that transactions involving land will be faster and less complex than they are at present.

4 Business Transactions and the Law of Contract

The "contract" is the most important legal mechanism for business activity. In essence a contract is an agreement which the law regards as binding on the parties who enter into it. Partnerships, tenancies, and sales of land are based on contract. Almost every transaction made by, with, or on behalf of a business will be based on and regulated by the principles of contract. Such transactions include the purchase of raw materials and other requirements, sale of goods, hiring of employees, acceptance or provision of services, appointment of salesmen or other agents, provision of credit and insurance, and granting of franchises and licences. This list is not exhaustive.

Freedom of contract

The common law view of contract is founded on the idea that people should be free to make whatever agreement they wish. Within well-defined limits, the parties are allowed to make "law" binding on themselves. It was believed in the nineteenth century that the maximum good could be obtained by interfering with people as little as possible. The courts felt that they should not interfere with freely negotiated contracts but should merely provide a machinery by which the intention of the contracting parties could be put into effect, or at least to provide a remedy against a party who failed to fulfil his undertaking. Notions of "freedom of contract" and "sanctity of contract" still account for many of the principles of contract law. Freedom of contract was, however, always subject to some limitation. Some agreements were not enforceable because they were illegal or contrary to the public interest or because of fraud, duress, mistake or lack of a required formality such as writing.

Protecting the weaker party

In the course of time it became all too obvious that complete freedom of contract put weaker parties, particularly consumers, in the power of big business endowed with bargaining strength or monopoly privilege. In contracts made by parties of unequal bargaining power, agreement becomes increasingly artificial especially with the widespread use of standard form contracts and exemption of liability clauses.

The State has been forced by such realities to interfere directly with freedom of contract to redress the balance in favour of the weaker party. We have examined statutory interference in tenancies in favour of tenants. There are many other legislative interferences with freedom of contract which affect, for example, sale of goods, hire-purchase, moneylending and employment contracts. The legislature achieves its objectives by implying terms, in favour of the weaker party, into these contracts regardless of the wishes of the parties. Despite these modifications, however, the law of contract is still essentially based on enforcement of the freely negotiated agreement of the parties themselves.

THE FORMATION OF A CONTRACT

In order to enforce a right under an alleged agreement a person must first satisfy the court that a contract giving such a right exists. Contractual rights and duties can only flow from the existence of a contract. In practice there will be no dispute about the reality of the agreement in the vast majority of cases. Although some contracts are made under seal or in writing, most are made without formality when, *e.g.* people buy goods in shops, order a meal in a restaurant, rent accommodation, take up employment, or use public transport. Most of us make such agreements every day without realising that we are making legally valid contracts. The common misconception, that an agreement has no legal significance unless it is in writing, is untrue. There are some agreements which the law will not enforce unless certain formalities are observed—contracts involving an interest in land, *e.g.* must be evidenced by a note or memorandum in writing. These are, however, the exceptions rather than the rule, although any contract may be put into writing if the parties so wish.

The three requirements for a valid contract
A typical commercial arrangement or agreement will usually be a legally enforceable contract. In the event of a dispute arising over the existence of the contract, the court must first determine this issue before it can adjudicate on any alleged liability arising from it. Using established principles of law, the court will examine negotiations between the parties to see if a contract was created.

There must be at least three essential interrelated elements to create a valid contract.

(1) There must be an *Agreement*, expressed or implied, between the parties. In the event of doubt about such agreement the court may examine the negotiations to see if there was a definite "offer" made by one party which was clearly accepted without qualification by the other side. Such matching offer and acceptance will be deemed to establish agreement between the parties.

(2) There must be an *Intention to create legal relations*. The parties must intend to contract, *i.e.* they must intend to be legally bound by their agreement, so that it will be enforceable in the courts if need be. In some cases this intention will be implied from the nature of the agreement – as in all business or commercial agreements. In other cases it must be established by evidence, as in the case of social or domestic arrangements, particularly within the family.

(3) There must also be *Consideration* which is some contribution or undertaking on both sides which suggests a bargain. A party cannot sue on a contract unless he can show that he gave consideration. For the moment we may say that a plaintiff gives consideration when he provides any benefit given or accruing to the other party or suffers or undertakes any loss or detriment to himself.

The Agreement

A contract is based on the agreement or mutual assent of the parties involved. At times some judges have sought genuine agreement or meeting of minds between the parties. This is sometimes referred to as *consensus ad idem* (agreement as to the same thing). Whereas this is the ideal, in fact the test of agreement applied by the courts is an objective one. The courts accept that the minds of the parties are out of reach of the court. The test is not whether the parties have really agreed but whether their words and conduct are sufficient to lead a reasonable person to assume that they reached agreement. Agreement is not in law a mental state but an inference from what the parties have said, written or done. This is further emphasised when the agreement involves standard form contracts or where the parties are of unequal bargaining power. In such cases a party may not understand the small print, or may have no choice but to accept the terms offered, but is still deemed by the court to have genuinely assented to such terms.

Contracts are formed, therefore, by "agreement" in this sense and to discover whether agreement was reached by the parties the court may, if necessary, analyse the negotiations into offer and acceptance. Let us suppose that John is negotiating with Tony for the sale of a car. John says that he would be prepared to take £5,000 for the car. This is merely a statement of intention and not an offer to sell at that price. Tony says he will give £4,500 for the car but might be prepared to go as high as £4,750. This is in effect an offer to buy the car for £4,500. John replies that he will sell for £4,750. This is a counter-offer. Tony agrees to buy the car for £4,750 and his agreement constitutes an acceptance of John's counter-offer. There is now a matching offer and acceptance and hence agreement. The law assumes that they intended to be bound by their undertakings, as people do not go around making bargains for fun. There is consideration involved as both have provided something of value. The three essential elements are present and so the court would conclude that they have made or entered a contract.

The Principles Governing Offer and Acceptance

(1) *No formality required*

As a general rule there is no special formality regarding the way in which an offer or an acceptance is to be made. They can be made by written or spoken words or merely by conduct as in the case of a purchase in a self-service supermarket. The offer or acceptance may be communicated by phone, telex, letter or any means of communication which is appropriate and reasonable in the circumstances. An "offer" must be intended as such before a contract can arise. A resolution at a corporation meeting, for example, was held not to be an offer (*Wilson* v. *Belfast Corp.*, Ir.C.A. 1921). Offers are frequently made on business order forms and may be made subject to any terms printed, or referred to, on the form.

(2) *Clear, unqualified, and matching*

The terms of an offer must be clear and unqualified. The acceptance must also be clear and unqualified and must exactly match the offer. If there is any vagueness or uncertainty in the terms the court may hold that there was a failure to make a complete agreement and may, in any event, be unable to give effect to the alleged agreement, in that no clear meaning can be determined. Thus an agreement to accept a reduced rent in return for "permanent improvements you have made, and have promised to make" was held to be too vague and uncertain (*Morgan* v. *Rainsford*, Ir.Ex. 1845). Failure to agree on all the issues or doubts about acceptance (*Central Meat Products* v. *Carney* H.C. 1944), or failure to agree on a means of establishing the price (*Carr* v. *Phelan* H.C. 1976) can mean that no contract exists. An agreement, however, in which the plaintiff was to acquire that part of a farm called "The Inches" was held to be enforceable as its boundaries were known and ascertainable by the court (*McGillycuddy* v. *Joy*, H.C. 1959).

A reply to an offer which adds a new term is not an acceptance but a counter-offer. Where, *e.g.* a tenant agreed to a lease but unilaterally provided that it should last for the life of the Prince of Wales there was held to be no agreement (*Wright* v. *St. George*, Ir. C. of Ch.1861). There may be situations, also, in which there is no real agreement, as where a buyer of three cattle did not realise that one was a malformed hermaphrodite having both male and female characteristics (*Gill* v. *McDowell* Ir.K.B. 1903).

(3) *Communication of offer and acceptance*

The offer must be communicated to the other party and so also, with some exceptions, the acceptance must be communicated to the offeror, as otherwise no enforceable agreement will exist between the parties. In general this is a straightforward and obvious requirement. If an offer is not communicated how can it be accepted when the other does not know it exists? It would be likewise unreasonable if a person who made an offer could be held bound by an acceptance not communicated to him. But there are hidden difficulties involved. Let us suppose, *e.g.* that a person advertises a reward for lost property. Another person, now knowing about the offer, finds the property and returns it of his own free will. If he subsequently discovers the reward offer and sues to recover it, his case must fail, as his act was not done in acceptance of the offer, so there is no contract and there can be no contractual obligation to pay the reward.

The principle that acceptance must be communicated can be seen in operation in the English case *Felthouse* v. *Bindley* (E.Ex.Ch. 1863). The plaintiff offered to buy a horse by letter stating that "if I hear no more about him, I consider the horse is mine at £30 15s." No acceptance was communicated. When the horse was sold in error by an auctioneer, a case by the plaintiff for conversion failed as there had been no contract of sale and he did not own the horse.

Although as a general principle there cannot be a binding contract unless acceptance has been communicated, there are two exceptions:

  (a) where performance or conduct is deemed to constitute acceptance, and

(b) where acceptance is made by post or telegram and the letter
or telegram is lost or delayed.

Where performance constitutes acceptance. One of the
situations in which performance may constitute acceptance is in the
case of a unilateral offer to the public at large. If a person advertises
an offer of reward to anyone who returns his lost property then any
person who returns the goods is entitled to the reward and he does
not have to communicate acceptance of the terms of the offer
beforehand. In law the performance of the required action is in itself
an acceptance, or at least performance and acceptance will be
deemed to occur simultaneously. In *Carlill* v. *Carbolic Smoke Ball Co.*
(E.C.A. 1893), the plaintiff recovered £100 reward from the
defendants by performing what was required in their advertisement,
which offered the reward to anyone who caught influenza after using
their product in the prescribed manner. There are precedents too for
the proposition that performance or conduct which can only be
attributed to acceptance and which is known to the offeror may also
constitute a sufficient communication of acceptance (*Saunders* v.
Cramer, Ir. C. of Ch. 1842; *Brogden* v. *Metropolitan Rly. Co.,* H.L.
1876).

Acceptance by letter or telegram. The other exception to the
rule that acceptance must be communicated to the offeror is when
acceptance is made by letter or telegram. Whereas an offer only
takes effect when and if received, an acceptance by letter takes effect
when posted and an acceptance by telegram takes effect when given
to the post office for transmission. The posting rule dates back to the
case of *Adams* v. *Lindsell* (E.K.B. 1818) in which it was held that a
contract for purchase of wool was effective when the plaintiff posted
his letter of acceptance and the defendant was in breach of contract
by selling the wool between the time of posting and receipt of the
letter. This decision was confirmed in *Household Fire and Carriage
Accident Insurance Co.* v. *Grant* (E.C.A. 1879) when the court ruled
that a subscriber for shares was bound by an acceptance in a letter of
allotment although the letter was never delivered. An insurance
policy posted from London to the broker agents of the plaintiff in
Dublin constituted an acceptance in London making it an English
contract (*Sanderson* v. *Cunningham* Ir. C.A. 1919).

The posting rule is not based on any great rule of justice or reason.
It is merely an accepted solution to a practical problem. It is
convenient perhaps in that it is easier to prove that an acceptance
was posted than that it was received. As was pointed out in *Grant's*
case the offeror, if he chooses, can always make formation of the
contract which he proposes dependent on the actual communication

to himself of the acceptance. As mentioned, the posting rule also extends to acceptances by telegram, but acceptances by telephone or telex are governed by the normal rule and are only effective from the time actually received. An offer may require an acceptance to be made in a certain way, *e.g.* by telegram. In such a case an acceptance by other means may be ineffective. If, however, the offer suggests rather than insists on a method of communication an equally fast method may be as good.

(4) Acceptance must be by the offeree or his agent

The acceptance of an offer can only be validly made by the person to whom the offer was addressed or his agent. A unilateral offer can be made to the world at large, as in *Kennedy* v. *London Express Newspapers* (S.C. 1931), where an English newspaper offered a free accident insurance policy to its registered readers. Otherwise, however, a bilateral offer may only be accepted by the party to whom it is addressed or his authorised agent. Where a member of a school management board accepted, without the board's authority, the employment application of a teacher, the acceptance was held not to create a contract (*Powell* v. *Lee*, E.K.B. 1908). In the same way an unauthorised communication or publication of an offer will not lead to a contract if accepted (*Wilson* v. *Belfast Corp.*, Ir.C.A. 1921).

When does an Offer End?

An acceptance made in reply to an offer has no duration in time. If it is a good acceptance it creates a contract there and then. An ineffective "acceptance" is no acceptance at all, or if it includes new terms it may be a counter-offer which may be accepted or rejected by the other party. An offer or counter-offer, however, must exist for some time, at least long enough to give the offeree the opportunity of replying to it. It would, of course, be unreasonable if the offeree could come back in six months' time and say "Yes, I accept your offer." There must be some duration for which the offer stands and is open to acceptance leading to a contract. An offer does not last indefinitely and can terminate in one of the following ways without maturing into a contract.

(1) Revocation

An offer can be revoked (withdrawn) by the offeror at any time before it has been accepted. This is true even when the offeror agrees to keep the offer open for a fixed time. Such a promise could not be enforced against the offeror because no consideration was given for it. If consideration is given in return for keeping the offer open this would create a separate legal contract or "option." Once an offer has been accepted, a contract is created and it is too late to withdraw the offer. Thus in *Billings* v. *Arnott & Co. Ltd.* (H.C. 1945) it was held that it was too late for the defendants to withdraw an offer to pay their employees half their salary up to £2 per week for joining the Defence Forces when the plaintiff had already accepted the offer.

Where an offer is to be withdrawn it is only fair that the offeree be informed, and this is the rule which the law has adopted. The revocation of an offer will only be effective if it has been communicated directly or indirectly to the offeree. It is not necessary that the offeror himself communicates the withdrawal of the offer. A revocation will be effective provided the offeree has sufficient notice of it (*Dickinson* v. *Dodds*, E.C.A. 1876). The revocation of an offer by post is only effective when the letter is delivered as it has more in common with an offer than with an acceptance (*Byrne* v. *Van Tienhoven*, E.C.P. 1880).

(2) *Rejection of the offer or a counter-offer*

If John makes an offer to sell his car to Tony for £5,000 and Tony rejects the offer the result is that John's offer is terminated. If Tony changes his mind and says that he will buy the car for £5,000, John may refuse to sell if he so wishes. In law Tony's statement is a new offer which John is free to accept or reject. A counter-offer, that is an offer made in response to an offer, has the same effect as a rejection. It terminates the offer (*Hyde* v. *Wrench*, E. Rolls C. 1840).

(3) *Lapse of time*

If an offer is made and stated to be open for a fixed time then the offer must be accepted within that time limit as this is a condition of the offer. The offeror is free to waive that condition or to renew his offer. There is no obligation on him, as we have seen, which prevents him from revoking his offer within the time specified. He may withdraw the offer at any time unless he has been given consideration for keeping the offer open which created an enforceable option contract.

If no time-limit is mentioned in the offer and if it is not lawfully revoked it is deemed in law to remain open for a reasonable time. How long a "reasonable time" is, depends on the nature of the contract and the circumstances of a particular case. If the offer relates to perishable goods, or commodities or securities which fluctuate in value, a reasonable period might be quite short. Put in another way, the offer will have lapsed when it may reasonably be argued that the offeror, not having had a suitably prompt reply, was led to assume that his offer had been rejected.

(4) *Failure of an express or implied condition*

If an offer is made subject to an express or implied condition then it cannot be validly accepted if the condition fails. This applies, for example, where an offer is made "subject to contract" or where a creditor agrees to a composition agreement provided it is signed by a majority of creditors (*Re Semple*, Ir. C. of Ch. 1846). A condition may also be implied from the nature of the offer. Suppose George offers to buy a consignment of fruit from Bernard for £6,000 and Bernard says he will let him know his answer on the following day. If the fruit is exposed to frost overnight and becomes worthless can Bernard accept George's offer? Obviously he cannot because the law implies that the fruit must remain in substantially the same condition until acceptance. A car offered on hire-purchase, for example, must remain in the same condition until the moment of acceptance (*Financings Ltd.* v. *Stimson*, E.C.A. 1962)

(5) *Death of the offeree*

Where an offer is made to a person and that person dies, can the offer be accepted on behalf of the deceased by his personal representative? The law has never authoritatively decided but it seems that he cannot because an acceptance can only be made by the offeree or his authorised agent. The death of the offeree, therefore, probably terminates the offer.

If, however, the offeror dies after making an offer, an acceptance by an offeree who does not know of his death will be valid provided that contract is not of a personal nature requiring the skills of the deceased. If the contract can be performed equally well by the deceased's personal representatives then they will probably be obliged to fulfil it.

Recognising an Offer

Offers and invitations to treat

Confusion can sometimes arise between an offer which can lead to a contract and an invitation to make offers, which latter is often referred to as an "invitation to treat" or "an offer to chaffer" (bargain). Displaying goods for sale, even with the price tag attached, is not a contractual offer to sell but is merely an invitation to the public to bargain or negotiate for the item. If the price is misleading the trader may be liable for an offence under the

Consumer Information Act 1978, but he will not be obliged to sell the goods if a member of the public attempts to accept his alleged "offer." The same rule applies to goods advertised for sale. The advertisement does not usually constitute a legal offer for sale but merely an invitation to bargain for the advertised goods. The person who thus advertises does not legally bind himself to provide the goods at the price mentioned. The difference between an advertisement which makes an offer and one which does not is, however, merely a difference as regards intention and related circumstances. When an advertisement makes an offer which is clear, definite, and explicit, and leaves nothing open for negotiation, it constitutes an offer, acceptance of which will complete the contract. In such advertisements traders often wisely take the precaution of limiting their offer, especially if the price is reduced, to a specified number of the particular items or "while stocks last." In the Irish case *Minister for Industry and Commerce* v. *Pim Bros. Ltd.* (H.C. 1966), it was held that a coat displayed for sale with a notice of the price attached did "not constitute an offer to sell which could be made a contract of sale by acceptance." This can be contrasted with a United States case, *Lefkowitz* v. *Great Minneapolis Surplus Store* (Minn. 1957) in which the defendant's advertisement was held to be a legal offer. The advertisement read: "Saturday 9 a.m. 2 brand new pastel mink 3-skin scarfs selling for $89.50. Out they go Saturday. Each . . . $1.00. 1 black lapin stole beautiful, worth $139.50 . . . $1.00. First come first served."

Quotations

Similar principles apply to the question of whether a quotation is an offer or merely an invitation to make an offer. The usual quotation is prima facie a furnishing of information and is regarded as being in the nature of an invitation to treat. This was the attitude of the court in *Boyers* v. *Duke* (Ir.K.B. 1905) where a quotation by the defendant canvas manufacturers was held not to be an offer which could be accepted by an order given by the plaintiffs. In *Dooley* v. *Egan* (H.C. 1938), however, a quotation was given which was subject to a standard condition that it was for "immediate acceptance only" and "subject to change without notice." The judge held that this made the quotation an offer subject to immediate acceptance. A wine merchant's price list has been deemed to be an invitation to treat (*Grainger* v. *Gough*, H.L. 1896).

Tenders and auction bids

A request for tenders to supply goods or services is not an offer but an invitation to others to make offers. The tenders made, however, are normally legal offers which lead to a binding contract. The party requesting the tender is, like any offeree, under no obligation to accept the lowest or any tender. If he accepts a tender he must accept it as tendered or there may be no agreement (*Navan Union* v. *McLoughlin* Ir.C.P. 1855).

In an auction sale the offers come from successive bidders and the auction takes place subject to any conditions brought to the notice of the bidders by catalogues, notices or by being read out at the auction. Failure to comply with conditions relating to payment, *e.g.* as in *Morrow* v. *Carty* (Ch.D.N.I. 1957) may result in a loss of the bargain. At a public auction the contract is concluded when the auctioneer accepts a bid by striking the bench with his hammer or by some other indication that the property has been sold. Independently of this contract, another one exists between the seller and all persons who, by bidding, accept his conditions of sale (*Tully* v. *Irish Land Commission*, H.C. 1961). If the auction is advertised as being "without reserve" this constitutes a firm offer to sell to the highest bidder.

Intention to Create Legal Relations

Contract law is based on the idea that the courts will give their support to freely negotiated agreements of the public. The law upholds agreements not only because of the bargain or consideration involved but also because the parties intended to contract, *i.e.* they intended to create legal relations. If there is no intention to create legal relations involved in their agreement, there is no enforceable contract. This can be seen, *e.g.* in the case of *Callaghan* v. *Callaghan* (1841). An Irish M.P., Daniel Callaghan, was in danger of being disqualified for lack of the required property qualification. He entered a written agreement for the lease of certain lands from his brother who died without executing the lease or parting with possession of the land. Daniel sued the heir at law of the deceased for specific performance. The action was dismissed on grounds that the purpose of the agreement was to give the plaintiff a parliamentary qualification and that the parties never intended that the agreement should be executed. A further appeal by the plaintiff to the House of Lords was likewise dismissed.

Regarding intention to create legal relations, the court does not seek to determine whether the parties intended in their minds to be bound by what they agreed to, although conclusions may be inferred by the court from the evidence. The test is whether from their words, conduct, and the circumstances of the negotiations a reasonable person would infer that they intended to be bound in law by their agreement.

Commercial or business-type agreements

Where the circumstances suggest that the negotiations were of a commercial, business or objective nature the court will presume that the parties intended to be legally bound by their agreement. This is the usual situation and the issue does not arise very often in practice. This presumption that the parties intended to create legal relations will be defeated, however, when the words used or conduct of the parties indicate a contrary intention. Thus in the English case, *Rose & Frank Co.* v. *Crompton Brothers Ltd.* (H.L. 1925), an agreement was made whereby the plaintiffs were to be the sole agents in the United States for the sale of paper tissues manufactured by the defendants. The agreement, however, was stated not to be a "formal or legal" one and would not be "subject to legal jurisdiction in the law courts" but one "to which they each honourably pledge themselves with the fullest confidence." The agreement was held to be binding in honour only and not enforceable as a contract as there was no intention to create a legally binding relationship. In another case in England an agreement concerning football pools was likewise held to be unenforceable as it was stated to be binding in honour only (*Jones* v. *Vernons Pools Ltd.*, Assizes 1938).

The most frequent situation in which there may be no intention to create legal relations is where an offer, an acceptance, or a memorandum of agreement is stated to be "subject to contract," or where phrases are used such as "agreement in principle" or "provisional agreement." When such phrases are used it is up to the court to decide whether or not a contract was created. The usual assumption is that such phrases indicate that the parties did not intend to be bound until a formal written contract had been signed. If that is the intention, the creation of a formal contract becomes a condition or term of the bargain and if it is not fulfilled there is no enforceable contract (*Thompson and Son Ltd.* v. *The King*, Ir.C.A. 1920; *Lowis* v. *Wilson*, H.C. 1949; *Black* v. *Kavanagh* H.C. 1974). If the evidence suggests that the parties intended to be bound by their preliminary agreement and merely wished to put it into a more formal shape it constitutes a binding contract from the beginning and the qualifying phrases will be ignored (*McInerney Properties Ltd.* v. *Roper*, H.C. 1979; *Irish Mainport Holdings Ltd.* v. *Crosshaven Sailing Centre Ltd.* H.C. 1980; *Branca* v. *Cobarro* E.C.A. 1947). Similarly a contract for the sale of land may be made subject to planning permission being obtained and in that event the contract is unenforceable until planning permission is obtained or the condition is waived (*O'Mullane* v. *Riordan*, H.C. 1978; *Maloney* v. *Elf Investments* H.C. 1979).

Collective agreements

Although it is generally assumed that collective agreements between workers' representatives and management are not legally binding, the same principles apply to such agreements. If the court finds that the parties intended to create legal relations it will hold that a contract was formed. In *Hynes* v. *Conlon* (H.C. 1939) the court accepted as enforceable an agreement between the Federation of Building Trade Employers and the I.T.G.W.U. The Supreme Court held, in *O'Callaghan* v. *Minister for Education* (1955), that certain rules relating to conditions of employment legally bound the Minister for Education. In England, however, two collective agreements were held not to be enforceable as contracts in *Ford Motor Co. Ltd.* v. *A.U.E.F.W.* (H.L. 1969) because by their nature such agreements were not intended to be legally binding. The decision has been criticised as having been influenced by political considerations. It was rejected by Kenny J. in *Goulding Chemicals Ltd.* v. *Bolger* (S.C. 1977) who upheld an agreement between Gouldings and the unions to be a valid enforceable contract. He referred with approval to the opinion of Justice Megaw in *Edwards* v. *Skyways Ltd.* (E.Q.B. 1964) that when an apparent agreement concerned business relations, the onus on the party who asserts that it was not intended to have legal effect is a heavy one. It should be noted, however, that whereas a union as an association or corporate body may be bound by such a collective contract, individual members of the union are not bound unless they expressly or impliedly consent to be bound under the terms of their employment contract (see p. 186).

Social or domestic agreements

If an agreement is of a social or domestic nature, such as an agreement between family members, there is a presumption that the parties did not intend legal relations to arise. This presumption can be defeated, however, by evidence to the contrary, and the existence of an enforceable contract depends on what inference can reasonably be made from the circumstances of the agreement.

The law will not readily enforce alleged promises to convey property where the parties are related unless the circumstances and words used clearly establish an intention to create legal relations. Thus Irish courts have refused to enforce a promise by a father to settle property on the marriage of his son (*Quinlan* v. *Quinlan*, Ir.Ex. 1834) and they have refused to enforce promises to leave property in a will (*Maunsell* v. *White* H.L. 1844; *Mackey* v. *Jones*, C.C. 1959).

Where, however, a grandmother of the bride promised to settle property in circumstances which showed an intention to be legally bound the agreement was enforced (*Saunders* v. *Cramer*, Ir. C. of Ch. 1842). Similarly where a mother promised to leave money in a will instead of a settlement on her daughter's marriage, the court held that there was an intention to make an irrevocable settlement (*Arthure* v. *Dillon*, Ir. C. of Ch. 1850).

In other domestic agreements the same principle applies. The court will not accept that there was an intention to create legal relations unless there is evidence to the contrary. The leading English case is *Balfour* v. *Balfour* (C.A. 1919) which is followed in Irish courts. The case involved an English civil servant stationed in Ceylon who agreed to pay £30 per month to his wife to maintain her in England during his absence. When the husband stopped making the payments he was sued by his wife for breach of contract. Her case failed in the Court of Appeal as their agreement was unenforceable. Such domestic agreements, Lord Atkin said, "are not contracts because the parties did not intend that they should be attended by legal consequences." Similar agreements between a mother and son (*Rogers* v. *Smith* S.C. 1970) and between a mother and daughter (*Jones* v. *Padavatton* E.C.A. 1969), were held not to create contracts as there was no evidence that the parties intended to create legal relations.

In some social and domestic agreements, however, the circumstances are such as to establish that legal relations were intended. If the husband and wife are separated, *e.g.* it is much more likely that any agreement, particularly in settlement of a possible legal action, will be intended to be binding. In *Bucknell* v. *Bucknell* (Ir. Rolls C. 1858) a husband who was threatened with divorce and alimony proceedings agreed to pay his wife £60 a year and one-quarter of his gross earnings as an engineer. The parties were separated and not on good terms. The court held that the agreement was enforceable. Similarly in *Courtney* v. *Courtney* (Ir.C.A. 1923) the court agreed with the principle set out by Atkin J. in the English case *Balfour* v. *Balfour*, referred to above, but nevertheless upheld a separation agreement between a husband and wife. The couple agreed to separate in the presence of a priest. The husband agreed to pay a lump sum of £150 to his wife and she was to return a watch and her ring. The fact that they were separated and intended to have no further dealings was held by the court to be evidence of an intention to be bound in law, and it was implied that the wife would abstain from proceedings for separation and alimony, which was consideration on her part. The circumstances showed that the parties intended legal relations so that it was in fact an enforceable contract though made between a husband and wife. An agreement between an estranged husband and wife was also upheld in the English case *Merritt* v. *Merritt* (E.C.A. 1970).

Consideration

In addition to agreement and an intention to create legal relations there must be consideration to create an enforceable contract. The best definition of consideration is that given by Lush J. in *Currie* v. *Misa* (E.Ex.Ch. 1875). A valuable consideration in law, he said, "may consist either in some right, interest, profit, or benefit accruing to the one party, or some forbearance, detriment, loss or responsibility given, suffered, or undertaken by the other." It is a principle of our law that a contract is not enforceable unless it involves consideration or "mutuality" as it is called in the older cases. This is sometimes referred to as the doctrine of consideration which states that a person cannot sue on a contract unless he can show that he gave consideration which was bargained for, or acceptable to the party he wishes to sue in exchange for what that party promised in return.

An agreement by a landlord, *e.g.* to reduce the rent on a farm was held not to be enforceable by the tenant because he provided no consideration (*Fitzgerald* v. *Lord Portarlington*, Ir.Ex. 1835). In a similar case a tenant could not sue because he had sold his interest and could no longer show consideration of any kind. "Taking the case as it now stands," the judge said, "we find no mutuality in the terms of the agreement" (*Morgan* v. *Rainsford*, Ir.Ex. 1845). A guarantee to pay premiums on an insurance policy taken out as security for an existing overdraft was held unenforceable as no new consideration was given for it (*Provincial Bank of Ireland* v. *Donnell*, C.A.N.I. 1933). A plaintiff cannot, therefore, sue on a contract unless he can show that he gave consideration.

Simple and speciality contracts

One exception to the rule that a contract must involve consideration is where the contract is made by deed or, as it is also called, is made "under seal." A contract contained in a deed is sometimes classified as a speciality contract as opposed to contracts which are not by deed and which are called "simple" or "parol" contracts. As regards simple contracts, a bare promise or *nudum pactum* for which nothing has been undertaken in return cannot give rise to a legal action because there is no consideration or "mutuality." A speciality contract by deed, however, does not require consideration and will be enforced if it complies with the requirements of a valid deed. It must be in writing, it is usually signed, and it must be sealed and delivered. Where a deed contains promises by one party only it needs to be executed by that party only and is called a "deed poll." A deed which is executed by two or more parties is sometimes referred to as an "indenture."

What is consideration

Let us suppose that Tony gives an order to John asking him to send him two instrument cabinets and John agrees to supply him. There is an agreement between them and, since it is a business deal, it is assumed that they intend to create legal relations by their agreement. But is there consideration? If John dispatched the cabinets at once and Tony refused to pay for them, there would be no doubt that John could sue for breach of contract as he had given consideration. The cabinets were provided by John and constitute his consideration as they are a benefit to Tony and a loss to him. But the definition of consideration does not state that the benefit has to be given. It is sufficient if the benefit is accruing to the other party or that a loss has been undertaken. John and Tony have undertaken obligations towards each other. There are mutual promises and this constitutes mutuality or consideration which is the hallmark of the enforceable agreement. John has promised to make and supply cabinets and Tony has undertaken to accept and pay for them. Both have provided consideration and either can enforce the contract. But, of course, only the consideration bargained for will suffice.

The Legal Rules Governing Consideration

(1) *Consideration must be recognised as good in law but need not be adequate*

Good consideration in law is anything of value which contributes to the bargain. Land, merchandise, goods, services and money are all good consideration. Many other undertakings which confer a benefit on the other party or which represent a loss to the plaintiff will also satisfy the consideration or mutuality requirement. Examples of good consideration include marriage, "the most valuable of all considerations" (*Saunders* v. *Cramer*, Ir. C. of Ch. 1842), a promise to settle a misdemeanour of a private nature (*Westby* v. *Westby*, Ir. C. of Ch. 1842) and an undertaking not to put a bid or offer on land for sale (*McGillycuddy* v. *Joy*, H.C. 1959). A quite trivial act or undertaking may be sufficient.

There are certain situations, however, in which the law will hold that there is no real consideration because the act or promise in question must be performed under the general law or an existing contract with the other party. A promise to do something, such as to give evidence, is not consideration if the person is already required to do it by law (*Collins* v. *Godefroy*, E.K.B. 1831). Similarly a promise to do something which your existing contract requires you to do is no consideration (*Stilk* v. *Myrick*, E.K.B. 1809). If, however, a person does more than the law requires such as a policeman providing more protection than reasonably necessary (*Glasbrook Bros. Ltd.* v. *Glamorgan C.C.* H.L. 1925) or an unmarried mother providing more than basic care for her child (*Ward* v. *Byham*, E.C.A. 1956; *Farrington* v. *Donohoe*, Ir.C.P. 1867), then there is something unique given which will be regarded as good consideration. Likewise, services due under an old contract provided the old one is superseded (*Hartley* v. *Ponsonby*, E.Q.B. 1857). A party may also enter contracts with two parties in which the consideration for both contracts is the same. He will have the option of suing on either contract, and possibly the option of recovering on both contracts (*Scotson* v. *Pegg*, E.Ex. 1861; *The Eurymedon*, P.C. 1974).

Good consideration, therefore, must provide something of value which contributes to the bargain made. But whereas it must have some value the consideration need not be "adequate" in the sense of being equal in value to that for which it is given in return. A person may, therefore, sell an article worth £1,000 for £100 in cash and the court will accept that consideration was given for the article unless there is evidence of fraud or unfairness in the transaction. In *Barry* v. *O'Grady* (Ir. C. of Ch. 1846), *e.g.* a sale of land by a man who died shortly afterwards, for an annuity of £308, was enforced by the court. The judge held that the contract was not affected by the inadequacy of the consideration. Similarly the court enforced a contract with a cousin although the consideration "was fairly and honourably reduced in consequence of relationship and affection" (*Moore* v. *Crofton*, Ir. C. of Ch. 1846). In the absence of fraud or unfair dealing, therefore, the inadequacy of consideration is irrelevant and the law will not protect a person of full capacity who makes a bad or foolish bargain.

(2) *The consideration must have been provided by the plaintiff*

Once it is accepted that an enforceable contract requires consideration it necessarily follows that a person cannot sue on a contract even when consideration has been provided by someone else on his behalf. Thus work done by a third party for the defendant on the proviso that the defendant paid the plaintiff was not consideration on which the plaintiff could sue (*Price* v. *Easton*, E.K.B. 1833). A plaintiff could not sue either on a contract made by his father and father-in-law whereby they each undertook to pay him a sum of money following his marriage (*Tweedle* v. *Atkinson*

E.Q.B. 1861). This principle was followed in Ireland also. In *McCoubray* v. *Thomson* (Ir.C.P. 1868) property given by another to Thomson provided he pay half its value to McCoubray was not consideration moving from the plaintiff, McCoubray, and he could not sue on the contract.

A person who has not contributed to the consideration cannot sue on the contract. It is said that such a person is not "privy" to the contract or that he is a "stranger to the consideration." A person who is "privy" to a contract is a party to it and has provided consideration. There is "privity" between him and the other parties so that he may sue or be sued under the terms of the contract. This principle is often referred to as the "privity of contract doctrine" and the doctrines of consideration and privity of contract are merely two aspects of the same idea. As a general rule privity of contract means that a person who is not a party to a contract (has not provided consideration) cannot sue on it. Thus, *e.g.* a manufacturer cannot sue to enforce a price maintenance agreement between his wholesaler and retailer (*Dunlop* v. *Selfridge & Co. Ltd.* H.L. 1915). Likewise the wife of a tenant could not sue the landlord for breach of a letting agreement (*Coughlan* v. *Corp. of Limerick*, C.C. 1977). Some exceptions to this rule arise by statutory law or under some principles in the law of trusts, property and agency, but as a general rule it holds true of all contracts.

(3) *The consideration must not have been provided prior to the agreement*

A person cannot sue on the basis of consideration which was given or completed before the agreement was made. "Past consideration is no consideration." As we saw, a guarantee given to a bank to pay premiums on an insurance policy was not enforceable because advances previously made by the bank were consideration given prior to the agreement and of no use (*Provincial Bank of Ireland Ltd.* v. *Donnell* C.A.N.I. 1933). The only apparent exception to this principle is where the past or executed consideration was done at the defendant's request. This is sometimes referred to as the rule in *Lampleigh* v. *Brathwait* (1616) where the plaintiff successfully sued the defendant for £100 promised to him after Lampleigh had already given "consideration" by obtaining a pardon for Brathwait from the King. The past consideration was held to be good as it had been given at the defendant's request. The modern interpretation of this rule is that the contract was made when the "past" consideration was requested and the parties understood that payment would be made. The later promise to pay does not create the agreement but merely fixes the price to be paid. The consideration is, therefore, not past consideration at all. This was the approach of the Irish Court of Exchequer in *Bradford* v. *Roulston* (Ir.Ex. 1858).

(4) *Consideration must not be illegal, vague, or impossible to perform*

If the consideration put forward by the plaintiff is illegal or immoral the court will not enforce the contract as it would be contrary to the public interest. If the consideration relied on is vague or impossible to perform the court may likewise refuse to enforce the contract in that it would indicate that there was either no real intention to contract or that no real agreement was reached.

(5) *There must be consideration given to enforce the waiving of a contractual obligation*

When a party to a contract waives, or gives up, a right which he has under the contract, wholly or in part, he is not bound by the waiver unless he has been given consideration for it. Let us suppose that George has paid £500 to Denis to have his house painted. If George tells Denis, when half the work is done, that he need not finish the work, George will have waived a contractual right but he will not be bound by it unless Denis gives him something of value as consideration. The waiver constitutes a new agreement and like any agreement it requires consideration to make it an enforceable contract.

When this principle is applied to the waiving of a contractual debt it leads to a rather absurd result. It is quite common for persons in business to accept the part payment of debts from doubtful debtors rather than risk getting nothing. In doing this they waive their right to the remainder. The waiver, however, is only binding on the creditor if he receives consideration for it. The part payment is not consideration as it is due under the original contract. The settlement is not binding, therefore, on the creditor and he can subsequently sue the debtor for the balance if he wishes. This was decided as long ago as 1602 in *Pinnel's Case* and was reaffirmed by the House of Lords in *Foakes* v. *Beer* (1884). To offset this injustice to debtors the courts began to find reasons, often trivial ones, to hold the creditor to his agreement. The creditor was held bound when he agreed to accept a smaller sum and requested payment at a different location, or at an earlier date, or accompanied by a chattel however insignificant. Similarly the creditor was held bound by a settlement of a debt when there was a dispute over the amount owed, or where payment was made by a third party or in a valid composition agreement with creditors. In such cases consideration of some kind could generally be shown.

Outside these situations the waiving of a contractual obligation still remained unenforceable in the absence of consideration. The same problem arose in relation to a promise to vary a contract or as regarding a promise as to future conduct, such as an undertaking not to enforce a bond as in *Jorden* v. *Money* (H.L. 1854). The only hope a person has to enforce such promises, in the absence of consideration, is under the principle of promissory estoppel. Under this principle, where a person promises to waive a debt or obligation, and where the other party acts on his promise, the promisor is estopped from acting inconsistently with his promise. This principle, adopted in *Hughes* v. *Metropolitan Railway* (H.L. 1877), was given a new lease of life when it was used by Denning J. in the *High Trees House case* (K.B. 1947). It has been followed by McVeigh J. in the Northern Ireland case of *Morrow* v. *Carty* (1957). It was likewise accepted and applied by Kenny J. in *Cullen* v. *Cullen* (H.C. 1962) where a father was equitably estopped from withdrawing permission given to his son to erect a house on a site which the father owned. The principle was also applied by Kenny J. in *Revenue Commissioners* v. *Moroney* (H.C. 1972).

Contracts which must be in a Special Form

As a general rule there are no formalities required for creation of a contract. There are, however, some exceptional cases where the law demands some formality such as a deed, writing or evidence in writing. Without such formality the contract may still be valid but it will not be enforceable.

Contracts which must be by deed

Certain contracts must be made by deed, *i.e.* in writing under seal, to be binding. These include agreements made without consideration, transfers of shares in ships, contracts granting any agent a power of attorney, conditional bills of sale which create a mortgage of personal property, and conveyances of freehold land. Other contracts which do not require to be made by deed may also be made in this way to give them extra effect.

Contracts which must be in writing

There are also some contracts which are required by statute to be in writing but not necessarily under seal. These include leases greater than ones from year to year (Deasy's Act 1860), share transfers (Stock Transfer Act 1963), Bills of Exchange and Promissory Notes (Bills of Exchange Act 1882), marine insurance contracts (Marine Insurance Act 1906), and the assignment of personal property by bill of sale (Bills of Sale Acts 1882 to 1891).

Contracts which must be evidenced by writing

There is an important group of contracts which do not have to be in writing but which must be evidenced by writing to be enforceable. This is a requirement for contracts under section 2 of the Irish Statute of Frauds 1695, namely:

(i) Contracts of guarantee in which a person promises "to answer for the debt, default or miscarriages of another person";

(ii) Any contract made in consideration of marriage, that is where the consideration given by one of the parties for the promise of the other is marriage, but does not include marriage itself;

(iii) Any contract relating to land or any interest in land; and

(iv) Any contract which is not to be performed within the space of one year.

No legal action can be brought in court to enforce these contracts "unless the agreement . . . or some memorandum or note thereof, shall be in writing, and signed by the party to be charged therewith, or some other person thereunto by him lawfully authorised." These contracts, therefore, may be in writing but that is not necessary. It is sufficient if the agreement was made orally and a written note or memorandum was made of it and was signed by the party to be sued or his authorised agent. If there is no written evidence the court will not enforce the contract unless it can do so under the equitable doctrine of part performance. In *Naughton* v. *Limestone Land Co. Ltd.* (H.C. 1952) the plaintiff's claim for damages for breach of an oral employment contract to last for four years three months was dismissed because it was a contract not to be performed within a year and there was no note or memorandum signed by the defendants to support it. Problems frequently arise in this respect relating to sales of land. The situation in *Hoon* v. *Nolan* (S.C. 1967) was typical. The Supreme Court held that a contract for the sale of a particular premises was a verbal one but as there was no sufficient memorandum in writing the contract was unenforceable. It should be noted that even in the absence of writing or part performance the contract is still valid and may be enforced in any legal way other than court action, as by forfeiting a deposit for example.

The note or memorandum in writing

The purpose of the Statute of Frauds was to ensure that there would be objective written evidence of those contracts and in this way avoid the need for oral evidence which might be fraudulent. For this reason the memorandum must contain all the essentials of the contract such as names or identity of the parties, subject-matter of the agreement, consideration provided, and all material (in the sense of "important") terms. If an additional term is agreed afterwards, however, and not included in the memorandum, the contract may still be enforced if it favours the plaintiff and he waives it, or if it favours the defendant and the plaintiff agrees to be bound by it (*O'Mullane* v. *Riordan* H.C. 1978).

By contrast, a lot of flexibility is allowed as to the nature of the memorandum. Any writing made after the contract and before the action is brought may suffice. It may consist of two or more documents which must expressly or impliedly recognise the existence of the oral contract. The signature may be stamped or printed or even a solicitor's headed paper may be sufficient (*Casey* v. *Irish Continental Bank* S.C. 1979). In absence of contrary evidence it may be assumed that a solicitor has authority to sign a memorandum (*Guerin* v. *Ryan* H.C. 1977). There need be no intention to create a memorandum at the time the writing was made.

If the memorandum relied on contains the words "subject to contract" a question arises as to whether the memorandum is sufficient to satisfy the Statute of Frauds. Although the answer is not settled it would seem that in general it is not (*Mulhall* v. *Haren* H.C. 1979) but it may still be sufficient in some circumstances (*Kelly* v. *Park Hall School Ltd.*, S.C. 1978).

Part performance

Whereas the common law courts had no option but to enforce the Statute of Frauds, the Court of Equity would not allow any statute to be used as a means to do an injustice. It developed the principle that if the plaintiff could prove that the defendant allowed him to do acts which were in part performance of a contract consistent with the one alleged, it would enforce the contract. These acts of part performance proved that the oral contract was made and it would be a wrong to the plaintiff not to enforce the contract even though there was no evidence in writing, particularly if it adversely affected him.

The act of part performance must point clearly to a contract consistent with the one the plaintiff seeks to enforce, but otherwise its adequacy depends on the facts of a particular case. In general, however, giving possession of property to the plaintiff under a contract is a good act of part performance, for to deny that it was done under a contract is tantamount to an allegation of trespass by the plaintiff (*Clinan* v. *Cooke*, Ir. C. of Ch. 1802; *Starling Securities Ltd.* v. *Woods*. H.C. 1977). A payment of money is not usually sufficient as it may be explained on a number of grounds. In *Lowry* v. *Reid* (C.A.N.I. 1927) the giving of his farm and a sum of money to his brother was a sufficient act of part performance by the plaintiff to enforce a verbal agreement by his mother that she would leave him two other farms in return.

Other contracts requiring evidence in writing

There are some other contracts which are required to be in a certain form before they can be enforced. These include sale of goods and hire-purchase contracts (see chapter 5). Moneylending contracts must also be evidenced by writing and, under section 3 of the Family Home Protection Act 1976, a conveyance by a spouse of any interest in the family home is void if done without the consent of the other spouse.

The Proper Law of the Contract

When we think of contract law we normally have in mind the principles of Irish law. It is important to remember that an Irish business may enter contracts with foreign buyers or sellers and that such contracts may not be governed by Irish law or be subject to the jurisdiction of Irish courts. The law which governs the many aspects of a contract, and the law which an Irish or foreign court will apply in determining the obligations under it, is called the "proper law of the contract." The basic rule is that the parties have a right to choose the law which is to govern their agreement. A contract made in Ireland for work to be done in Ireland was held to be governed by the English courts and laws because it contained a clause that it should "in all respects be construed and operate as an English contract, and in conformity with English Law" (*Mayor & Corp. of Limerick* v. *Crompton* Ir.C.A. 1910). The parties may also agree that part of their agreement is to be governed by foreign law, such as a life assurance policy, which was expressed to be governed by the synopsis of a section of a British statute printed on the back (*Griffin* v. *Royal Liver Friendly Society* H.C. 1942).

Where the intentions of the parties are not expressly or impliedly made known and the contract contains a foreign element the court decides the proper law on the basis of which law has the most real connection with the contract (*Cripps Warburg* v. *Cologne Investments* H.C. 1979).

THE CONTENTS OF THE CONTRACT

A contract is created, we have seen, where three essential elements are present, namely, agreement, intention to create legal relations, and consideration. Before a person can be certain that the contract will get the backing of Irish courts he must also ensure that any special contract formality has been fulfilled.

In many cases, however, parties to an agreement will freely admit that a contract exists between them, but they may completely disagree concerning the contents of the contract. The stipulations contained in any contract are called the terms of the contract and these regulate the rights, obligations, and rules by which the parties are to be bound in their agreement. For a person to enforce rights under a contract he must discover the exact terms. There are two sources from which contractual terms can arise – from the parties themselves or implied by law. The former are called express terms, and the latter are called implied terms. The terms of a contract whether express or implied must be carefully distinguished from statements not intended to form part of the contract. Such statements are called mere representations or non-contractual representations and although not enforceable under the contract they are not without legal significance.

The express terms of the contract

The words used by the parties when making their agreement, whether written or spoken, and by which they intended to be bound are express terms. They are called "express" terms because they were expressly agreed to, orally or in writing. A contract may have been created entirely by spoken words, or it may have been made in writing, or it may be a combination of both. If a dispute arises concerning the contents of an oral contract it can only be resolved by evidence produced before the courts. There are, however, certain rules which apply to all written contracts.

Signed contracts

It is settled law that a person is bound by the terms of a written contract which he signed. This is true regardless of whether the party has read the contract or not. The only situations in which persons may not be bound by their signature are where it was obtained by fraud, or misrepresentation, or where the signer was fundamentally mistaken regarding the nature of the document. The plea of mistake in such a case is known as *non est factum*. If the person who signs a document is mistaken as to its nature and the other party is aware of the mistake, the transaction may be held to be void (*Foster* v. *McKinnon*, E.C.P. 1869). Where, *e.g.* a defendant without negligence signed a guarantee in the honest belief that it was a different type of document, he was held not bound by it (*Bank of Ireland* v. *McManamy*, Ir.K.B. 1916). There is a tendency for the courts to restrict the scope of this defence and it may not be available, to a person who signs a document without taking ordinary care to examine its contents (*Saunders* v. *Anglia Building Society* H.L. 1970).

Other documents and notices

A person will also be generally bound by terms contained in any other document or notice which is brought sufficiently to his attention. Thus conditions and terms contained on purchase order forms and similar provisions contained in acceptances of such orders will be valid terms. Terms referred to or included in tickets or catalogues,' or prominently displayed on notices, may likewise become terms. The actual terms do not even have to be given to the party as the law holds that they will bind a party to a contract if he has been given sufficient notice of their existence. This principle was clearly established in the English case *Parker* v. *South Eastern Rail Co.* (C.A. 1877) concerning conditions referred to on a parcels office ticket.

Supplementing the written documents

Problems arise where one party claims that the whole of the contract is not contained in the written documents, or that the documents do not correctly record the contract. The general principle applied by the courts is that the written documents prima facie contain the contract as agreed. Under the "parole evidence rule" the parties will not usually be allowed to produce evidence outside the written documents to add to, vary, or contradict what the written contract contains.

The court will, however, allow extrinsic evidence to show that the contract was invalid due to misrepresentation, mistake, or incapacity. It will allow such evidence where a party wishes to have the contract rectified on grounds that it does not correctly record a prior oral contract as intended. In *Nolan* v. *Graves* (H.C. 1946) lands were sold at public auction for £5,500, but £4,550 was inserted in the memorandum of the agreement by mistake. The court ordered that the memorandum be rectified in favour of the seller.

The court will allow parole evidence to prove that the written agreement was not the whole agreement. This occurs *e.g.* where a collateral contract was made at the same time but was not incorporated into the written contract. In the English case *De Lassalle* v. *Guilford* (C.A. 1901), the plaintiff concluded a lease agreement only on an assurance that the drains were in order. This term was not included in the written lease but the court held that it was a term of a collateral contract existing side by side with it.

The implied terms of the contract

In addition to express terms agreed to by the parties orally or in writing, a contract may contain implied terms. The implied terms of a contract are terms implied by law either—

  (i) to give effect to presumed intentions of the parties, or
 (ii) to supply a term inherent in the nature of the contract, or
(iii) in accordance with the provisions of some statute.

(i) To give effect to the intentions of the parties.   Generally, the law is very reluctant to find implied terms and it tries to avoid "making" the contract for parties. The general presumption is that parties have expressed every material term by which they intended to be bound, whether the contract is an oral one or in writing. The law recognises, however, that in certain contracts it will appear obvious that the contracting parties must have intended incorporation of a particular term or condition but failed to express it. The court will imply the necessary term into the contract to round it out, or give it "efficacy," on the theory that it is giving effect to the presumed intentions of the parties. In the leading case, *The Moorcock* (E.C.A. 1889), the court implied a term that the wharf made available by the defendants would be a safe berth for the plaintiff's ship. The objective of the court in applying a term was to give to the transaction "such efficacy as both parties must have intended it should have." The Irish High Court continues to do likewise (see *Massarella* v. *Massarella* H.C. 1980).

It must be a necessary inference.   The court will not imply a term merely because it is just and reasonable to do so. The implied term must be a necessary inference from the expressed terms of the agreement. The test is not easy to apply. In *Ward* v. *Spivack* (S.C. 1955) the High Court and Supreme Court came to different conclusions as to whether a term should be implied in a contract of agency that commission continue to be paid, after the termination of the contract, on all sales to customers acquired during the period of the agency. The Supreme Court refused to imply such a term as to do so would be to make a new contract for the parties.

The terms which may be implied in contracts will depend on the unique circumstances of particular cases. There are some terms, however, which may be implied into all contracts in the absence of a contrary intention. These include a term that neither party shall prevent the other party from performing the contract, that any work to be done will be carried out competently and, in the absence of a specified time limit, that the contract will be performed in a reasonable time.

(ii) Terms normally implied in particular contracts. The court's reluctance to imply terms will not operate as regards terms inherent in the nature of certain classes of contract, such as contracts of employment or building contracts. In any contract involving work and materials, *e.g.* building or engineering, there will be an implied term that the materials used will be of good quality and, if chosen by the contractor, there will be an implied term that they will be fit for their purpose (*Brown* v. *Norton* H.C. 1954; *Norta Wallpapers* v. *John Sisk Ltd.* S.C. 1978). There will be an implied term that the building or other job will be done in a proper manner (*Johnson* v. *Longleat Properties* H.C. 1976) and that a dwelling when finished will be fit for human occupation as a residence (*Siney* v. *Dublin Corp.* S.C. 1979).

Implied terms are likewise imposed on employers and employees so that they may be regarded as duties rather than terms open to negotiation. The same applies to other standard contracts such as agency, sale, and carriage. The law will also imply a term on the basis of a custom or usage adopted in the particular trade to which the contract relates. In these situations the rigorous test concerning implied terms is not used. These standardised terms are always implied unless expressly excluded and are practically duties imposed by law.

(iii) Terms implied by statute. Some implied terms were used so frequently by the courts in certain classes of contract that they became embodied in statutes intended to codify the law. Many terms once implied at common law are now contained in the Partnership Act 1890, Sale of Goods Act 1893, Landlord and Tenant Amendment Act 1860, and Bills of Exchange Act 1882, and may be, or must in some cases, be implied into the contracts in question. Other terms must be implied into certain contracts by statute to protect the weaker party.

Non-contractual representations

The terms of a contract must be distinguished from statements and opinions expressed during the negotiations but not intended to be part of the contract. Whether a statement is a term of a contract or a non-contractual representation depends on the intention of the parties. The test is based on what a reasonable person would understand the intention of the parties to be. In deciding the issue the court may be influenced by the requirements of fairness between the parties.

In *Cody* v. *Connolly* (H.C. 1940) a party was held liable for statements made concerning a mare when he discouraged the buyer from obtaining a veterinary examination by saying "what do you want to do that for? Didn't I tell you she was all right?" Likewise the statements of a person in a position of superior knowledge or skill are likely to be taken as contractual terms as it is reasonable for the other party to rely on them. (*Oscar Chess Ltd.* v. *Williams* E.C.A. 1957; *Dick Bentley Productions* v. *Harold Smith (Motors) Ltd.* E.C.A. 1965).

THE LEGAL SIGNIFICANCE OF CONTRACT TERMS

The terms, whether express or implied, may be classified into conditions, warranties, and exemption or limitation of liability clauses. Where it is not clear whether a particular term is a condition or a warranty it is sometimes called an innominate term.

Distinguishing conditions from warranties

When a term of a contract is broken or "breached" it is sometimes important to know whether the breached term was a condition or a warranty. A breach of a condition entitles the other party to repudiate the contract, that is to treat himself as free from having to fulfil his own obligations, whereas a breach of warranty does not.

Parties may misuse the terminology so the fact that they have referred to a term as a "condition" is no guarantee that it is a condition in the eyes of the law (*Schuler* v. *Wickman Machine Tool Sales Ltd*, H.L. 1973). If the parties agree that breach of a particular term will give the other party the right to repudiate the contract then, of course, that term must be a condition. Similarly where one party's promise need only be performed provided the other party does some act or fulfils some promise, then that act or promise must likewise be a condition. A term is also a condition where a party makes it clear that it is of such vital importance that he is not prepared to contract without it.

Where an implied term is described as a condition or a warranty in a statute, such as the Sale of Goods Act 1893, the term must be regarded as such by the courts.

Conditions and warranties defined

A condition is a vital term of a contract whereas a warranty is merely subsidiary to the main purpose of the contract. (See Fletcher Moulton L.J. in *Wallis* v. *Pratt* (H.L. 1911)). Thus an actress who failed to turn up for the first week of a performance of a London operetta was held to be in breach of a condition (*Poussard* v. *Spiers*, E.Q.B. 1876). A singer who missed three out of six days' rehearsals before a concert tour was held to have breached a warranty only (*Bettini* v. *Gye*, E.Q.B. 1876).

Breach of a condition gives the wronged party a right to rescind the contract (*Carson* v. *Jeffers*, H.C. 1961) but he has the option to affirm it. Regardless of whether he rescinds or affirms the contract the wronged party may claim damages for losses incurred. A breach of warranty does not entitle the wronged party to repudiate the contract but it does allow him to claim damages.

Conditions precedent and conditions subsequent

A contract may also be made subject to a condition precedent. If the condition is not fulfilled the contract does not come into operation at all. Similarly a contract may be made subject to a condition subsequent. If the condition occurs the contract is dissolved but without either party incurring any liability.

Innominate terms

There has been a tendency in recent years to move away from traditional classification of terms into conditions and warranties. It is argued that in the interests of justice, the right of a party to repudiate a contract for breach of a term should depend on the gravity of the breach and its consequences rather than on whether it is classified as a condition or warranty. (See *Hong Kong Fir Shipping Co. Ltd.* v. *Kawasaki Kisen Kaisha Ltd.* (E.C.A. 1962) and *Cehave N.V.* v. *Bremer Handelsgesellschaft M.G.L.* (E.C.A. 1976).

Exemption and limitation clauses

An exemption of liability clause is a term which seeks to exempt one or more of the parties from a liability which might arise out of adoption or performance of the contract. A limitation of liability clause seeks to limit the scope or amount of such liability. They are sometimes called "exclusion clauses."

These clauses are all phrased so as to exclude or limit the liability of a party for breaches of contract or tort. Clothes may be accepted for cleaning, *e.g.* "on condition that the company is not liable for any damage howsoever arising."

The courts and exemption clauses

The courts have been caught between conflicting objectives when dealing with such clauses. Contract law is based on the idea that courts will enforce the freely negotiated agreements of the public so that they feel obliged to give effect to exemption clauses if the parties agreed to such terms. But the courts are also aware that such clauses have come into widespread use in standard form contracts and "contracts of adhesion" in which the stronger party produces standard terms to which he requires the weaker party to adhere if he wishes to do business. Agreement to such clauses may be fictitious as the consumer has no real choice and must accept these terms or go without the goods or services.

The courts have tried to redress the balance in favour of the weaker party. They may

   (i) attempt to exclude the clause from the contract;
  (ii) strictly construe it against the party who relies on it, or
 (iii) defeat the clause on the grounds of fundamental breach of contract.

The legislature has also intervened so that in certain classes of contracts these clauses are restricted by statute.

(i) Eliminating the clause from the contract. An exemption or limitation clause becomes a term of a contract in the same way as any other term. It may be binding on a person who has signed a written contract even when the party to be bound has not read it as in the case of an English café proprietress in *L'Estrange* v. *Graucob Ltd.* (E.K.B. 1934). The clauses may be contained on a separate ticket or notice and they will bind a party to the contract provided the existence of the clauses has been brought sufficiently to his attention (*Parker* v. *S.E. Ry.*, E.C.A. 1877 and *Early* v. *Gt. S. Rys. Co.*, S.C. 1938). A person may also exempt himself from liability by making it a condition of a verbal contract but this is rarely done.

Exemption and limitation clauses have been held not to apply where their effect was misrepresented, and also where the party to be bound did not know of them, and their existence was not brought sufficiently to his attention. There was held to be inadequate notice, *e.g.* where a ticket containing or referring to the clauses was given as a receipt (*Chapelton* v. *Barry U.D.C.*, E.C.A. 1940); where the ticket was folded, although this was not enough to defeat a clause when notice was otherwise given (*Shea* v. *Great S. Ry. Co.* C.C. 1944); where notice came too late – after a person had signed into an hotel, for example (*Olley* v. *Marlborough Court Ltd.* E.C.A. 1949); although a person will be bound by an exemption clause in a memorandum of the agreement which he signs after the contract was made (*Slattery* v. *C.I.E.* H.C. 1968); where the ticket was dispensed by a machine so that the terms of the contractual offer could not easily be rejected (*Thornton* v. *Shoe Lane Parking* E.C.A. 1971).

It is no excuse to say that one did not read the notice (*McFarland* v. *Burns* 1897). A person cannot plead inadequate notice if he knows, or should have known, that such clauses apply from similar contracts entered into in a previous course of dealing with the party in question (*Kendall* v. *Lillico*, H.L. 1968).

(ii) Strict construction of the clause.   Where exemption or limitation clauses cannot be eliminated from the contract they will be strictly construed by the courts against the party seeking to use them to avoid liability. Where a person wishes to exclude liability for his own negligence he must make his intention clear as otherwise the clause will be construed as applying to liability arising from causes other than negligence. An ambiguous exemption clause did not, therefore, exempt the defendants in *Alexander* v. *Irish National Stud Co. Ltd.* (H.C. 1977) when the plaintiff's horse sustained fatal injuries through their negligence.

Other rules of law will also be used to defeat exemption clauses. If a contract with a minor contains a sweeping exemption clause depriving him of his rights it may be repudiated by him as detrimental to his interests. Such a clause was not allowed to hinder a minor from suing for injuries caused to his greyhound by the negligence of the defendants (*Harnedy* v. *Nat. Greyhound Racing Co. Ltd.* H.C. 1943).

Where a contracting party gives an oral undertaking which conflicts with an exemption clause it may be held to supersede it (*Couchman* v. *Hill*, E.C.A. 1947; *Evans* v. *Andrea Merzario Ltd.*, E.C.A. 1976). A person who is not a party to the contract may be personally unable to rely on an exemption clause (*Cosgrave* v. *Horsfall*, E.C.A. 1945), unless he can claim privity of contract in that a party to the main contract acted as his agent, thus making him a party to the agreement (*New Zealand Shipping Co. Ltd.* v. *A. M. Satterthwaite & Co. Ltd.* P.C. 1975).

(iii) Fundamental breach of contract.   Every contract may be said to have a fundamental obligation. If this is not fulfilled there is said to be a fundamental breach and the party responsible may not be able to avail of an exemption clause.

In Ireland it has been accepted as a rule of law that exemption and limitation clauses cannot be relied on to escape liability for fundamental breach. Where a consignment of scampi to be shipped from Dublin to Liverpool perished because of a failure to load them into a refrigerated hold, it was held that there was a fundamental breach, and the defendants could not rely on an exemption and limitation clause in the contract (*Clayton Love & Son (Dublin) Ltd.* v. *B. & I.*, S.C. 1966). It should be noted, however, that an Irish court might choose to regard this as a rule of construction as happened in England (*Photo Production* v. *Securicor Transport* H.L. 1980).

Statutory restrictions

There is a limit to the courts' power to protect weaker parties from oppressive use of exemption and limitation clauses. The legislature has intervened via the Sale of Goods and Supply of Services Act 1980 (see p. 129).

MISREPRESENTATION

Many things may be said during negotiations leading to the formation of a contract. Statements of opinion, puffs, and sales talk are not usually of any legal significance. Such expressions as "every home should have one," detergent that washes "whiter than white," come into this category. A contracting party will be liable, however, for statements of fact which are not true and which induce the other party to enter the contract. These untrue statements are misrepresentations. They may also be included in the terms of the contract if this is the express or implied intention of the parties. In that event the innocent party can sue either on the grounds of misrepresentation or breach of contract.

What constitutes misrepresentation

A party to a contract will be liable for misrepresentation provided the false statement purported to be one of fact and not of opinion or intention, and provided it was relied upon by the other party so that it influenced him to enter the contract.

It must be a false statement, or indication, of fact

A statement of opinion is not sufficient. In a case in England the seller of a farm in New Zealand stated that it could support 2,000 sheep, but as both parties were aware that the seller did not carry on sheep farming there, it was held to be merely a statement of opinion which did not constitute misrepresentation (*Bisset* v. *Wilkinson* P.C. 1927). A person will not usually be responsible for a misstatement of his intentions but a misstatement of present intentions may nevertheless amount to a misrepresentation where it fraudulently induces the other party to enter the contract (*Eddington* v. *Fitzmaurice*, E.C.A. 1885).

Even silence of a party may constitute an actionable misstatement where there is a failure to reveal changes in circumstances relevant to the contract. There was misrepresentation when a doctor failed to reveal the deterioration in value of a practice he was selling (*With* v. *O'Flanagan*, E.C.A. 1936), and when a bank official remained silent as to the true cash position of an investor in a joint investment undertaking (*Northern Bank Finance Corp. Ltd.* v. *Charlton* S.C. 1978).

The false statement must have been relied on

If the false statement did not induce the other party to enter the contract he has no claim to a remedy. Where a person makes his own investigation or where he enters the contract for other reasons, as where roofing material was bought because it was specified by the architects (*Southern Chemicals Ltd.* v. *South of Ireland Asphalt Co. Ltd.* H.C. 1976), there is no misrepresentation. The plaintiff must show that he relied on the misstatement. The purchaser of a house which turned out to have woodworm infestation was held not to have been induced to purchase by a misstatement that it was in "excellent structural and decorative repair" (*Smyth* v. *Lynn* Ch.D.N.I. 1950).

Where a person is given an opportunity to investigate the statements made and fails to do so he is not necessarily barred from suing for misrepresentation if the statements are false. A statement in the contract that a party is not to rely on the representations made by the other party will not be any protection against a claim for fraudulent misrepresentation (*Pearson & Son Ltd.* v. *Corp. of Dublin* H.L. 1907).

Contracts requiring positive disclosure

Some contracts require a party to make a full disclosure of relevant facts known to him. These include insurance contracts, and contracts made between principals and agents, between partners, between promoters and the companies they promote, and contracts involving a relationship of trust between the parties such as exists between a parent and child. In such cases a party may be liable for failing to disclose relevant facts, in addition to the normal liability for misrepresentation.

Type of misrepresentation

A misrepresentation can be

(1) fraudulent,
(2) negligent, or
(3) innocent

depending on the state of mind of the person making the false statement.

(1) Fraudulent misrepresentation. A misrepresentation is fraudulent when the false statement is made knowingly, or without belief in its truth, or recklessly, careless whether it be true or false (*Derry* v. *Peek* H.L. 1889). There is fraudulent misrepresentation when a vendor purposely exaggerates the turnover of a licensed premises he is selling and this misstatement is relied on by the purchaser (*Early* v. *Fallon* H.C. 1976). The party who is misled in this way may be allowed to rescind the contract and sue for damages for the tort of deceit (*Carbin* v. *Somerville*, S.C. 1933). The plaintiff may not want rescission and it may not be allowed if it is not appropriate, as when the parties cannot be restored to their previous position (*Fenton* v. *Schofield* S.C. 1965; *N.B.F.C. Ltd.* v. *Charlton*).

(2) Negligent misrepresentation. Only since the decision in *Hedley Byrne & Co. Ltd.* v. *Heller & Partners Ltd.* (H.L. 1964) has English law recognised that a non-fraudulent misrepresentation could be negligent and not just innocent. It was held that the defendant bankers, except for a disclaimer of liability, would have been liable for negligent misrepresentation in that they caused loss to the plaintiff advertising agents by providing them with a favourable credit reference for a company that went into liquidation. The decision established a principle that anyone with special knowledge or skill who applies it for the assistance of another, in contract negotiations or otherwise, owes a duty of care towards that person or to persons likely to be affected by it.

The principle was approved in Ireland in *Securities Trust Ltd.* v. *Hugh Moore and Alexander Ltd.* (H.C. 1964) although in that case faulty articles of association were held not to give rise to a misrepresentation as there was no duty of care owed by the defendant to the plaintiff. This duty of care can arise where one contracting party has such expertise that the other may be expected to rely on it. Thus Esso were held liable for negligent representations as to annual petrol consumption figures given for a garage which it leased (*Esso* v. *Marden* E.C.A. 1976).

The duty of care is owed not only to the person to whom it is given but to anyone "to whom it might reasonably be expected that the information would be conveyed" (*Stafford* v. *Mahony* H.C. 1980). A person who is induced to enter a contract on the basis of a negligent misrepresentation may be allowed to rescind the contract and in any event will be entitled to damages in tort for loss incurred as a result.

(3) Innocent misrepresentation. If the person making the false statement was neither fraudulent nor negligent, the misrepresentation was innocent. It was made without negligence and in honest belief that it was true. If the misrepresentation related to a material fact the injured party may rescind the contract, or if rescission is not possible he may instead be indemnified by a money payment. If the innocent misrepresentation becomes a contractual term damages may be awarded for any loss that results (*Bank of Ireland* v. *Smith* H.C. 1966).

Statutory remedy for misrepresentation

Part V of the Sale of Goods and Supply of Services Act 1980 provides additional remedies for misrepresentation in contracts for the supply of goods by sale, hire-purchase, or lease, and in contracts for the supply of services. Under section 45 (1) damages may be awarded for loss resulting from a non-fraudulent misrepresentation unless the defendant can prove that "he had reasonable ground to believe and did believe up to the time the contract was made that the facts represented were true." This section creates a new type of "negligent" misrepresentation in that the person making the statement will not be liable if he acts with due care. (See *Howard Marine & Dredging Co. Ltd.* v. *A. Ogden & Sons Ltd.* E.C.A. 1978, based on section 2 of the English Misrepresentation Act 1967 on which the Irish provisions are based.) Under section 45 (2) of the 1980 Act the court may award damages instead of rescission for negligent or innocent misrepresentation in the contracts specified where "it would be equitable to do so." No exclusion of liability or remedies for misrepresentation in such contracts are enforceable unless it is shown such an exclusion is fair and reasonable.

Duress

A contract is voidable on grounds of duress where it was made because of the actual or threatened violence to, or the false imprisonment of, the contracting party, his or her spouse, parents or children. The pressure exerted must involve a crime or tort, or a threat to commit a crime or tort. A threat to a person's goods, or a threat to take proceedings to assert a lawful right (*Headfort* v. *Brocket* H.C. 1966), is insufficient.

Undue Influence

A contract may also be avoided where subtle pressure, "undue influence," has been brought to bear on one of the parties to make him enter the contract.

If there is no special relationship between the parties there must be some unfair or improper conduct to establish undue influence

(*Allcard* v. *Skinner*, E.C.A. 1887). This includes cheating, conmanship and threats not necessarily amounting to duress.

Where, however, parties are in a special relationship with each other there is a presumption of undue influence, and the person in the dominant position must show that the other party exercised free and independent judgment otherwise the contract will be avoided if challenged. Special relationships include solicitor-client, doctor-patient, trustee-beneficiary, parent-child and religious superior-subordinate.

A contract of guarantee executed by a daughter on reaching 21 years of age, for the benefit of her mother who had managed the daughter's property during her minority, was avoided in *McMackin* v. *Hibernian Bank* (Ch. Div. Ir 1905). In *Provincial Bank of Ireland* v. *McKeever* (H.C. 1941), however, a mortgage in favour of a third party executed by a beneficiary on the inducement of his trustee, and which conferred a voluntary benefit on the trustee, was upheld as it could be shown to be the result of the free exercise of the beneficiary's independent will.

Unconscionable Bargains

Closely related to the doctrine of undue influence is a broader equitable principle that a court will intervene in a contract or other transaction to protect the weaker party from being victimised. There must be something unconscionable about the contract as where an advantage is taken of a weak, distressed, or mentally deficient person. It is said of such cases that there is "inequality of bargaining power" (*Lloyds Bank Ltd.* v. *Bundy*, E.C.A. 1975). A contract under seal, *e.g.* executed by a man of weak intellect, was set aside by the court in *Grealish* v. *Murphy* (H.C. 1946).

The person who seeks to validate the contract must establish its fairness but, if it is found to be unconscionable, it will be set aside. An impetuous contract to sell a farm, dwelling and tractor at an undervalue, which was made by a farmer who was not able to manage his affairs, was set aside as an unconscionable bargain in *Buckley* v. *Irwin* (Ch.D.N.I. 1960). Similarly in *Smelter Corporation* v. *O'Driscoll* (S.C. 1977) specific performance of a contract to sell property was refused where the vendor was wrongly led to believe that she had no real choice as her property would otherwise be acquired by compulsory purchase.

Such contracts will be upheld if shown to be fair. The secret purchase of a farm by a tenant, from a man who had received hospital treatment for depression, was upheld where the price paid was reasonable and there was nothing to indicate that the seller was unable to protect his own interests (*Haverty* v. *Brooks* H.C. 1970). Similarly a sale of a reversionary interest in a piece of land, by a nephew to his uncle, who already had a life interest, was upheld as it was conducted fairly although it was challenged on the grounds of undue influence and unconscionable bargain (*Smyth* v. *Smyth* H.C. 1978).

Mistake

A contract may be void or voidable on the grounds of mistake where the parties are at odds in their perception of the material terms, or where, unknown to them, the contract as agreed is impossible to perform.

Mistake as to material terms

A contract will be void or voidable because of mistake where a party is deceived by a rogue or conman into believing that he is dealing with a reputable party. If the person would not deal with the rogue and did not intend to do so, any purported contract is void from the beginning (*Cundy* v. *Lindsay* H.L. 1878). But if a person contracts with a party, and intended to do so, although deceived by his false pretences, there is a voidable contract which remains good until avoided. There was, therefore, a voidable contract where a supplier intended to contract with a person though a rogue (*King's Norton Metal Co.* v. *Eldridge, Merrett & Co. Ltd.* E.C.A. 1897), or to sell a car (*Lewis* v. *Averay* E.C.A. 1972) in person to a party who falsely pretended to be somebody else, or to exchange a car (*Anderson* v. *Ryan* H.C. 1976) with such a person. Although such a contract can be avoided for fraudulent misrepresentation, the contract is valid until this is done and the rogue can pass a good title in the goods to a purchaser buying in good faith.

If the parties are at odds concerning other material terms there will likewise be no contract. Where the parties bargain for completely different things, or where one party knowingly exploits a mistake in respect of the terms made by the other party, any alleged contract is void on grounds of mistake. A contract remains valid, however, where one party erroneously misinterprets the contract through no fault of the other party provided there is nothing ambiguous about the bargain. There was no mistake, *e.g.* when a purchaser bought a property believing that it contained two plots which were not included in the sale (*Tamplin* v. *James* E.C.A. 1880), or where a person took out a policy in the belief that he could get an interest-free loan but where there was in fact 5 per cent. interest payable on it (*Jameson* v. *Nat. Benefit Trust Ltd.* Ir.K.B. 1901).

Mistake as to possibility of performance

There may also be what is called "common" or "mutual" mistake because both parties do not realise the subject-matter of the contract does not exist or because it lacks some quality they believed it had. The contract is void if at the time it was made the subject-matter, *e.g.* a premises (*Hoban* v. *Bute Investments Ltd.* H.C. 1980), was not owned by the seller as they had believed. The contract is likewise void when the subject-matter was already destroyed or missing, or voidable where a fishery was already owned by the lessee (*Cooper* v. *Phibbs* H.L. 1867).

Where the parties are mistaken concerning some quality in the thing bargained for, it has been held in a number of English decisions since *Bell* v. *Lever Bros. Ltd.* (H.L. 1932) that such contracts are voidable rather than void and may be set aside on such terms as the court thinks fit. Where it was wrongly believed that there was planning permission to let premises as office space (*Laurence* v. *Lexcourt Holdings Ltd.*, E.Ch.D. 1978), the contracts were held to be voidable on terms, provided the misapprehension was fundamental, and the party seeking to set it aside was not himself at fault.

Loss of right to rescind

Although a contract may be voidable a party may lose his right to rescind. Rescission is a discretionary remedy and may not be given or may be allowed only on such terms as the court thinks fair and equitable. Rescission will not usually be allowed where the person affirms the contract, where it is not possible to restore the parties to their pre-contract position, or where it would be unfair to innocent third parties who have acquired rights deriving from the contract. The court may alternatively order rectification of the contract to eliminate the mistake (*Monaghan Co. Co.* v. *Vaughan* H.C. 1948).

Illegality

There are a number of situations in which an otherwise valid contract will be held to be unenforceable because it is in conflict with some statutory regulation, or because it is prohibited under common law because it is contrary to the public interest.

Contracts unenforceable by statute

Wagering or gambling agreements are unenforceable under the Gaming and Lotteries Act 1956. These agreements are not illegal in themselves but the law will not help the parties to enforce them. The Act also prohibits any action to recover money lent for betting purposes (*Anthony* v. *Shea*, C.C. 1951).

Other contracts likewise fall foul of statutory restrictions. Examples include an agreement to transport greyhounds for reward contrary to the Transport Acts (*O'Shaughnessy* v. *Lyons* C.C. 1957); a contract to convey a family home without the consent of the spouse as required by the Family Home Protection Act 1976 (*H.* v. *S.*, H.C. 1979).

A contract may also be temporarily unenforceable where permission required to pay for goods in foreign currency has not been given or has expired. The court cannot order payment for the goods as it is prohibited by law. The contract itself is valid but must await a time when such payments are no longer prohibited (*Namlooze Venootschap De Faam* v. *Dorset Manufacturing Co. Ltd.* H.C. 1948; *Fibretex* v. *Beleir Ltd.* S.C. 1949).

Contracts unenforceable at common law

Contracts which will not be enforced because they are contrary to public policy include contracts to commit a crime, tort, or fraud; contracts to frustrate the administration of justice, or to stifle a prosecution involving a matter of public interest (*Parsons* v. *Kirk*, Ir.Ex. 1855; *Nolan* v. *Shiels* C.C. 1926). The courts will not give effect to a contract which defrauds the revenue (*Starling Securities Ltd.* v. *Woods* H.C. 1977) or one promoting corruption in public life or fostering sexual immorality. The courts have regarded it as in the public interest to preserve the dignity of marriage and this duty is reinforced by article 41 of the Constitution. Separation agreements between estranged spouses are nevertheless enforceable (*MacMahon* v. *MacMahon* 1913; *Lewis* v. *Lewis* H.C. 1940) as are ante-nuptial agreements which limit the father's right to decide the religious education of his children (*Re Tilson* S.C. 1951)

Contracts in restraint of trade

These are contracts which restrict the freedom of a person to carry on whatever business, trade, or profession he chooses. The rule applies to contracts in which an employee is restricted in his liberty to compete against his employer on leaving his job. It applies to situations in which the seller of a business with goodwill restricts his own freedom to compete against the purchaser. Other types of contracts such as solus agreements, contracts for exclusive supply of goods or services, and even mortgages, may be invalid if unreasonably in restraint of trade.

All contract provisions in restraint of trade are prima facie void but they may be shown to be valid if they are reasonable in protecting the interests of the parties and provided they are not contrary to the public interest (*Nordenfelt* v. *Maxim* H.L. 1894;

Continental Oil Company of Ireland v. *Moynihan* H.C. 1977). If the restraint is excessive or contrary to public policy it will be declared void by the courts.

Restraints on employees

In contracts of employment a restraint on an employee will be upheld if it is reasonable in protecting the employer's trade secrets, or his business contacts such as a solicitor's clients (*Fitch* v. *Dewes* H.L. 1921). If, however, the restraint on the employee is excessive as regards the prohibited trades, the geographical area to which the restraint applies, or the time for which the restraint is to last, it will be invalid. A restraint on a solicitor that he should not set up practice within a 30-mile radius of Ballina and Charlestown and 20 miles of Ballaghadereen, was held to be unenforceable (*Mulligan* v. *Corr* S.C. 1925). A restraint on a hairdresser that he should not practise his profession within one mile of his employer's premises, during his employment or three years thereafter, was held to be unnecessarily wide and unenforceable (*Oates* v. *Romano* C.C. 1949).

Restraints on the seller of a business

The courts will more readily uphold a restraint on the seller of a business in favour of the buyer as the seller is paid for the goodwill of the business and it would be unfair to the buyer if he could set up in competition with him. The restraint on the seller must be reasonable in the circumstances (*Nordenfelt* v. *Maxim* H.L. 1894). Reasonable protection to the buyer extends only to the business interest bought and must not be excessive. It must give no more than adequate protection to the buyer, it must be justified in relation to the benefits given to the party restrained, and it must not be contrary to the public interest.

Restraints in Other Contracts

Similar principles have been applied to restraints in contracts for exclusive supply or purchase of goods and services. They have been applied to rules relating to the supply of milk to creameries (*McEllistrim* v. *Ballymacelligott Co-Op.*, H.L. 1919), to solus agreements to purchase petrol from one supplier only (*Esso* v. *Harpers Garage* H.L. 1968; *Irish Shell and B.P. Ltd.* v. *Ryan* H.C. 1966), and to contracts for exclusive services.

If the restraint of trade agreement is valid, it is normally enforced by an injunction and damages (*Arclex Optical Corp. Ltd.* v. *McMurray* H.C. 1958). Where such a contract is severable and the severed portion is reasonable, that part may be enforced (*Skerry* v. *Moles*, Ir.Ch.D. 1907).

Incapacity to Contract

Certain persons have limited legal capacity to enter contracts. These include young people who have not reached the age of majority (presently 21 years of age) who are called "minors" or "infants," persons incapacitated through drink or mental disorder, and corporations.

Minors
Young persons below the age of majority have limited contractual capacity.

(1) Minors may enter valid contracts for necessary goods and services and they may enter beneficial contracts of employment or apprenticeship. Necessary goods or "necessaries" are goods suitable to the condition in life of a minor and which are actually required by him at the time of sale or delivery. The contract will not be enforceable if the minor has enough of the goods already as where an undergraduate with sufficient clothes ordered more including 11 fancy waistcoats (*Nash* v. *Inman* E.C.A. 1908). A minor is only required to pay a reasonable price for necessaries and this may be less than the contract price. Trade goods bought for resale are not necessaries.

Beneficial contracts of employment or apprenticeship are also binding if they may reasonably be regarded as for the benefit of the minor (*Doyle* v. *White City Stadium Ltd.* E.C.A. 1935). If the terms are too harsh they will be invalid. (*De Francesco* v. *Barnum* E.C.A. 1890).

(2) Certain long-term contracts may be avoided by the minor while still a minor or within a reasonable time of reaching the age of majority. These include contracts involving an interest in land, or the acquisition of securities on the stock exchange, or a partnership agreement. Although he may repudiate such contracts, he may not be able to recover money paid if he has received consideration such as enjoyment of a lease (*Blake* v. *Concannon*, Ir.Ex. 1870) or the shares contracted for (*Steinberg* v. *Scala (Leeds) Ltd.* E.C.A. 1923).

(3) Under the Infants' Relief Act 1874 loans, contracts for goods other than necessaries, and book debts are "absolutely void." In practice, however, they are regarded by the courts as being merely unenforceable against the minor or voidable although he will not be allowed to recover back what he has already given where he has received consideration for it.

Although a minor is normally liable for torts such as negligence, he will not be liable where the effect would be to make him liable on a contract which is not binding on him (*Fawcett* v. *Smethurst* E.K.B. 1914).

Drunkenness and Mental Disorder

If a person, when he contracts, is so mentally disordered as to be unable to understand the nature of a contract, or if he is in such a state of drunkenness as not to know what he is doing, the contract is voidable if it can be shown that his condition was known to the other party.

Corporations

Statutory corporations and companies formed under the Companies Acts may have limited powers or *vires* to enter contracts. If they make contracts which are beyond their powers the contracts are said to be *ultra vires* and void. This rule has been modified, however, in that contracts made in good faith with directors of companies are deemed to be valid. If the contract is *ultra vires* it will still bind the company but the director himself will be liable to his company for any loss sustained thereby (Companies Act 1963, s.8; European Communities (Companies) Regulations 1973). A contract may still be *ultra vires* and unenforceable where the creditor is supplied with a copy of the memorandum and mistakenly believes it to authorise the transaction (*Northern Bank Finance Corp. Ltd.* v. *Quinn*, H.C. 1979).

THE TERMINATION OR DISCHARGE OF A CONTRACT

Performance

A contract is not usually discharged by performance unless that which is done exactly matches that which was agreed to be done under the contract. Anything less than full performance is a breach of contract and may mean the party responsible will not be able to sue on the contract to recover payment or other benefits.

In the interests of justice, however, an incomplete performance will still entitle a party to sue to recover payment for a completed part of a severable contract. Likewise, where completion of the contract is prevented by the other party, a person may bring an action in damages for breach of contract, or he may sue on a *quantum meruit* to recover reasonable payment for work done. A person may also sue on an incomplete performance of the contract where the partial performance is accepted by the other party, or where the contract is in fact substantially performed.

Where a partial performance has been accepted the law assumes thereby a willingness and intention to make a reasonable payment for the work done, and an action may be brought on a *quantum meruit*. Where a person has no choice but to accept the partial performance there may be no implicit promise to pay. An agricultural worker who agreed to work for the defendant for a year but who voluntarily quit the job could not recover wages due or payment on a *quantum meruit* (*Creagh* v. *Sheedy*, C.C. 1956). A person may likewise have no option but to accept a partially constructed house built on his own land and an agreement to pay for the work done cannot be inferred from such acceptance (*Coughlin* v. *Moloney* Ir.C.A. 1904).

A person who has substantially performed his obligations is likewise entitled to sue on the contract. It would be unfair to a person who has substantially performed what he contracted to do to deprive him of all payment. The court can, however, make deductions from his remuneration to cover the costs of rectifying any defects, *e.g.* defects in the repair of a house (*Dakin* v. *Lee*, E.C.A. 1916).

Where it is a condition in a contract that it be performed within a certain time, it is said that "time is of the essence" of the contract. Time will be of the essence where that is an express or implied term of the agreement or if time is vital considering the nature of the contract. Time may be made of the essence also where a party has delayed in performance and has been notified that if he does not complete the contract by a specified reasonable date the contract will be treated as breached (*Hynes* v. *Independent Newspapers* S.C. 1980).

Performance can be carried out vicariously by someone other than the contracting party when it does not involve personal skill, integrity or artistic ability. The contracting party, however, remains liable for any defects in performance.

Agreement

Contracts are formed by agreement and may also be varied or terminated by agreement. Some contracts of a continuing nature such as employment contracts, contracts of agency or franchises may be terminated by agreement when one or other of the parties gives the required notice. If no period of notice is specified, such contracts may be terminated by either party giving reasonable notice. An agreement to discharge or vary a contract is itself a new contract subject to the rules governing consideration. The agreement may involve the transfer of one party's obligations to some third party. A tripartite agreement of this nature, where one contract is substituted for another, is referred to as novation.

Frustration

The parties to a contract are excused further performance of their obligation if some event occurs during the currency of their contract, without fault of either party, which makes further performance, as envisaged by the parties, impossible.

Performance may be frustrated where the subject-matter of the contract is destroyed (*Taylor* v. *Caldwell* E.Q.B. 1863) or where further performance would be illegal as where pension rights were claimed in respect of a judicial office which had been abolished by statute (*O'Crowley* v. *Minister for Justice* H.C. 1934). There is frustration of contract also where further performance would be in appearance only, as the real or substantial purpose of the contract cannot be fulfilled (*Krell* v. *Henry*, E.C.A. 1903). A contract to perform personal services is frustrated by sickness but it is not frustrated if vicarious performance is possible (*Flynn* v. *Great Northern Ry. Co.*, H.C. 1953; *Belfast Banking Co.* v. *Hamilton* Ir.C.A. 1883).

It is not sufficient if the alleged frustrating even merely causes hardship, loss, or inconvenience or where *e.g.* the contract proved more difficult due to shortages of skilled labour and building materials (*Davis Contractors Ltd.* v. *Fareham U.D.C.*, H.L. 1956). There will be no frustration if the event has been provided for in the contract, or if it was foreseen or reasonably foreseeable so that it should have been covered by a contractual term.

The parties must as a rule suffer any losses under the contract that have accumulated up to the moment of frustration. A party may, recover money paid where there has been a total failure of consideration, *i.e.* where he has received no benefit at all from the agreement.

Breach

A contract may end by actual breach when a party fails to perform the contract, or it may end by anticipatory breach when he makes it clear that he is not going to, or renders himself unable to, perform the contract. No discharge of the contract occurs until the innocent party rescinds by choosing to treat the contract as at an end. The innocent party is entitled to ignore the breach and to tender performance on his part, and in any event is not entitled to rescind if the other party is merely in breach of warranty see *White and Carter (Councils) Ltd.* v. *McGregor*, H.L. 1962).

Remedies for Breach of Contract

Where a contract has been breached the innocent party can apply to the court for a legal remedy provided he acts without delay. Under the Statute of Limitations 1957 an action on a simple contract must be brought within six years of the date when the cause of action arose, or within 12 years where the contract was by deed. An action for personal injuries must be commenced within three years, however. The limitation period may be extended where the plaintiff was under some disability, as where he was a minor or of unsound mind, or where the plaintiff did not discover the breach because of fraud or mistake.

Rescission

Where there has been a breach of condition the innocent party may accept the breach as discharging the agreement. If he is in doubt about his right to rescind, or where he requires the return of a deposit, he may apply to the court for an order of rescission (*Hughes* v. *Carter* H.C. 1978).

Regardless of whether the innocent party rescinds the contract he may sue in addition for damages.

When rescission takes place the contract is terminated at the time of rescission whereas in the case of misrepresentation the contract is deemed never to have existed if rescission is allowed. The right to rescind may be lost where the innocent party cannot restore benefits received under the contract and he must be content with damages. If rescission is allowed the parties must restore any benefits received except in the case of a deposit given as an "earnest" or guarantee of performance (*Sepia Ltd.* v. *M. & P. Hanlon Ltd.* H.C. 1977).

Damages

The purpose of damages is to put the innocent party, by an award of money compensation, into a position equivalent to the one he would have been in if the contract had been performed.

The contract itself may specify a sum to be paid by way of liquidated damages in the event of a breach of contract. If the specified sum is a genuine pre-estimate of damages it will be recoverable, but if it is a penalty to secure performance it will be void and unenforceable. Guidelines to distinguish one from the other were formulated by Lord Dunedin in *Dunlop Pneumatic Tyre Co. Ltd. v. New Garage and Motor Co. Ltd.* (H.L. 1915). Where the specified sum, for example, is extravagant or unconscionable compared with the conceivable loss, or where it is greater than a money debt due under the breach, it will be held to be a penalty. It is also presumed to be a penalty when the same sum is recoverable for a variety of breaches, great or trivial (*Laird Bros. v. City of Dublin Steam Packet Co.*, N.P. 1899). The fact that it is difficult to pre-estimate a loss is, however, no obstacle to the specified sum being recoverable as liquidated damages.

The loss for which damages may be recovered

Where there is no designated sum provided for in the contract, or where such a sum is void as a penalty, the court must determine what losses resulting from the breach are compensatable. Under the rule in *Hadley v. Baxendale* (E.Ex. 1854) the court will grant compensation for losses resulting naturally from the breach or which may reasonably have been in the contemplation of the parties, when they made the contract, as likely to result from a failure to perform it. On these principles the plaintiff, Hadley, failed to recover £300 for loss of profits, from the defendant carrier who was five days overdue in delivering a broken crankshaft from the plaintiff's flour mill in Gloucester to an engineer in Greenwich, where it was needed as a pattern for a new one.

These principles have been reconsidered in more recent times (*Koufos v. C. Czarnikow Ltd.* H.L. 1969) but remain the basis on which the courts decide which losses are not too remote from the breach to be compensatable. In *Maye v. Merriman* (H.C. 1980), for example, the purchaser of a farm failed to recover £19,400 in damages where the vendor was two weeks late in closing the sale and the price of cattle to stock the farm had increased in the meantime. The judge held that the loss had not arisen as a natural consequence of the breach and the price of cattle could just as easily have fallen. The vendor had not, by implication or otherwise, undertaken that he would be liable for such a loss.

Quantifying the damages

The amount of the damages is assessed on the basis of a reasonable and fair estimation of the plaintiff's loss. This may be determined by a comparison with market prices (*Whitecross Potatoes v. Coyle* H.C. 1978). The plaintiff is required to produce evidence of his loss, but if such evidence is unavailable, the court will not hesitate to speculate on his loss and award damages accordingly.

A party is entitled to compensation for incidental expenses caused by the defendant's breach (*Murphy* v. *Mulligan* H.C. 1976) and for normal loss of profits, but not for special unspecified profits (*Victoria Laundry (Windsor) Ltd.* v. *Newman Industries* E.C.A. 1949).

A plaintiff is also entitled to damages for physical inconvenience arising from the breach of contract. Until recently no damages were awarded in breach of contract cases for mental distress and loss of enjoyment. This rule changed, however, following an English decision which awarded such damages arising out of a breach of warranties made in relation to a ski-ing holiday in Switzerland (*Jarvis* v. *Swan's Tours Ltd.*, E.C.A. 1973). Similar cases involving breaches of contract by tour operators have arisen in Ireland. Damages for loss of enjoyment can be awarded for breach of other types of contract also as where the loss arises from defects in a dwelling-house built by the defendant (*Johnson* v. *Longleat Properties (Dublin) Ltd.* H.C. 1976; *Quin* v. *Quality Homes Ltd.* H.C. 1977).

Mitigation of loss

The rules concerning quantification of damages are subject to the principle that the plaintiff must take reasonable steps to mitigate or moderate his loss otherwise his compensation must be reduced in fairness to the defendant. In *Johnson* v. *Longleat Properties* the plaintiff was allowed the cost of making good defects in his house at the lower rate prevailing when the contract was breached and not at the rate prevailing at the date of the litigation because the extra cost arose from the plaintiff's failure to effect the repairs at an earlier date. Where, however, it would be unreasonable to expect the plaintiff to do some act in mitigation of his loss he will not be penalised if he fails to do it (*Quinn* v. *Quality Homes*).

Other factors may also affect the amount of damages awarded. In relevant cases the amount of damages may be reduced to take into account any sums claimed for out of which income tax would have been paid (*Glover* v. *B.L.N. Ltd.*, H.C. 1973). Where the plaintiff is a foreigner an award may be made in a foreign currency or the Irish currency equivalent (*Damen & Zonen* v. *O'Shea* H.C. 1977). An award of damages may be set aside where the loss arose indirectly from bad faith or unreasonableness on the part of the plaintiff (*McCord* v. *E.S.B.*, S.C. 1980). A defendant who makes a profit as a result of a breach of contract will be deprived of it but only where he has acted in bad faith (*Hickey and Co. Ltd.* v. *Roches Stores (Dublin) Ltd.* H.C. 1976). In awarding damages the court will take account of inflation where it is necessary to adequately compensate the plaintiff and where the inflationary loss was a reasonably foreseeable consequence of the breach (*Hickey and Co. Ltd.* v. *Roches Stores (Dublin) Ltd.* (No. 2.), H.C. 1980).

Specific Performance

Specific performance is a court decree ordering a contracting party to perform a contract he has made. Damages may be awarded instead of, or as well as, specific performance. If the court is of opinion that damages would be adequate compensation it will not order specific performance. Contracts for the sale of land are usually enforced in this way, but sale of goods contracts are not, unless the goods in question are rare or unique.

Specific performance is an equitable remedy. It will only be given at the discretion of the court and is not available as a legal right. The court is guided by established principles and will only grant this remedy where it would be just and equitable in all the circumstances of the case (*Conlon* v. *Murray* C.A.N.I. 1958). It will not be given as a remedy to enforce a contract of a personal nature such as an employment contract (*Fitzpatrick* v. *Nolan*, Ir. C. of Ch. 1851; *Gillis* v. *McGhee*, Ir. Rolls C. 1862) or where it could not theoretically be ordered against the plaintiff himself. A plaintiff may not be granted an order of specific performance where he himself has been in default of his obligations as where he deliberately delays the completion of a sale (*O'Brien* v. *Seaview Enterprises Ltd.* H.C. 1976) or where the contract involves an attempt to defraud the revenue (*Starling Securities Ltd.* v. *Woods* H.C. 1977), or where in the circumstances the court believes it is unsuitable (*Carthy* v. *O'Neill* H.C. 1979).

Injunction

An injunction is a court decree ordering a person to do, or not to do, a certain act. It can be given as a remedy to restrain a party from committing a breach of contract, particularly to enforce a valid restraint of trade. It is a discretionary remedy which will only be given when it is fair to the parties and in circumstances in which an order for specific performance might have been made.

It is a suitable remedy in a contract of an on-going nature as where the court granted a mandatory injunction ordering an oil company to supply petrol quotas (*Westward Garages* v. *B.P. Irl.* H.C. 1979). An interlocutory injunction is also very useful in preserving the status quo pending a court hearing. It will be typically granted where the plaintiff establishes a prima facie case (*T.M.G. Group* v. *Al Babtain Trading Co.* H.C. 1980) or where it is appropriate on a balance of convenience in dealing justly with the parties (*Lift Manufacturers Ltd.* v. *Irish Life Assurance Co. Ltd.*, H.C. 1979).

Other Remedies

Where a person may be unable to claim a remedy for breach of contract he may instead be able to recover on the basis of a *quantum meruit* or in quasi-contract.

A claim may be made on a *quantum meruit* ("as much as he has deserved") where the contract makes no express provision for price or remuneration in return for goods sold or work done. If there is an express provision for the price or remuneration to be paid, a claim on a *quantum meruit* cannot replace the expressly agreed provisions. If, however, the contract was void or rescinded such a claim could be made. Where a contract of employment was void because the required sanction of the Minister was not obtained, the employee was entitled to six months' salary on a *quantum meruit* for work done (*O'Connell v. Listowel U.D.C.*, C.C. 1956). Similarly, if the contract is unenforceable because either it was not fully performed by the plaintiff or because it did not comply with the Statute of Frauds, and the defendant accepted the work done, a claim may be made on a *quantum meruit*.

Where one person has become unjustly enriched at the expense of another, the wronged party may sue in quasi-contract to recover money due to him.

5 Sales and the Law

Almost all business activity is concerned with buying and selling. Special rules govern supply of goods by sale, lease, and hire-purchase. Buying and selling are frequently conducted through the medium of agents.

Agency

If a housewife gives a £1 to a youngster (John) with instructions to buy sugar from the local grocer and John accepts the task, the relationship of agency exists between them. The housewife who has delegated authority is called the principal and John, who agrees to act on her behalf, is called the agent. If John goes to the shop and asks for a kilo of sugar for the housewife, and the grocer gives him the sugar, a binding contract has been made between the grocer and the housewife. John has no rights or obligations under the contract he has arranged for his principal. John as agent has affected the legal position of the housewife who is his principal and the fact that he has the authority to do this means the relationship of agency exists between them. The person with whom the agent deals on behalf of his principal is often referred to as the third party.

In this hypothetical situation John has undertaken to act as agent without any reward. There is no consideration involved and therefore no contract. This is a gratuitous agency. If the housewife promised to pay 10 pence to John for his services the agency relationship between them would now be based on a contract. This agency contract between principal and agent should be distinguished from any contracts which the agent creates for his principal with third parties.

Agency, then, is the relationship which arises when one person called an agent has authority in law to bind another person called a principal by making contracts or property arrangements with others on the principal's behalf.

Modern commercial life is based on specialisation and large work units owned by companies. Such business cannot be conducted without agents to manage, buy, sell and provide specialist services.

The Existence of Agency is a Question of Fact

When the average person thinks of an "agent" he probably envisages a dealer who stocks a particular manufacturer's products. In law, however, these dealers are not usually agents in the legal sense but merely traders on their own account who stock a particular manufacturer's goods under a special contract called a franchise or concession. These traders cannot normally contract with their customers so as to create legal relations between the customers and the manufacturer. They are not, therefore, the agents of the manufacturer in the legal sense and the manufacturer is not their principal.

If a manufacturer can control and regulate a dealer's actions the dealer will not be an independent trader but will be deemed to be an agent. Whether a person is or is not another's agent is a question of fact to be determined on all the circumstances of the case (*Williamson* v. *Rover Cycle Co.*, Ir.C.A. 1900).

The Classification of Agents

(1) *General and special agents*
If an agent has authority to conduct a series of transactions in the ordinary course of his trade, business or profession, or to act for his principal in all matters of a particular nature or trade, then he may be called a general agent. A special agent, by contrast, is one who is authorised to carry out a prescribed set of transactions only. An estate agent instructed to sell a property could be called a special agent.

(2) *Mercantile agents, factors and brokers*
Factor is the old name for any agent entrusted with possession of goods for purposes of sale in either his own name or in his principal's name. Factors were typically agents residing abroad or at a distance from the owner and were given possession of the goods, or documents of title to the goods, so that they might be sold on the appropriate market.

A *broker* of goods is an agent who negotiates for the sale of goods in the principal's name but does not have possession of the goods or of documents of title to them. The commission paid to such agents for their services is called brokerage.

The law relating to agents who negotiate the sale of goods was amended by the Factors Act 1889. This Act uses the term *"mercantile agent"* which is defined as any agent:

> "having in the customary course of his business as such agent authority either to sell goods, or to consign goods for the purpose of sale, or to buy goods, or to raise money on the security of goods."

The term "mercantile agent" therefore includes both the factor and broker of goods. In fact it would seem that the law will quite readily declare an agent to be a mercantile agent who will attract the protection of the statute. See *e.g. Lowther* v. *Harris*, E.K.B. 1926; *Midwood* v. *Kelly*, Ir.C.A. 1901).

(3) *Estate agents*

An *estate agent* negotiates sale or purchase of land, including buildings, on behalf of his principal. He is normally employed by owners of property to obtain offers from prospective purchasers. He has no usual or implied authority to conclude a sale for his principal (*Roony* v. *Thomas* H.C. 1947), or to prepare a memorandum or agreement for the sale of land (*Lynch* v. *Bulbulia* H.C. 1980). Most cases concerning an estate agent's authority were considered by Kenny J. in *Law* v. *Roberts & Co. (Irl.) Ltd.* (S.C. 1964), whose conclusions were endorsed by the Supreme Court. Among other propositions he pointed out that an owner who puts his property on the books of an estate agent, or who informs him of the lowest price he will accept, does not by such actions authorise him to conclude a contract. If the owner instructs the estate agent to sell at a fixed price then the agent is authorised to conclude an open contract at that price. Where the estate agent is expressly authorised by the owner to accept an offer made to the agent, he has authority to conclude an open contract with the purchaser. An open contract is one in which the terms, except for the essential ones, are left to be implied by the general law, especially as regards title.

An estate agent will not usually be entitled to commission unless he does what he was employed to do, namely, to obtain a purchaser. If sale of the property did not really and substantially proceed from the agent's efforts he has not earned commission (*Brandon & Co.* v. *Hanna*, Ir.C.A. 1906; *Judd* v. *Donegal Tweed Co. Ltd.* H.C. 1935). The owner must pay commission where he wrongfully refuses to complete the sale (*Rohan* v. *Molony*, Ir.K.B. 1905; *Cusack* v. *Bothwell* C.C. 1943) or where he wrongfully terminates the agency and the sale is completed by a new agent (*O'Hanlon* v. *Belfast Inns Ltd.* H.C.N.I. 1961). If two estate agents are employed by the seller and both are instrumental in making a sale the owner will be liable to both (*Etchingham* v. *Downes*, C.C. 1945). If no express term for commission has been agreed, the estate agent will be entitled to reasonable remuneration for the work performed (*Henehan* v. *Courtney* H.C. 1966).

(4) *Del credere, confirming and forwarding agents*

A *del credere agent* undertakes to indemnify his principal should the third party to whom he sells the principal's goods fail to pay for them. In return the agent usually gains a higher rate of commission, a *del credere* commission. Such agents are especially useful to exporters who can sue the *del credere* agent for loss if the buyers, whom they may not know personally, fail to pay for the goods. Because the agent is connected with the sale of the goods he is held to indemnify rather than guarantee the transaction. A *del credere* contract does not therefore have to be evidenced by writing under the Statute of Frauds, and the agent is only responsible for the price of the goods when the buyer fails to pay for them. He guarantees the buyer's solvency and this gives him a sufficient interest to sue the buyer on a bill of exchange accepted by him.

To some extent the *del credere* agent has been replaced in modern times by the *confirming or export agent* who may not only guarantee payment but also undertake liability for actual performance of the contract. If these so called "agents" actually purchase the goods and then resell them at a profit to foreign importers they are acting on their own account and not as agents. When, however, they buy as agents for a foreign importer they may undertake liability to the seller of the goods for the price and the performance of the contract and thus provide a service similar to that provided by the *del credere* agent. Both are also mercantile agents under the Factors Act.

International overseas trade involves arrangements for carriage, insurance, and transfer of title in goods. A *carrier* is not usually an agent for the shipper or consignor of goods but agrees to transport them for reward under a contract of carriage. An exporter will often employ a *forwarding agent* to look after the problems of arranging carriage. He will be the agent of the owner of the goods unless he contracts with him as a carrier in his own right.

The General Principles of Agency

How agency arises

(i) Actual authority, express or implied. Agency is usually created under a contract of agency, enforceable between principal and agent, which determines their respective rights and duties. The contract may be made by express words, whether spoken or written, or it may be implied from the conduct of the parties. In most cases no formality is required. An agent cannot, however, execute a deed for his principal unless it is done in the presence of his principal and at his direction, or unless the agent is himself given this authority in a deed, when he is said to have powers of attorney.

Because an agent is acting on behalf of his principal he need not have full contractual capacity provided the principal himself has capacity to enter the contract arranged by his agent. A person with limited capacity, such as a minor, cannot, however, circumvent his incapacity by appointing an agent not affected by his handicap. A mentally disordered person cannot validly appoint an agent while in that state.

Implied agency. An agency relationship may also arise from the conduct of the parties. If they consented to an arrangement which amounted to agency in law then an implied agency will be held to exist between them. Where a motor accident victim consulted the insurance company's solicitor rather than his usual one, he was held to have adopted him as his agent (*Kearney* v. *Cullen* H.C. 1955). It was held that there was prima facie a relationship of agency between the Festival of Kerry Committee and owners of beagles, where the committee organised a drag hunt, and sheep were later killed by some of the dogs (*Crean* v. *Nolan* C.C. 1963).

But even where there is an express agency terms may be implied into the agreement by the courts. Every agent has implied authority, in the absence of express provisions to the contrary, to do everything necessary and incidental to the performance of his instructions and in accordance with the usual way in which the particular business is conducted. The court must sometimes rule on whether a local custom (*O'Connor* v. *Faul* C.C. 1956), or a custom of trade (*Wilson & Strain Ltd.* v. *Pinkerton* Ir.Q.B. 1897), or a certain right to commission (*Ward* v. *Spivack Ltd.* S.C. 1957; *Hilton* v. *Helliwell*, Ir.Q.B. 1893) is an implied term of the contract. A term may be implied that a sole distributing agent would not deal in goods belonging to competitors of his principal (*Irish Welding Ltd.* v. *Philips Electrical (Ir.)* H.C. 1976).

(ii) Usual authority implied by law. Persons who occupy positions which normally carry the authority to act for a principal will be deemed to have the usual authority associated with their position in absence of notice to the contrary. Directors, partners, estate agents, solicitors and others may have such authority to act as persons of that class usually have. A third party is entitled to assume that they have such authority and in absence of notice it is usually irrelevant that they have been deprived of their usual authority. A railway booking agent or clerk has usual authority to make contracts with customers and in absence of notice it is irrelevant that his authority to do so had been limited by his principal (*Anderson* v. *Chester and Holyhead Ry. Co.* C.P. Ir. 1854).

A wife has authority implied by law to pledge her husband's credit for necessary goods and services appropriate to her customary lifestyle. The husband and wife must be living together or if they live apart it must not be through any fault on the part of the wife. The wife's right is based on a presumption that she is expressly or by implication the agent of her husband for this purpose, but this presumption can be rebutted. It also applies to a mistress, where the man and woman appear to the outside world to be husband and wife. The wife's agency never applies to anything other than necessary goods and services, and it may be rebutted by showing that her husband forbade her to pledge his credit or that he gave her a sufficient allowance (*Morel Bros. & Co. Ltd.* v. *Earl Westmoreland* H.L. 1904). If there is evidence that she was not acting with her husband's authority (*Moylan* v. *Nolan* Ir.Q.B. 1864) or that the tradesman gave credit to the wife as principal (*Saul* v. *Nelson* H.C. 1962) the husband will not be liable. Where, however, a husband has turned his wife out of the house and she is living apart from him against her will and without means, the wife can buy necessaries for herself and her family and the husband will be liable. In this case the husband has an obligation to his family and he cannot renounce it. A husband was held liable for necessaries bought by his wife where she had to leave her husband's home because of the abuse she received from her sister-in-law (*Devine* v. *Monahan* H.C. 1932), and where the husband, who had failed to get an annulment, refused to allow his wife back to his house (*Johnston* v. *Manning* Ir.Q.B. 1860). In such circumstances the husband will be liable also for the legal costs where the wife is justified in bringing proceedings for a legal separation even if the action fails (*Bradley* v. *Bradley* H.C. 1971).

(iii) Apparent authority by estoppel. If one person by words or conduct represents another as having authority to act on his behalf he will be bound by the apparent agent's acts as if he had expressly authorised them. The alleged principal will be estopped from disputing the agency though in fact no agency really existed. Estoppel in agency prevents a person, because of his conduct, from asserting something which is true (that no agency exists) in order to deal justly with a third party who relied on his misrepresentation.

A plaintiff must prove that the alleged principal represented expressly or by implication that the agent had authority to act for him. In general, the courts exercise caution in finding that there was agency by estoppel. No matter how many times an agent is specially authorised to act for his principal that never of itself makes him a general agent with ostensible authority to act for his principal in all like cases (*Foley* v. *Garden* Ir.K.B. 103; *Barrett* v. *Irvine* Ir.K.B. 1907).

(iv) **Authority of necessity.** In some situations the law confers an authority on one person to act as the agent of another without requiring the principal's consent. The courts will uphold an agent by necessity provided his actions were reasonably necessary in the circumstances; it was practicably impossible to communicate with the principal; and provided the agent acted bona fide in the principal's interests.

(v) **Retrospective authority by ratification.** If a person, without authority to do so, contracts with a third party on behalf of a so-called "principal," that "principal" can subsequently adopt the contract by ratifying it. Retrospective ratification is only possible where the agent contracts on behalf of a named or identified "principal". The contract when ratified dates back to the time negotiated by the agent (*Bolton & Partners Ltd.* v. *Lambert*, E.C.A. 1889; *Athy Guardians* v. *Murphy*, Ir. C. of Ch. 1895). Ratification is usually achieved by the express written or spoken words of the principal which indicate his acceptance of the agent's actions. There may also be implied ratification when the principal adopts the contract by dealing in the goods. A principal may likewise ratify an act done in excess of the agent's authority, expressly or impliedly by, *e.g.* accepting payments out of the purchase price of a property sold by the agent (*Barclays Bank* v. *Breen* S.C. 1956). There will be no implied ratification where the alleged principal seeks to compromise an action brought on a disputed agency (*Barrett* v. *Irvine*).

The Agency Relationship

The relationship between principal and agent is usually based on an express or implied contract. But even where there is no contract, as in a gratuitous agency, the law always imposes a fiduciary relationship. The agent is required to exercise his authority in good faith for the benefit of his principal. He will not be allowed to personally profit from his position without the principal's permission.

The primary duties of an agent come from the express or implied agreement which he has with his principal. He cannot exceed his authority, and he is obliged to obey his principal's instructions provided they are lawful and reasonable and fall within the scope of their agreement. He must perform the principal's business with reasonable care and skill, and if the agent has any special skill or training he must use it where it is relevant to the conduct of the principal's affairs.

The fiduciary duties imposed on the agent are more rigorous still. He must not become involved in any other activity which conflicts with the best interests of his principal. He cannot make a secret profit or take any indirect benefit without the principal's permission. The agent may, however, acquire a profit or benefit, where it has been disclosed, and the principal has consented expressly or impliedly (*Sherrard* v. *Barron* C.A.N.I. 1923).

There is an obligation on an agent not to delegate authority without the principal's permission. This is sometimes referred to as the maxim *delegatus non potest delegare* (a delegate cannot delegate) (*Maxwell* v. *Parnell* Ir.Ex.Ch. 1869).

The Legal Consequences of the Agent's Contracts

A contract made by an agent can bind (1) the principal and third party only or (2) the agent and the third party only or (3) both the principal and third party, and the agent of the third party.

(1) *Principal and third party only*
The existence of a relationship between the principal and the third party may depend on whether the agent disclosed or did not disclose the involvement of the principal to the third party. A principal is called a disclosed principal when his existence is known to the third party at the time of contracting. If the third party knew his name he is a named (disclosed) principal. If he knew there was a principal but did not know his name then the principal is an unnamed (disclosed) principal.

As a rule a disclosed principal, whether named or unnamed, is liable and entitled on the contract and the agent is not. However, words used, conduct, or the surrounding circumstances may show that the agent is liable and entitled either instead or as well as the principal.

Undisclosed principal. A principal is undisclosed when his existence is not known to the third party at the time of contracting. Although the third party intended to deal with, and believed he had dealt with, the agent only, the undisclosed principal may sue and be sued on the contract provided certain conditions are fulfilled:

(i) The agent must have had authority from the principal to make the contract.

(ii) An undisclosed principal cannot sue on a contract where the third party can show that he wanted to deal with the agent for reasons personal to the agent such as his skill, solvency, or artistic ability, or because they would not have contracted with the agent if they knew who he was acting for (*Said* v. *Butt*, E.K.B. 1920).

(iii) If the contract made by the agent can be construed as having in it an express term that the agent is really the principal, then the undisclosed principal has no right to sue on it.

(2) *Agent and third party only*

As a general rule an agent is neither liable nor entitled under a contract he makes on behalf of his principal.

An agent will be liable, however, if he shows an intention to undertake personal liability, or where he contracts under seal without authority, or where he contracts as the principal's trustee. He will, of course, be liable where he is really acting for himself or where the principal is non-existent. An agent will be strictly liable for breach of warranty of authority where he causes loss by falsely representing himself as having the principal's authority (*McDonnell* v. *McGuinness*, S.C. 1939).

(3) *Principal and agent liable to third party*

The third party may sue both principal and agent where the circumstances, words, or conduct of the agent result in both parties being contractually bound. The third party has the option of suing either the principal or the agent, but he cannot sue both (*Jordie & Co.* v. *Gibson*, Co.Ct. 1894).

Debts Paid to The Agent

As a rule when the principal owes a debt and gives the money to his agent to pay it and he fails to do so, the principal will still be liable to pay the debt provided the third party knew that the agent who contracted the debt did so for his principal.

Ending the Agency Relationship

Where an agency relationship is based on contract it may terminate in the same way as any contract can end by performance, agreement, frustration or breach. The agency contract, like an employment contract, is unusual in that it may be an on-going arrangement with no time fixed for its termination. In such cases the contract may be ended by agreement, by either side giving the required notice, or where no time is fixed, by giving reasonable notice. Failure to give notice without justification is a breach of the agency contract.

SALE OF GOODS

The general principles of contract apply

Contracts for the sale of goods are regulated by two principal statutes. These are the Sale of Goods Act 1893 (the 1893 Act) and the Sale of Goods and Supply of Services Act 1980 (the 1980 Act). The latter Act amends and extends the 1893 Act and also regulates other areas of law, particularly contracts for the provision of services and contracts for the provision of goods by lease and hire-purchase, with a view to providing better legal protection for the consumer. References in this chapter to the 1893 Act will generally be to that Act as amended by the 1980 Act. These two statutes do not contain all the rules governing sale of goods. They contain only the partly modified common law rules peculiar to contracts for sale of goods, and all other matters are governed by the ordinary rules of contract. In addition, the parties to a sale of goods contract are not generally bound to accept the provisions of the 1893 Act. Except as regards certain implied terms relating to the seller's title and to the quality and fitness of the goods, the parties are quite free to make their own agreement and to exclude most of the statutory provisions (s.55(1)).

A sale of goods contract is therefore like any other contract in law, except that the provisions of the Sale of Goods Act 1893 as amended may apply to it. It is up to the parties to make their own bargain. The Act for the most part merely sets out the rules which will apply where some detail of their arrangement is not covered by express agreement.

What is a Sale of Goods Contract?

Definition

The 1893 Act concerns the sale of goods contract which is defined as "a contract whereby the seller transfers or agrees to transfer the property in goods to the buyer for a money consideration, called the price." It may be a sale between one part-owner and another as where a firm sells goods to a partner or where the goods are owned in common by seller and buyer (s.1(1)). A barter or exchange of goods will not be governed by the Act (see *Clarke* v. *Reilly*, C.C. 1962; *Flynn* v. *Mackin*, S.C. 1973).

In addition a sale of goods contract must be one for "goods" which are defined as including all chattels personal other than things in action and money (s.62). This definition is based on the traditional classification of *chattels personal* (that is all personal property except leasehold land) into two categories

   (i) *things, or choses, in action* such as debts, shares, patents and cheques, and

   (ii) *things or choses in possession* which consist of physical, tangible, movable articles of property such as merchandise, cattle, cars and furniture.

A sale of goods contract must involve physical movables which can range from purchase of a bar of chocolate to elaborate contracts for the supply of raw materials, machinery, aircraft or ships. Growing timber (*Gilmore* v. *O'Connor Don* S.C. 1947) and non-industrial crops such as fruit, grass and clover, are part of the land, that is they are real property, until severed, but then become chattels personal. Growing turnips (*Dunne* v. *Ferguson*, 1837), and a letting of meadowing (*Scully* v. *Corboy* H.C. 1948), have been held to be goods by the Irish courts. Whereas money is excluded from the definition of goods if the money has some unique attribute for the collector and is not just a currency, it may be the subject of a sale of goods contract.

Contracts for services and hire-purchase contracts

A contract for work and materials will usually involve transfer of ownership of material goods but it is a contract for services and is not governed by the Sale of Goods Act. The distinction between the two types of contract is based on whether the main object of the agreement is to sell goods or to provide labour or other services. If a person buys ready-made fitted kitchen units which have to be installed by the seller, he is contracting to buy goods although there is labour involved. If, however, he hires a carpenter to make and instal fitted kitchen units from materials supplied by the carpenter, he will have acquired ownership under a contract for work and materials governed solely by contract law and not the 1893 Act.

Similarly a person who acquires goods on hire-purchase cannot invoke the Sale of Goods Act, as the agreement is not one of sale but a contract to hire the goods for a rental with an option to buy them. A credit sale agreement, by contrast, will be governed by the Act provided the buyer buys or commits himself to buying the goods. These distinctions have, however, become less important since some of the implied terms in the Sale of Goods Act have been extended to contracts for the provision of services, and to contracts for the provision of goods by hire and hire-purchase, under the Sale of Goods and Supply of Services Act 1980.

Two Types of Sale of Goods Contract – Sales and Agreements to Sell

The 1893 Act divides contracts for the sale of goods into two types. Where ownership (called "property" in the Act) passes immediately under the contract, the transaction is called a *"sale."* But where ownership of the goods is to pass at a future time, or subject to some condition thereafter to be fulfilled, the transaction is called *"an agreement to sell"* (s.1(3)).

The significance of the distinction

A sale of goods contract can be absolute or conditional (s.1(2)). If the conditions are not fulfilled then the agreed consequences follow. Goods, *e.g.* may be sent on approval, or may be sold subject to a condition that the seller may resell them if they are not collected and paid for within a specified time.

If a sale of goods contract is a sale, the transaction has two features. It is a contract and it is a conveyance which passes property (ownership) in the goods from seller to buyer. If the transaction is an agreement to sell it is merely a contract and property (ownership) remains for the time being in the seller.

The importance of the distinction is that the rights of the buyer and seller depend to some extent on who owns the goods at the significant time. If the goods are destroyed, the loss normally falls on the person who owns them. If there is a breach of contract, the party owning the goods has normally rights in the property as well as personal rights against the defaulter. In a sale, therefore, where ownership has passed to the buyer, the seller can sue for the price of the goods "bargained and sold," even if there has been no delivery, *i.e.* no transfer of possession. The buyer can, of course, sue for breach of contract, but he can also sue in tort for conversion or detinue if ownership has passed to him and the goods have not been delivered. In an agreement to sell, the parties have only personal rights for breach of contract.

Forming The Contract

Formation of a sale of goods contract is largely governed by the ordinary rules of contract not specifically mentioned in the 1893 Act. There must be agreement between the parties, an intention to create legal relations and consideration. The contract may be made by deed, in writing, spoken words, by the conduct of the parties, or a mixture of these (s.3).

Formality required

Where goods are valued at £10 or over the contract cannot be enforced unless one of the following conditions is fulfilled (s.4):

(i)   There has been acceptance and receipt of part of the goods by the buyer; or

(ii) he has given something in earnest to bind the contract or in part payment; or

(iii) there is a written note or memorandum containing the terms of the contract and signed by the party to be sued or his agent.

(i) Acceptance and receipt.   An oral contract for goods valued at £10 or more will be enforceable where part or all of the goods have been accepted and received by the buyer. "Acceptance" is defined by the 1893 Act and is deemed to occur when "the buyer does any act in relation to the goods which recognises a pre-existing contract of sale whether there is an acceptance in the performance of the contract or not." The buyer may reject the goods as unsuitable, or as being not in accordance with the contract, but his action will still be an "acceptance" for the purposes of this section, as long as it recognises that a contract was made.

"Receipt" is not defined by the 1893 Act but is interpreted as a delivery of the goods into the actual or constructive possession and control of the buyer. There will be delivery if the buyer removes any part of the goods, if they are given to a carrier deemed to be acting as agent for him, if the seller or some other third party holds the goods as bailees for the buyer, or even if they happen to be already in the possession of the buyer who now acts as the owner of the goods. An alleged constructive delivery, however, must change the nature of that possession from owner to bailee (*Jennings* v. *MacAulay*, H.C. 1936).

(ii) Earnest or part payment.   Although an earnest or deposit need not technically be a money payment, it is usually a nominal sum given to the seller as a token that the parties are in earnest in concluding the contract. The sum given may be separate from, and in addition to, the purchase price, or it may be given as a part payment which will be deducted from the purchase price, but which will also make the contract binding. A contract for the sale of seven acres of meadowing was enforceable where the buyer gave the seller £5 as part payment. The court held that the meadowing which was fit and ripe for cutting should be defined as goods and not an interest in land, so that it was governed by the 1893 Act (*Scully* v. *Corboy*

H.C. 1948). The earnest must be given by the buyer, but it must also be willingly taken by the seller (*Kirwan* v. *Price* C.C. 1958).

(iii) Note or memorandum in writing. The memorandum must contain all essentials of the contract such as names or identity of the parties, goods involved, price if it has been agreed, and any other significant term. Invoices were held not to be a sufficient memorandum in an action for non-delivery of whiskey because they omitted significant terms (*Mahalen* v. *Dublin and Chapelizod Distillery Co. Ltd.*, Ir.Q.B. 1877).

The memorandum can be any kind of writing made between the time the contract was created and the bringing of the action, which has been signed by the party to be sued or by his agent. It may consist of a number of documents provided they are attached together or refer to each other. The signed documents must acknowledge the contract alleged to have been made (*Haughton* v. *Morton*, Ir.Q.B. 1855). If the terms of the contract are not clearly stated or if the note is not signed the memorandum is not sufficient (*Russell* v. *Hoban* Ir.C.A. 1921). Where the signed memorandum contains a term not alleged to be in the contract sought to be enforced it is not a sufficient memorandum (*Jennings* v. *MacAulay & Co.* H.C. 1936) although there must be a doubt about this where the term benefits the defendant and is accepted by the plaintiff.

In modern business practice there will usually be a memorandum of the contract where purchase order forms, invoices, and acknowledgment slips are used routinely by the parties. In over-the-counter sales the buyer usually accepts and takes the goods away with him, or else puts a deposit on the goods or makes a part payment by way of earnest. The deposit or earnest is normally a guarantee that the buyer will complete the sale so that prima facie he loses the deposit if the sale is not completed through his fault. Whether the deposit or earnest is or is not returnable depends on the intentions of the parties when the arrangement for the deposit was made.

The Terms of the Contract

The contents of the contract of sale will be determined by the normal principles of contract as previously examined.

The Express Terms

In a typical sale of goods contract the parties will expressly agree on the basic terms of their agreement. These will normally include the amount, quality, and (where technical goods are concerned) a detailed specification of the goods, the price to be paid, and the time and method of delivery. In the absence of express agreement some of these terms will be governed by the Sale of Goods Act 1893.

The goods

The goods which are the subject-matter of the contract may be "existing goods" which are owned or in the possession of the seller. They may alternatively be "future goods" which have yet to be manufactured or acquired by the seller and, as such, the contract for their sale may be subject to a contingency (s.5) *e.g.* the sale of a crop provided it grows.

Existing goods or future goods may be "specific," "ascertained," or "unascertained" depending on whether or not the goods have been identified and agreed to as the goods forming the basis of the contract.

The price

It is not essential to the contract that a price be agreed by the parties provided they agree on a feasible method of fixing the price. Section 8 of the 1893 Act states that the price may be fixed by the contract "or may be left to be fixed in a manner thereby agreed, or may be determined by the course of dealing between the parties." If a price is not determined in any of these ways then the buyer must pay a price which is found to be reasonable in the circumstances of the case.

Where it is agreed that a price is to be fixed by a valuer who cannot or will not make a valuation, then, under section 9, the contract is avoided but a reasonable price must be paid for any goods delivered. A reasonable price will normally be the market price of the goods. If the valuer's failure to settle a price is caused by the seller or buyer, the party not at fault can sue for damages.

If, however, the parties intend to fix a price by further negotiation, or if the "agreed" method of price determination is too vague to be given effect, the court may hold that no contract was created as they failed to conclude their agreement.

Conditions of sale

A common business practice is for the seller, or buyer, or both to contract on the basis of their own standard conditions of sale or purchase. These conditions are usually contained in, or referred to, on their standard forms. Where the goods are of a technical nature these conditions can be elaborate, and may cover everything from quality and delivery to insurance and infringement of patents.

The Implied Terms

The 1893 Act

Important terms, concerning the title or quality of the goods, may be implied into a sale of goods contract under sections 12 to 15 of the 1893 Act as amended. Section 12 implies a condition in all sale of goods contracts that the seller has a right to sell the goods and a warranty that they are free from undisclosed charges. A seller with a limited title may sell goods but in that event there are implied warranties that all charges have been disclosed and that the buyer will have quiet possession except as regards the charges disclosed to him.

Where goods are sold by description, which they usually are, there may be an implied condition that the goods correspond with the description (s.13). When goods are sold in the course of business there is an implied condition that the goods are of merchantable quality. They must be fit for reasonable use subject to the price, description and other relevant circumstances. This condition does not apply, however, to defects which are specifically drawn to the buyer's attention, or to defects which he ought to have seen when he has examined the goods before buying them (s.14 (2)(3)).

If the buyer expressly or by implication makes known to a business seller his purpose in buying the goods then there is an implied condition that the goods supplied are reasonably fit for that purpose. This condition will not apply, however, where the seller can show that the buyer did not rely on the seller's skill and judgment, or that it would have been unreasonable for him to rely on the seller's skill and judgment (s.14 (4)).

In a contract for the sale of goods by sample there may be implied conditions under section 15 that the bulk shall correspond with the sample, that the buyer shall have a reasonable opportunity of comparing the bulk with the sample, and that the goods shall be free from any defect not apparent on a reasonable examination of the sample which would make the goods unmerchantable (see p. 169).

The 1980 Act

Under section 12 of the Sale of Goods and Supply of Services Act 1980 there is an implied warranty in contracts for the sale of goods that the seller will make available, for the specified period if any, such spare parts and "adequate aftersale service" as are stated in any offer, description or advertisement given by the seller, or given by him on behalf of the manufacturer. The Minister for Commerce and Trade is empowered by the Act to define by order what a reasonable period will be in relation to any class of goods.

There is an implied condition, under section 13, in all sales of motor vehicles, except when the buyer is a dealer, that at the time of delivery, the vehicle is free from any defect which would render it a danger to the public, including persons travelling in the vehicle. This term will not be implied when, in a fair and reasonable agreement, it is agreed that the vehicle is not intended to be used in its condition of delivery, and a document to that effect is signed and given to the buyer by the seller. Similar terms are implied into contracts for the supply of goods by lease and hire-purchase.

The Significance of the Contract Terms

Conditions and warranties

The terms of a sale of goods contract, whether express or implied, can be classified into conditions, warranties, or exemption and limitation of liability clauses under the normal principles of contract.

If the buyer and seller intended, or are deemed by the court to have intended, themselves to be bound by a particular statement, then it will be a term of their contract. If a term is regarded as vital to the contract it will be a condition, but if it is only subsidiary to the main purpose of the contract it will be merely a warranty. The terms implied by statute are classified into conditions or warranties by the 1893 Act and the 1980 Act.

Whether a non-statutory stipulation in a contract of sale is a condition or warranty depends in each case on the construction of a particular contract. A stipulation may be a condition although called a warranty. A breach of condition gives the innocent party a right to repudiate the contract, but a breach of warranty is a minor breach which gives rise to a claim for damages only.

Where there has been a breach of a condition by the seller the buyer may either waive the condition entirely and treat the contract as fulfilled, or he may choose to treat the breach of condition as a breach of warranty and sue for damages while still treating the contract as being in existence (1893 Act, s.11).

If, however, a contract is not severable, and the buyer has accepted a part or all of the goods, then he must treat any breach of a condition by the seller as a breach of warranty unless he is otherwise entitled by an express or implied term of the contract (s.11(3)). The situations in which a buyer will be deemed to have accepted the goods are set out in section 35 (see p. 132).

Exemption and limitation clauses

Widespread use of exemption clauses and the growth of the

consumer movement brought demands for change in the United Kingdom, leading to introduction of two statutes there, the Supply of Goods (Implied Terms) Act 1973 and the Unfair Contract Terms Act 1977. Similar provisions were adopted in Ireland as part of the Sale of Goods and Supply of Services Act 1980.

It is no longer possible for a seller of goods to totally exclude the statutory implied terms from the sale of goods contract. Under section 55 of the 1893 Act, as amended, any term of the contract which exempts a party from the provisions of section 12, concerning the seller's title, is void.

Any term exempting a party from the provisions of sections 13, 14 or 15 or the 1893 Act, concerning implied terms as to quality and fitness of the goods, will be void where the buyer deals as consumer, and in any other case will not be enforceable unless it is shown to be "fair and reasonable."

Similarly, any term exempting the parties from the provisions of sections 12 and 13 of the 1980 Act, concerning spare parts, aftersale service, and the safety of motor vehicles, is void. As regards contracts for the supply of goods or services it is only possible, as we shall see, to exempt or limit a party's liability for misrepresentation where it can be shown that it is fair and reasonable to do so (1980 Act, s.46). A person will generally be dealing as a consumer when he is actually and apparently acting in a private or non-business capacity. A test as to what is a "fair and reasonable" exclusion is set out in a Schedule to the 1980 Act and is based on section 11 of and Schedule 2 to the United Kingdom Unfair Contract Terms Act 1977 (see p. 172).

The provision in section 55 of the 1893 Act which regulates any attempted exclusion of the implied terms under sections 12 to 15, concerning title, quality and fitness of the goods, do not apply to genuine international contracts for the sale of goods (s.61(6)). A new section 55A is, however, inserted into the 1893 Act to prevent the parties from getting around the provisions in section 55 by choosing an unrelated foreign law to govern their contract.

Defects in a Sale of Goods Contract

The sale of goods contract may be unenforceable unless the formalities specified in section 4 of the 1893 Act have been fulfilled. The contract will be subject to the normal rules concerning capacity to contract and to transfer and acquire property (s.2). The usual principles concerning mistake will apply. Where specific goods have perished without the knowledge of either party at the time the contract is made, the contract is void (s.6). This provision contained

in section 6 is believed to embody a decision in *Couturier* v. *Hastie*
(H.L. 1856) where a buyer and, therefore, the defendant agent, were
held not liable on a contract for the sale of a cargo of corn which had
in fact been sold in transit at the time the contract was made, as it
was deteriorating due to the weather. Specific goods are goods
identified and agreed upon at the time the contract was made
(s.62(1)).

Misrepresentation

Some alterations were made to the law relating to misrepresentation by Part V of the Sale of Goods and Supply of Services Act 1980.
They are modelled on the English Misrepresentation Act 1967.

A person who has a right to rescind the agreement for negligent or
innocent misrepresentation no longer necessarily loses that right
because the misrepresentation was made a term (that is a warranty)
of the contract, or because the contract has been performed, or
because both of these things have happened (1980 Act, s.44).

Where a party to a contract suffers loss from a non-fraudulent
misrepresentation he will now, in these contracts, be entitled to
damages, but only if the other party was "negligent." The party
making the misrepresentation can escape liability if he proves that
he had "reasonable grounds to believe and did believe up to the time
the contract was made that the facts represented were true"
(s.45(1)).

Where a party is entitled to rescission for non-fraudulent
misrepresentation and seeks such a remedy, the court may
nevertheless uphold the contract and award damages instead, if it
would be equitable to do so, considering the nature of the
misrepresentation and the possible loss to both parties (s.45(2)).
Damages awarded in lieu of rescission must be taken into account in
assessing any damages claimed for loss caused by the misrepresentation (s.45(3)). Any provision excluding or restricting liability for a
misrepresentation, or excluding or restricting another party's
remedies for a misrepresentation will not be enforceable unless
shown to be fair and reasonable in accordance with the criteria set
out in the Schedule to the 1980 Act (see p. 172).

Discharging the contract

A sale of goods contract terminates in the same way as any other
contract by performance, agreement, frustration, or breach.

Performance

Part III of the 1893 Act specifies in detail what will constitute
performance of a sale of goods contract.

The seller has a duty to deliver the goods, *i.e.* to transfer possession of them, and the buyer is obliged to accept and pay for them, and both must do so in accordance with the terms of the contract (s.27). Unless otherwise agreed, the handing over of the goods (delivery) and payment are concurrent conditions (s.28). The parties must be willing to perform, and it is no excuse for a seller to refuse to send wool sold, for example, because no cheque was sent or money tendered by the buyer (*MacAuley* v. *Horgan* H.C. 1924) unless this is a term of the contract.

The place and date of delivery

Whether the buyer must come and take possession of the goods, or whether the seller must send them to the buyer depends on the contract. A merchant was held to be in breach of contract for not delivering coal at the places specified (*Board of Ordnance* v. *Lewis* Ir.Q.B. 1855).

Where no place of delivery is agreed it is assumed that the goods will be handed over at the buyer's place of business, if he has one, or his residence, or at some other place if it is known that the goods are stored there. A specified date of delivery is usually held to be a condition of the contract, but, in the absence of an agreed date, delivery must be made within a reasonable time and in a reasonable way, and the seller must put the goods into a deliverable state. If the goods are held by a third party, there will be delivery, that is a transfer of possession, when the third party acknowledges that he holds the goods for the buyer (s.29).

Delivery of wrong quantities

If less than the contract quantity of the goods is delivered the buyer may reject them, or accept the lesser quantity and pay at the contract rate. If the seller delivers more than the contract quantity, the buyer may reject the lot, or accept the contract quantity and reject the excess, or accept the whole amount and pay for them at the contract rate. Where sellers delivered £65 worth of flags instead of £28 worth, the buyer was held to be justified in rejecting the lot (*Wilkinson* v. *McCann, Verdon & Co.*, Ir.Q.B. 1901).

Similarly, where goods contracted for are sent mixed with others which were not ordered, the buyer may either reject the whole, or accept the goods contracted for and reject the rest (s.30).

Instalment deliveries

A buyer need not accept delivery by instalments unless this is specifically agreed. A Dublin firm were held entitled to reject a delivery of carpets and other floor covering from a Glasgow company because the whole order had not been tendered together in one lot. Some of the order which was subsequently sent was retained and paid for but this was held to be, in effect, a new contract (*Norwell & Co.* v. *Black* C.C. 1930). Where part of an instalment is not in accordance with the contract the buyer may reject the whole instalment (*Tarling* v. *O'Riordon*, Ir.C.A. 1878).

Delivery through a carrier

Sections 32 and 33 of the 1893 Act deal with responsibilities of the parties for shipment, insurance and deterioration of the goods during transit.

Delivery of goods to a carrier is prima facie deemed to be a delivery to the buyer but it depends on whether the carrier or other bailee of the goods is acting as agent for the seller or the buyer. In a C.I.F. (Cost, Insurance and Freight) contract, Irish port, cash against documents, it was held that the French sellers had not delivered yarn until the carriers had landed the goods at Dublin, which was after the delivery date, so that the Irish buyer was entitled to reject them (*Michel Freres Société Anonyme* v. *Kilkenny Woollen Mills* H.C. 1959). A buyer was held liable, however, to pay for paper although it was destroyed by fire in a warehouse, where it had been temporarily stored by the seller's carriers, on the instruction of the buyers (*Spicer-Cowan Ireland Ltd.* v. *Play Print Ltd.* H.C. 1980).

Acceptance by the buyer

If the buyer accepts delivery he is no longer entitled to go back on his action and to reject the goods for breach of a condition by the seller, unless he is empowered to do so by an express or implied term of the contract (s.11(3)). The buyer can reject the goods, however, before acceptance, for breach of condition including the grounds for rejection specified by the 1893 Act. For this reason, if he has not previously examined the goods, there is deemed to be no acceptance until he has a reasonable opportunity of examining them to see if they are in conformity with the contract (s.34). In *Marry* v. *Merville Dairy Ltd.* (C.C. 1954) it was held reasonable for a dairy to defer acceptance of milk until tested at their premises.

Subject to this right to examine the goods for the first time, the buyer is deemed to have accepted them if he lets the seller know that he has accepted them, if he treats the goods as his own, or if he retains them "without good and sufficient reason" without letting the seller know he has rejected them (s.35). A buyer may therefore lose his right to reject the goods, as by allowing the unloading of a load of turf to continue after it was obvious that it was not of the quality contracted for (*Gill* v. *Heiton & Co. Ltd.* H.C. 1943).

Where the buyer rightfully rejects the goods he does not have to see to their return, unless otherwise agreed, but need only inform the seller (s.36). If the buyer wrongfully refuses to take delivery within a reasonable time he becomes liable to the seller for any loss caused and for storage during the period the seller was forced to retain the goods for him (s.37).

Discharge of the Contract in Other Ways

A sale of goods contract may end by agreement where the parties decide to give up their rights under it, or where they vary the contract to such an extent that they end the old contract and create a new one. The normal contract principles apply and there must be consideration to make the new agreement enforceable.

The doctrine of frustration applies to contracts for the sale of goods and they will be terminated in accordance with the usual principles where further performance is illegal or impossible. The contract is avoided under section 7 of the 1893 Act when specific goods perish, without fault of the buyer or seller, between the time of contracting and the passing of the risk to the buyer. A contract was terminated by frustration where the contract goods were known to be only obtainable from a country which became enemy territory, making any trade therewith illegal (*Ross Bros. Ltd.* v. *Shaw & Co.* Ir.K.B. 1917).

A sale of goods contract will end by breach of condition where the innocent party rescinds the contract. Breach of contract also gives the party who suffers loss a right to a remedy.

Remedies for Breach of Contract

The buyer and seller are entitled to the appropriate and usual contractual remedies. Sale of goods contracts are, however, unusual in that the seller has also rights which do not derive from the contract, but are property rights which give the seller in possession of goods sold a security for their price.

Contractual Remedies

The seller
The seller's usual contractual remedies are rescission, an action for the price, and damages for non-acceptance of the goods.

Rescission is only available where the buyer is in breach of a condition of the contract.

A seller may bring an *action for the price* when the buyer "wrongfully neglects to pay" for the goods, and provided either property in the goods has passed to the buyer or, where the price was payable irrespective of delivery on a certain date, that date has passed (s.49). This is the usual action brought by the seller and is usually defended on the ground that there was breach of contract by the seller in that the goods were defective or on the grounds of misrepresentation, as in *Southern Chemicals Ltd.* v. *South of Ireland Asphalt* (H.C. 1980) which involved roofing materials.

Where the buyer "wrongfully neglects or refuses to accept and pay for the goods" the seller may sue him for *damages for non-acceptance* (s.50).

The buyer

Likewise where the seller "wrongfully neglects or refuses to deliver" the goods, the buyer can sue for *damages for non-delivery* (s.51). Damages are assessed by following the normal contract principles taking into account the loss sustained on the basis of the market for the goods, if any, at the relevant date. Thus the damages awarded for failure by a Cahirciveen seller to deliver wool was based on the price of wool on the Dublin market less the cost of carriage to Dublin at the time of refusal to deliver (*McAuley* v. *Horgan* H.C. 1925).

If the contract is for specific or ascertained goods the court has discretion to order *specific performance* on such terms as the court thinks just (s.52). In practice, however, specific performance is only ordered where damages would be inadequate as where the goods are relatively unique in some respect.

The buyer too may be entitled to reject the goods and *rescind* the contract where the seller is in breach of a condition. He cannot do this however where, as we have seen, he has accepted the goods under section 35, or for breach of warranty. If, for example, the goods delivered are not the goods contracted for, the buyer is free to reject them. In *American Can Co.* v. *Stewart* (Ir.K.B. 1915) it was held that the defendant, who refused to accept and pay for 30 adding machines, which would not do precisely what they were represented to do, was not liable on the contract. The buyer must exercise his right to reject the goods within a reasonable time, or he will lose the right but without prejudice to his right to sue in damages for breach of the contract by the seller (*C. E. MacAulay & Co. Ltd.* v. *Lannon* S.C. 1954).

The Unpaid Seller's Security Through Possession

In addition to his contractual remedies, the unpaid seller who has actual or constructive possession of the goods can hold them as security for the price. An unpaid seller is one to whom the whole price has not been paid or tendered, or who has received conditional payment by means of a cheque, for example, which has been dishonoured. The seller's agent, if he is in the position of the seller, can also exercise security over the goods (s.38).

Retention or lien

The unpaid seller in possession of the goods can retain them if property has not passed to the buyer, or he can exercise a lien over the goods or any part of them where property in them has passed, provided there was no stipulation as to credit, or the buyer's credit has expired or he has become insolvent (s.41). Under these conditions the unpaid seller is entitled to hold on to the goods until the price is paid or tendered. This right ceases, however, on delivery of the goods to a carrier without reserving a right of disposal, or when the buyer or his agent lawfully obtain possession of the goods, when the goods are paid for or the seller waives his lien, or where an innocent third party has acquired a good title to the goods.

Stoppage in Transit

When the buyer becomes insolvent the unpaid seller has a right of stoppage in transit, *i.e.* a right to resume possession of the goods and to retain them until paid for, provided the goods are in transit (s.44). Transit ceases, in general, when the buyer or his agent obtains possession or when the goods are held by a carrier or other bailee as agent for the buyers (s.45).

Right to Resell

The seller in possession of the goods who has not been paid may also resell them where he reserved the right to do so, or where the goods are perishable, or where he gives notice of his intention to resell and the buyer does not pay or tender the price within a reasonable time. A resale by the seller rescinds the original contract but the buyer remains liable for damages (s.48).

Where the buyer lawfully holds documents of title to the goods and transfers them to a person who takes them in good faith and for valuable consideration, then, if the transfer is by way of sale, the seller's rights of retention, lien, and stoppage in transit are defeated, or if it is by way of pledge, the seller's rights are subject to the rights of the transferee (s.47).

Transfer of Property in the Goods

The Sale of Goods Act 1893 is not concerned with the contract of sale alone, but also deals with the personal property problems involved in a sale. The unique feature of a sale of goods contract is that it involves a conveyance, *i.e.* a transfer of property or ownership in the goods from seller to buyer.

Importance of the transfer of property
Whether property in the goods remains with the seller or has been transferred to the buyer is important for a number of reasons. If the goods are lost or damaged, then, as a rule, the person who has property in the goods is the one who must suffer the loss. The buyer's right to claim the goods if the seller becomes bankrupt, and the right of the buyer's creditors to the goods in the event of the buyer's bankruptcy will generally depend on whether or not the property in them has passed to the buyer. As we have seen, the seller can sue the buyer for the price of the goods if property has passed (s.49). If the buyer resells the goods to a third party he will usually give him a good title only if he himself has property in the goods, but there are exceptions to this rule. Finally, the separation of property or ownership from possession allows the seller to deliver the goods subject to title reservation.

The Time when Ownership is Transferred

The moment at which property or ownership in goods is transferred from seller to buyer depends partly on whether the goods are specific, ascertained, or unascertained.

Specific goods are defined as "goods identified and agreed upon at the time a contract of sale is made" (s.62). Thus where the parties have agreed that particular and unique articles are the ones being contracted for, and none other, then the goods are specific ones. When the goods are identified and agreed upon after the contract is made they become, and are called, ascertained goods.

Unascertained goods, can be either generic goods, such as any 50 cartons of Carrolls No. 1 cigarettes, or goods forming part of a larger consignment or bulk such as 20 tons of unselected coal from a heap in the coal merchant's yard.

Where the Goods are Specific or Ascertained

In the case of specific or ascertained goods, the property in them is transferred to the buyer at such time as it appears that the parties intended it to be transferred, judging by their conduct, the terms of the contract, and other circumstances (s.17).

If, as it often happens, the intention of the parties is not clear, then, unless it appears otherwise, it will be presumed that they intended property to pass in accordance with the rules in section 18.

Rule 1

Under the first rule property in the goods passes to the buyer when the contract is made, provided the contract is an unconditional one for the sale of specific goods, which are in a deliverable state. In such a case it is immaterial whether the time of payment for the goods, or delivery, or both, are postponed until later. In *Clarke* v. *Reilly & Sons* (C.C. 1962), the plaintiff had been involved in an accident and had damaged a second-hand car which he had previously traded-in, but which the garage allowed him to use pending delivery of a new one he had purchased. The court held that ownership had passed to the defendant garage proprietors as soon as the contract was made. As the plaintiff was merely a bailee of the car and had taken reasonable care of it, the defendants must bear the loss.

It should be emphasised that the rule will not apply if a different intention appears from the contract. It has been said that it does not take much to give rise to an inference that property is to pass only on delivery or payment.

Rules 2 and 3

Rules 2 and 3 concern situations in which the goods are specific goods but the seller has to either

(i) Put the goods into a deliverable state (rule 2), or
(ii) although the goods are deliverable, he must weigh, measure, test or do some other act to determine the price (Rule 3).

In these situations the property in specific goods (again, in the absence of a contrary intention) does not pass until such act or thing is done and the buyer is notified. Where a car is bought on the basis that panel beating will be done to it, property will not pass until this is done, as only then will the goods be in a deliverable state (*Anderson* v. *Ryan* H.C. 1967).

A "deliverable state" is defined as "such a state that the buyer would under the contract be bound to take delivery . . . ." (s.62(4)).

Rule 4

Where goods are sent to a prospective buyer "on approval" or "on sale or return," property in the goods passes to the buyer:

    (a) When he signifies his approval or acceptance to the seller or does any other act (pawns them for example) adopting the transaction.

    (b) If he does not signify his approval or acceptance but retains the goods without giving notice of rejection, then, if a time has been fixed for the return of the goods, on the expiration of such time, or if no time has been fixed, on the expiration of a reasonable time, the property in the goods passes to the prospective buyer.

If the goods are damaged during the approval period the prospective buyer will be liable if it happens through his fault. If the damage is without fault of either party the seller must bear the risk. If the buyer retains the accidently damaged goods beyond a reasonable period property passes to him and he must pay for them.

Note, however, that these principles are now subject to section 47 of the Sale of Goods and Supply of Services Act 1980 which provides that in certain cases unsolicited goods will be deemed to be an unconditional gift to the recipient.

Unascertained goods – Rule 5

Where the contract is for unascertained goods (such as 20 tons of wheat from a larger bulk cargo, or any 20 barrels of Guinness) no property in the goods passes to the buyer unless and until the goods are ascertained (s.16).

In addition under rule 5 of section 18, in order to pass property in unascertained or future goods, there must be

    (a) an unconditional appropriation of specified goods to the contract by either the seller or the buyer and

    (b) the express or implied assent to this appropriation by the other party.

There will be an unconditional appropriation of the goods to the contract only when the party intends to attach them irrevocably to the contract. The time at which this happens depends on the circumstances and it may occur when the goods are assigned to a carrier at the buyer's request. In such circumstances the risk of deterioration (not the risk of loss or damage) remains with the buyer unless otherwise agreed (s.33). If, however, the goods begin to deteriorate before delivery the seller must bear the risk of deterioration as in the case of a Valentia Island fish exporter who sent 20 boxes of mackerel to a London buyer but the fish began to deteriorate because of delay before they were appropriated to the contract at Holyhead, by the railway officials, at his instructions (*Healy* v. *Howlett*, E.K.B. 1917).

Where an item, such as a barge, is being constructed over a period of time, property in the portion finished may pass progressively to the buyer if that is the intention of the parties (*Howden Bros. Ltd.* v. *Ulster Bank Ltd.* Ch.D.N.I. 1924).

Title Reservation

Property or ownership in specific or ascertained goods passes from seller to buyer when the parties intend it to pass and is a matter for contractual agreement. In the absence of an express or implied intention regarding the transfer of property, the matter is regulated by the rules in section 18. Since the parties may agree on the time at which property is to pass it is possible to defer or reserve the passing of ownership as a means of giving security to the seller for the price of the goods or other debts due to him.

This right is recognised in section 19 of the 1893 Act in that the seller may reserve the right of disposal of the goods so that property does not pass until any conditions imposed by the seller are fulfilled. Where the goods in a bill of lading are deliverable to the order of the seller or his agent, it is prima facie assumed that the seller has reserved the right of disposal. Property in the goods will not pass to the buyer unless he honours a bill of exchange for the price, sent to him with the bill of lading.

Romalpa and Re Interview Ltd.

The potential value of these provisions as a means of giving the sellers of goods better security for trade debts due to them has only recently been realised due to two important but independent decisions made in the English and Irish courts. In the English case, *Aluminium Industrie Vaassen BV* v. *Romalpa Aluminium Ltd.* (C.A. 1976), a Dutch supplier succeeded in recovering a stock of aluminium foil sold to an English company in receivership, under a contract which provided that property in the goods would not pass until all money owing to the Dutch company was paid. It was entitled also to £35,000 held by the receiver representing the proceeds of sales of aluminium to customers.

In the Irish case *Re Interview Ltd.* (H.C. 1975) part of the stock held by Interview Ltd. which was in liquidation had been acquired from an associated company, Electrical Industries of Ireland Ltd. (E.I.I.), who had in turn bought the goods from a German supplier, A.E.G., under a contract in which A.E.G. was to retain ownership in the goods until paid for. E.I.I. therefore could not pass ownership to Interview Ltd. when they did have property in the goods themselves, nor were Interview Ltd. innocent purchasers (see s.25 below) as they were aware of the terms on which the goods had been supplied to E.I.I.

The implications of these decisions are far-reaching. Title reservation has great potential in giving security to the seller of goods in the event of the buyer's insolvency in that he could recover possession of his goods not disposed of by the buyer, and where the buyer could be considered to be placed in a fiduciary position regarding the goods, the seller could recover the proceeds of sub-sales of the goods under the equitable doctrine of tracing. On the other hand it could lead to problems of insurance, an over-valuation of a company's credit-risk and be rather unfair to other unsecured creditors, or even to a creditor secured on a floating charge.

The limits of title reservation

Subsequent decisions have shown that the courts are prepared to put some limits on title reservation. In the English case *Re Bond Worth Ltd.* (1979) ownership of Acrilan fibre was held to have passed to the buyer as the seller had only reserved "equitable and beneficial ownership" in the goods. This resulted in the equivalent of a floating charge, which was held to be void as against other creditors since it was not registered under the Companies Acts, as required.

Four different title reservation clauses were upheld by McWilliam J. in *Re Stokes & McKiernan Ltd.* (H.C. 1978). One of these involved the reservation of the equitable and beneficial ownership in the goods, and in a later case McWilliam J. implied that if he had then the benefit of the judgment of Slade J. in *Re Bond Worth Ltd.* he would have held that it created a registrable equitable charge only. A straighforward reservation of title to goods still in the buyer's possession will still be effective (*Frigoscandia Ltd.* v. *Continental Irish Meat Ltd.* H.C. 1979). See also *Borden (U.K.) Ltd.* v. *Scottish Timber Products Ltd.*, E.C.A. 1979.

Transfer of Title

The final personal property problem dealt with by the 1893 Act concerns the title, or rights to goods, which persons can obtain when they buy the goods from a person who has no property in them.

The basic rule is that a seller, or an agent acting for the seller, can give no better title to the goods than the seller himself has. This is often expressed as *nemo dat quod non habet* (no one gives what he has not got). There are exceptions to the rule.

Estoppel

A buyer may obtain a good title to goods by estoppel where the owner by his words or conduct led the buyer to believe that the seller had authority to dispose of them (s.21(1)).

Statutory or common law power of sale

The buyer will also gain a good title where the seller has power at common law or under statute to dispose of goods as if he were the true owner (s.21(2)). Valid sales can be made in certain cases by pawnees, sheriffs, trustees in bankruptcy, and hotel proprietors (Hotel Proprietors Act 1963) among others.

Sales in market overt

A person buying goods in market overt, according to the usage of the market, acquires good title provided he buys in good faith and without notice of any defects in the seller's title (s.22). A market overt is a market established by statute, charter, or long-standing custom.

Sales under a voidable title

A seller of goods who has a voidable title will pass a good title to a buyer who buys in good faith and without notice of the defect, provided the seller's title has not been avoided at the time of the sale (s.23) (see *Anderson* v. *Ryan* H.C. 1967, or *Lewis* v. *Averay* E.C.A. 1971). Where the goods were obtained by fraud they will not revest in the owner merely because of the conviction of the offender. If the seller obtained the goods by larceny, however, the goods revest in the owner on the offender's conviction (s.24).

Disposition by a seller in possession

Where a person having sold goods is still in possession of them or of their documents of title, he passes a good title if he disposes of them to a person who takes them in good faith and without notice (s.25(1)).

Disposition by a buyer in possession

A buyer who obtains possession of the goods or their documents of title with the seller's consent, and if he disposes of them to a person who takes in good faith and without notice, the effect is the same as if the goods had been disposed of by a mercantile agent under the Factors Act. The third party gets a good title provided the buyer or his mercantile agent has possession and acts in the ordinary course of his business (*Newtons of Wembley* v. *Williams* E.C.A.1965). If the sub-purchaser has notice of the defects in the buyer's title he gets no better title than the buyer had (*Re Interview*).

Sale by a judgment debtor

Where a writ of execution is issued against the goods of a judgment debtor it binds the property as soon as it is delivered to the sheriff. If the judgment debtor subsequently disposes of the goods the person acquiring them in good faith, for valuable consideration, and without notice of the writ, gets a good title (s.26).

FINANCING THE ACQUISITION OF GOODS

In a consumer economy sale is only one of the methods of acquiring or distributing goods. Customers without ready cash can obtain use or ownership of goods by taking them on hire or by availing themselves of different types of credit arrangement. Available schemes can be classified into three groupings from a legal viewpoint.

  (1) There are those which involve sale but with credit facilities;
  (2) Those which involve a hiring or lease of goods; and
  (3) Hire-purchase which combines both hiring and a sale option.

(1) Sales on credit

Short-term trade credit is in common use as a matter of convenience. More sophisticated ways of giving credit include credit cards, budget accounts, instalment credit, and personal loans repayable by instalment.

Credit-sales under the Hire-Purchase Acts. The legal implications of these transactions depend on the type of security demanded for the credit given. A simple sale of goods on credit without security is generally an ordinary sale of goods contract in which payment is deferred by agreement. If, however, payment is to be made in five or more instalments and the value of the goods exceeds £5 then, although the transaction is regulated by the Sale of Goods Act 1893, it is also subject to some of the provisions of the Hire-Purchase Acts (see p. 149).

Title-reservation. The seller may give himself security for payment, as we have seen, by title reservation. In this case the contract is a "conditional sale," or "agreement to sell," because property in the goods is not to pass to the buyer until certain conditions are fulfilled. The buyer may not own the goods, for example, until they are paid for or until all debts due to the seller are paid. In the meantime he may be merely a type of bailee of the goods although the contract is governed by the Sale of Goods Act 1893 because the buyer has not got the option to return the goods.

Personal loans. Other forms of credit arrangement may involve two or more transactions. Most banks and finance houses provide personal loans for the purchase of goods. The money is provided as a separate transaction if the client is a good credit risk or if he can provide security. The loan is repayable by instalments. The agreement normally provides that the whole debt becomes payable if the borrower defaults in making repayments. The borrower may also be required to provide security by way of a bill of exchange which can be negotiated and used as a convenient method of suing the borrower for the amount due. In this way the lending institution segregates itself from the market place and avoids problems of liability for defective products which might arise in a hire-purchase transaction. The customer gets the loan and in a separate transaction buys the goods under an ordinary sale of goods contract from the dealer. If, however, money borrowed to buy goods is paid to the seller by a finance house, and the buyer deals as a consumer, then the finance house and seller are jointly and severally liable on the contract (Sale of Goods and Supply of Services Act 1980, s. 14).

Security given for credit facilities. Any provision of credit whether by way of trade or financial borrowing may involve a requirement that the borrower provide security for the repayment of the debt. The security provided may give a right against property, or a personal right of action against some person other than the borrower.

Securities involving property rights. Securities involving rights over property include a pledge or pawn of goods, and a mortgage of real or personal property. A pledge, or pledge in pawn, occurs where possession of goods is given to the pledgee or pawnbroker as security for the payment of a debt or the performance of an obligation. On default being made the pledge may be sold.

It is possible to grant a mortgage of personal property. A mortgage of goods is a transfer of property in them from the mortgagor to the mortgagee in order to secure a debt. There is no legal reason why a mortgage of goods cannot be made orally but if it is in writing it will normally be governed by the Bills of Sale (Ireland) Acts 1879–1883, which regulate the validity of any document intended to give effect to the grant of chattels absolutely, or by way of mortgage, where the grantor remains in possession of them.

Bills of Sale Acts.   The Bills of Sale Acts were enacted to protect creditors who might be induced to lend money or to extend credit to persons who appeared to own valuable goods which they had in their possession, but who had in fact already granted the legal or equitable ownership of them to others. Protection was given by providing that bills of sale would not be fully effective in granting legal or equitable ownership of goods which remained in the grantor's possession unless they were registered under the Acts.

A note or memorandum of a sale of goods contract, not made in the ordinary course of business, or an auctioneer's memorandum of a sale, may be bills of sale requiring registration for their full effectiveness where the seller remains in possession of the goods. If such a bill of sale is not registered, the transaction remains valid as between the parties, but the goods will be subject to any bankruptcy or execution order against the seller, or any assignment in trust for his creditors.

Personal security.   The usual method of providing security for sale of goods transactions is for the lender to insist that the borrower provides some third party who may be sued in a personal action for the debt in the event of default in making the repayments.

This may be achieved by making another person a principal to the transaction so that both the borrower and his surety become jointly, or jointly and severally, liable on the agreement. Alternatively a dealer who supplies the goods, or a director of a company seeking credit, may be asked to indorse a bill of exchange so that they also become liable on it. Finally, a third party, preferably one of substance, may be required to enter a contract of guarantee to underwrite the debt.

Contracts of guarantee.   A contract of guarantee, or surety contract, is one in which a person called a guarantor or surety makes himself collaterally liable for the payment of the debt of another person, or for the performance of a contract by another person. The guarantee is collateral or supplemental to a primary debt or contract between a principal debtor and a principal creditor. The guarantee is a contract between the guarantor and the principal creditor that the guarantor will pay the debt, or assume liability on a contract, if the principal debtor fails to do so. The guarantor or surety only becomes liable if the principal debtor defaults. Contracts of guarantee must be in writing or be evidenced by writing (Statute of Frauds 1695).

A contract of indemnity, which is similar to a guarantee, does not have to be evidenced by writing to be enforceable. An indemnity is a contract whereby a person, sometimes called an indemnifier, makes himself directly liable to the principal creditor for any loss he suffers out of the credit given, or contract entered with another party. The indemnifier accepts primary liability for the debt or contract involved, whereas the guarantor only becomes liable on the failure of the primary debtor to discharge his obligation.

If a guarantor or surety satisfies an obligation for which he made himself liable he is entitled to recover the amount from the principal debtor. If where there are a number of guarantors and one of them is compelled to pay the whole amount or more than his share he is entitled to contribution from his fellow guarantors.

(2) The hiring and leasing of goods

The use of goods can also be acquired without purchase by means of a hiring or lease agreement under which the owner allows another to use goods in return for rental payments. Such agreements vary from short-term hire of goods for a few days or weeks to long-term financial or operating leases. Almost all types of non-consumable goods may be acquired in this way, including dress-suits, televisions and cars.

A hiring or lease agreement is not, of course, a contract of sale as no property in the goods passes, or is intended to pass, to the person acquiring the goods. These agreements are bailments of goods for reward.

Bailment. A bailment of goods is a delivery of possession of them to another for some purpose. There is an express or implied condition that the goods will be returned to the person who gave them (the bailor), or be dealt with in accordance with his directions, by the person to whom the goods were delivered (the bailee), when the purpose for which the goods were bailed is completed. Bailment occurs when goods are lent, hired for reward, deposited for storage or for repair, or when given to another by way of security.

The rights and obligations of the bailor and bailee depend on the nature of the bailment and any express agreement between them. The bailee is always expected to take reasonable care of the goods and the degree of care required of him depends on the agreement made and the type of bailment involved. He will be liable if he fails to return "empties" such as returnable mineral water bottles (*Cantrell & Cochrane Ltd.* v. *Neeson* C.A.N.I. 1926); for negligence where a lorry left in for repair is damaged by a mechanic who uses it without authority (*Morgan* v. *Smith* H.C. 1955); for the negligence of a sub-contractor where repair work has been delegated (*McElwee* v. *McDonald* H.C. 1969); where the goods are negligently destroyed by fire (*Keenan* v. *McCreedy* C.C. 1955); or where a watch sent in the post without permission is lost (*Morgan* v. *Maurer & Son* C.C. 1964; or for failing, contrary to the contract, to insure a car which was destroyed in a garage fire (*McNeill* v. *Millin & Co. Ltd.*, Ir.C.A. 1907).

Financial and operational leasing.   In long-term hirings there are two widely recognised types of agreement.

In an operational or contract hire lease the lessor or owner undertakes to maintain and to insure the goods, and the agreed leasing period is usually shorter than the expected life of the goods. The rentals do not cover the original capital cost of the items leased and they are sold off by the owners when the lease has expired.

Financial leasing is provided by finance houses such as the industrial banks and the lessor does not undertake responsibility for repair or maintenance. Separate service contracts may be possible, however, through the manufacturers, distributors, or their agents, depending on the type of goods involved. The rentals paid by the lessee will usually cover both the original capital cost of the goods and the lending institution's profit. As a result the goods, if still useful, are usually re-let to the user at a nominal rent after the primary lease period is concluded. Alternatively the parties may negotiate for the outright purchase of the goods at that time.

The hiring or lease contract.   Until recently the hiring contract was governed only by the ordinary contract principles of the common law. The courts have tended to imply certain terms into contracts for the hire of goods where they did not conflict with express terms, or had not been excluded by agreement.

There is at common law an implied warranty that the hirer will have quiet possession and that it will not be disrupted by any lack of title in the "owner." Among other terms there is an implied condition that the goods will be fit for their purpose.

The Sale of Goods and Supply of Services Act 1980 has greatly added to the protection available to the hirer. In this Act a person acquiring goods by hire, lease, or hire-purchase has been given virtually the same protection as has been given to the buyer of goods under the Sale of Goods Act 1893 as amended. All such contracts now have statutorily implied terms as regards title, quality, fitness, and where applicable terms as to spare parts and aftersale service. These terms cannot be excluded in consumer contracts and can only be excluded in other contracts if the exclusion is fair and reasonable (1980 Act, Part III, s.38).

(3) Hire-purchase

Bailment with an option to purchase. A hire-purchase agreement is a contract in which the owner gives possession and the use of goods to the hirer in return for the payment of rental instalments, and in which the hirer is given an option to buy the goods by paying the final instalment or by paying a nominal sum in addition to the instalments. It is not a sale but it is a type of bailment of goods with an option to purchase. Property in the goods remains in the owner until the option to buy is validly exercised.

The hire-purchase agreement may be made between a dealer in the goods and the customer, but more commonly the credit is provided by a finance house which is usually an industrial bank or a specialist hire-purchase finance company. In the latter situation the customer negotiates with the dealer for the goods and, if he requires hire-purchase facilities, there must be two transactions. The dealer sells the goods to the finance house, and the finance house, which now owns the goods, transfers them to the customer under a hire-purchase agreement which involves a finance charge for the use of the capital involved.

Block discounting. A variation of the above methods arises where the initial hire-purchase arrangements are made between the dealer and his customers, and the dealer then assigns his interest in the agreements to a finance house for cash. If he assigns a number of small agreements together the operation is referred to as block discounting. The relationship between the dealer and the finance house is usually regulated by a special contract, often called a recourse agreement, in which the dealer may have to undertake to indemnify the finance house for loss suffered where the hirer defaults in making his repayments.

The dealer may also be liable to the finance house for any loss caused to the finance house by his misrepresentations or breach of the terms of any implied collateral contract between them. In *Lombank Ltd.* v. *P. MacElligott and Sons Ltd.* (C.C. 1963) the defendant motor dealer in Co. Kerry was held liable to the plaintiff finance company for misstatements which induced the plaintiffs to enter a hire-purchase agreement with a hirer who defaulted in making his repayments.

Hire-purchase contracts at common law. In hire-purchase transactions the hirer was generally at the mercy of the dealer, who supplied the goods, and the finance house which supplied the credit. The rights of the hirer were based on a contract which was drafted to give all the advantages to the owner. It was generally provided that the hirer should bear the loss in the event of accidental destruction of the, goods by fire for example (*Crane & Sons Ltd.* v. *Galway* Ir.K.B. 1905). The agreement usually gave the owner a licence to enter the hirer's premises to "snatch-back" the goods for breach of the agreement. Such a licence was lawful at common law as long as it was used reasonably and not exceeded (*Weiner* v. *H. B. Phillips (Belfast) Ltd.*, Ir.C.A. 1914). In the event of the hirer's insolvency it was usually provided that the owner could recover the goods and arrears of instalments, and also a specified sum as compensation for the premature ending of the hiring (*Re Celt Co. Ltd.* H.C. 1926). Even when the hirer had given bills of exchange for the total amount of the instalments as collateral security and these had been discounted by the owner, there was held to be no transfer of ownership or conditional sale, so that the owner was still protected in the event of the hirer's bankruptcy (*Re Rankin and Shilliday* C.A.N.I. 1927).

The hirer's rights. At common law the hirer had difficulty in suing the dealer who supplied defective goods. The hirer, at least in legal theory, acquired the goods from the finance house as owners so that they had no right of action against the dealer (*Dunphy* v. *Blackhall Motor Co. Ltd.* C.C. 1953). In addition the goods were not acquired under a contract of sale so that the hirer could not rely on implied terms as to quality or fitness under the Sale of Goods Act 1893 (*Irish B.P.* v. *Smyth* C.C. 1931) and conversely the owner could not sue for the balance of the price of goods sold as there was no sale involved until the hirer exercised his option to buy (*Singer Manufacturing Co.* v. *Collins* Co.Ct. 1897).

These restrictions on the hirer have now been swept away. Under the Sale of Goods and Supply of Services Act 1980 the equivalent terms as to title and quality of the goods in sale of goods contracts are now implied into hire-purchase and hiring contracts also. Where the hirer deals as a consumer the person who conducted the "antecedent negotiations," such as a dealer or retailer who supplied the goods, is now deemed to be a party to the hire-purchase contract and is jointly and severally liable with the owner for breach of the agreement or for misrepresentations made (1980 Act, s. 32).

The Hire-Purchase Acts 1946 and 1960. The position of the hirer at common law was so poor that it was necessary to protect his interests by statutory intervention. Hire-purchase agreements are now regulated by the Hire-Purchase Act 1946 as amended by the Hire-Purchase (Amendment) Act 1960 and the Sale of Goods and Supply of Services Act 1980.

The Hire-Purchase Act 1946, in spite of its title, deals in fact with two types of instalment credit agreements, hire-purchase and credit sales.

Hire-purchase is defined as an agreement for the bailment of goods under which the bailee may buy the goods or under which the property in the goods will or may pass to the bailee. Where the same effect is achieved by two or more agreements they are deemed to constitute a hire-purchase agreement made at the date of the last one. This is designed to prevent evasion of the Act.

A credit sale agreement for the purposes of the Act is an agreement for the sale of goods under which the purchase price is payable by five or more instalments (1946 Act, s.1, see above).

Agreements relating to livestock or agreements between the Irish Sea Fisheries Association Ltd. and its members are excluded from the provisions of the Act (1946 Act, s.2; *An Bord Iascaigh Mhara* v. *Scallon* H.C. 1973).

Provisions Applying to Hire-Purchase and Credit Sales

Details of the cash price

The usual rules relating to the formation of contract apply to hire-purchase and credit-sale agreements. There must be agreement between the parties, an intention to create legal relations and consideration. There will be no contract, *e.g.* where the hirer withdraws his offer before the finance company has accepted it.

Certain formalities are required, however, to ensure that the hirer or purchaser knows the price he is paying for the credit and the main terms of the agreement. In the case of hire-purchase agreements, and where a credit-sale agreement involves a total purchase price exceeding £5, the owner must ensure that the hirer or buyer respectively is informed of the cash price of the goods. He may do this by informing the customer in writing; or by having a ticket or label clearly stating the cash price in any catalogue, price list, or advertisement from which the goods have been selected. If this provision is not complied with the owner or seller, as the case may be, cannot enforce the agreement, or any contract of guarantee relating to it, or any security provided. In the case of a hire-purchase agreement the owner cannot enforce any right to recover the goods.

Note or memorandum of the agreement

A note or memorandum of the agreement must be made and signed by the hirer or buyer as the case may be, and by or on behalf of all other parties to the agreement. This note or memorandum must contain a statement of the hire-purchase or total purchase price as appropriate, the cash price, the instalment amounts and the dates of payment, and a list of the goods. In the case of a hire-purchase agreement, the note or memorandum must also contain a prominent notice as set out in the Schedule to the 1946 Act. This notice informs the hirer of his right to terminate the agreement and the restrictions (there are special ones in relation to motor vehicles) on the owner's right to recover the goods. Both in the case of hire-purchase and regulated credit-sale agreements a copy of the note or memorandum must be delivered or sent to the hirer or buyer within 14 days.

If no note or memorandum of the agreement is made and signed the contract is not enforceable. A failure to include the specified details in the note or memorandum, or a failure to include the notice, or to send a copy to the customer, may also render the contract unenforceable unless the court is satisfied that the customer was not prejudiced thereby and that it would be just and equitable to dispense with the requirements (1946 Act, ss. 3, 4 as amended).

Where the parties to a hire-purchase agreement made a new oral contract covering the balance due on a rotovator, it was held to be unenforceable because there was no note or memorandum in writing. The judge was of opinion that all the terms required to be stated in the note could not be dispensed with by the court in view of the fact that such a note or memorandum was required in the first place (*United Dominions Trust (Commercial) Ltd.* v. *Nestor* H.C. 1962). The note or memorandum must be made and signed at the time of the agreement and it is not sufficient if it is made after the agreement is made but before the action is brought (*British Wagon Credit Co.* v. *Henerby* H.C. 1962). The court would not dispense with these requirements where in a hire-purchase agreement for a car, the required particulars were not filled in when the hirer signed the agreement, and the copy of the agreement sent to the hirer differed materially from the agreement originally signed. The hirer was lawfully in possession of the car under an agreement that was unenforceable against him (*Mercantile Credit Co. of Ireland Ltd.* v. *Cahill* C.C. 1964). A hire-purchase contract for a combine harvester was likewise unenforceable where there was no date fixed for the instalment payments and the copy changed to conceal the error; where the statutory notice was relegated to "the obscurity of the small print"; and a judgment for arrears of rent had been obtained in default of the hirer's appearance by wrongly swearing that the statutory requirements had been complied with (*B.W. Credit Corp. Ltd.* v. *Higgins* H.C. 1968).

The provision of information
At any time before the final payment has been made under a hire-purchase or credit-sale agreement, the hirer or buyer who provides 5p by way of expenses is entitled, on a written request, to be supplied with a copy of any note or memorandum of the agreement and a statement giving details of sums paid by him, sums now due, and future instalments. If any person entitled to enforce the agreement against the hirer or buyer fails to comply with this request within seven days' without reasonable cause, he cannot enforce the agreement, or any guarantee or security relating to the agreement, or recover the goods in the case of a hire-purchase agreement, while the default continues. If the default continues for one month the defaulter is guilty of an offence and liable to a fine not exceeding £10 (1946 Act, s.7 as amended). In both hire-purchase and credit-sales agreements any provisions purporting to exclude the liability of the owners or sellers for the acts of their agents, are void (1946 Act, s.6).

Implied terms
Under section 9 of the Hire-Purchase Act 1946, which has been repealed by section 26 (4) of the Sale of Goods and Supply of Services Act 1980, there were provisions by which terms relating to the owner's title, the merchantable quality and fitness for purpose of the goods, would be implied into every hire-purchase agreement. The implied condition relating to the fitness of the goods could only be excluded or modified by a provision which was clearly brought to the attention of the hirer (see *Butterly* v. *United Dominions Trust (Commercial) Ltd.* H.C. 1963). These provisions have now been replaced by implied conditions and warranties which are the equivalent of those implied in contracts for the sale of goods.
The new implied terms introduced by the 1980 Act relating to the provision of spare parts and aftersale service, and to the safety of motor vehicles, are also applied to hire-purchase agreements. Persons conducting "antecedent negotiations" (such as a dealer, his servants, or agents) as well as the owner (finance house) are made jointly and severally liable on the agreement where the hirer deals as a consumer.
The amendments to the law relating to misrepresentation contained in Part V of the 1980 Act apply to hire-purchase agreements. Similar terms are implied into credit-sale agreements by virtue of

the fact that they are sale of goods contracts and are governed by the Sale of Goods Act 1893.

Provisions Applying to Hire-Purchase Agreements Only

Hirer's right to terminate

Many of the abuses prevalent in hire-purchase transactions at common law are prohibited by the 1946 Act as amended.

The hirer is entitled to terminate the agreement, except in the case of a hiring of industrial plant or machinery for use in an industrial process with a cash price of over £200. The agreement can be ended at any time before the final payment falls due, by the hirer giving notice in writing to the owner or person entitled or authorised to receive payments. When the hirer terminates the agreement he becomes liable (irrespective of any liability which has already accrued, such as instalments due) to pay a sum which will bring his total payments up to one half of the hire-purchase price (which may include installation charges) if this amount is not already due and payable, or such lesser sum if specified in the agreement.

The hirer will also be liable to pay damages if he has failed, as a bailee of the goods, to take reasonable care of them. If he wrongfully retains possession of the goods, the court, in an action by the owner for repossession, may order the hirer to deliver them to the owner, without giving the hirer the option to retain them by paying their value, unless satisfied that this would not be just and equitable (s.5).

The hirer is also protected in that any provision in the hire-purchase agreement is void which excludes or restricts his right to terminate the agreement, or which imposes any liability on him in addition to that allowed by the 1946 Act for terminating the agreement as allowed by the Act or in any other way (s.6).

The liability of a guarantor is similarly restricted where the goods are returned to the owner, and any provision in a hire-purchase agreement which imposes a greater liability than that allowed is void (1960 Act, s.17).

Where the hirer has more than one hire-purchase agreement with the same owner he may decide which agreement is to be credited with any payment he makes which is not sufficient to discharge the total amount then due (1946 Act, s.10; 1960 Act, s.18).

Restrictions on The Owner's Rights

Restrictions on right to enter premises

The owner of hired goods can no longer give himself a licence to recover the goods in any way he wishes. Except in relation to motor vehicles, any term authorising the owner or his agent to enter premises to recover goods, or which relieves them from liability for such entry, is void (1946 Act, s.6).

This restriction does not apply to the owner of a hired motor vehicle or his agent who is authorised to enter premises, other than a dwelling or any building within its curtilage (courtyard), to recover a motor vehicle or who is relieved from liability for such entry (1960 Act, s.16).

In any situation, of course, the owner can enter premises and repossess goods with the hirer's consent.

Restrictions on right to recover the goods

Save for a limited right in relation to motor vehicles, the owner cannot enforce a right to recover possession of goods except by legal action, where one-third or more of the hire-purchase price has been paid or tendered.

If the owner recovers possession of the goods in contravention of this provision, the hire-purchase agreement ends and the hirer is released from all liability and may recover back any money paid by way of instalments or given as security. Any guarantor can likewise recover any money paid or given by way of security. This right does not apply where the hirer had terminated the agreement (s.12), or where he voluntarily returns the goods. In *McDonald* v. *Bowmakers (Ireland) Ltd.* (H.C. 1949) the defendants terminated a hire-purchase agreement under which the plaintiff hirer had paid in excess of one-third of the hire-purchase price on a lorry. The owners demanded the return of the lorry and threatened legal proceedings. The plaintiff returned the vehicle voluntarily and sued for the return of his instalments paid. The owners were held not liable as they were not in breach of the provisions of the 1946 Act.

Recovery of motor vehicles

In the case of motor vehicles the owner may still enforce a right to recover, although in excess of one-third of the hire-purchase price has been paid, provided he has commenced an action to recover possession of the vehicle and it is likely to be damaged or unduly depreciated due to its being abandoned or left unattended. He may then retain the vehicle pending a court order relating to its disposition. He is obliged to make an application to the court within 14 days of taking possession, or otherwise the hirer shall be free of all liability and be entitled to recover instalments paid as under section 12. If the court finds that he was not entitled to repossess the vehicle it may award damages to the hirer (1960 Act, s.16).

The owner's remedies

Where there has been a breach of a condition of the hire-purchase agreement by the hirer, the owner (finance house) is entitled to rescind the contract and he has a number of options:

(i) If less than one-third of the hire-purchase price has been paid he can repossess the goods provided he does not contravene the 1946 Act by entering premises without permission.

(ii) The owner may claim the return of the goods or their value, and damages from the hirer for failure to take reasonable care of the goods.

(iii) Where the hirer fails to return the goods or has transferred them to another party, the owner may claim damages for conversion (*British Wagon Co. Ltd.* v. *Shortt* H.C. 1960).

(iv) The owner may decide not to rescind the contract and can claim arrears of instalment payments instead.

If the hirer is not in breach of a condition of the hire-purchase contract the owner is not entitled to rescind but he will be entitled to claim arrears of instalments. Where the hirer has a duty to keep the goods in his possession or control he is obliged to inform the owner of the location of the goods on his request and may be fined for failing to do so without reasonable cause within 14 days (1946 Act, s.8).

The discretion of the court

The court has considerable discretion in dealing with an action by the owner to recover possession of goods after one-third of the hire-purchase price has been paid. The court can

(i) Order the hirer to deliver the goods to the owner;

(ii) or order the hirer to deliver the goods but with a postponement to allow the hirer or any guarantor to pay the unpaid balance of the price in such a manner and subject to such conditions as the court thinks just;

(iii) or to apportion the goods, if possible, between the owner and hirer subject to such terms as to further payments, if any, as the court thinks is justified (1946 Act, s.13).

The court may apportion the goods where they are divisible into parts on an application by the owner for judgment where the hirer does not appear. The owner is then obliged to furnish evidence of the value of the goods or the hirer may otherwise be given the option to retain the goods on payment of the balance where the balance due is relatively small (*United Dominions Trust Ltd.* v. *Byrne* H.C. 1955).

Although the hirer's liability on terminating the hire-purchase contract is limited by section 5 of the 1946 Act, it should be remembered also that his liability may be limited still further at common law. Where the owner rescinds the contract for the hirer's breach of condition he is only entitled to claim specified sums by way of "agreed depreciation" if such sums are a genuine pre-estimate of liquidated damages and not a penalty (*Lombank Ltd.* v. *Kennedy* C.A.N.I. 1961). Where the hirer exercises a right to terminate the contract he may be required to pay such a specified sum, up to the statutory maximum, as the agreed price of exercising his option to end the agreement (*Lombank Ltd.* v. *Crossan* C.A.N.I. 1961).

Hire-purchase and the transfer of ownership

The hirer of goods under a hire-purchase contract has no property in the goods until he validly exercises his option to purchase. In the meantime he is merely a bailee of the goods and any third party who acquires the goods from him does not usually get a good title under the rule that nobody gets a better title than that which the transferor had (the "nemo dat" rule). Where a defendant bought land reclamation machinery from a hirer he was held liable to the finance house for its detention or conversion and was not entitled to counterclaim for repairs to the machinery (*British Wagon Co. Ltd.* v. *Shortt* H.C. 1960). A purported sale by a hirer who has no property in the goods will not affect a subsequent valid sale and rehiring (*H. W. West Ltd.* v. *McBlain* K.B.N.I. 1950).

If, however, the hirer is a dealer in the type of goods hired, and if he sells the goods in the ordinary course of business, the sale will be as valid as if it had been authorised by the owner provided the buyer buys in good faith and without notice of the hirer's lack of authority (1960 Act, s.28). The principles relating to sales in market overt will likewise apply to sales by the hirer.

NEGOTIABLE INSTRUMENTS

Choses in action

Choses in action are non-physical property rights such as debts, shares, patents or cheques.

The assignment of choses in action

Commercial activity requires that property be easily transferable; this applies not only to goods but also to choses in action. The transfer of a chose in action is referred to as an assignment. Whether contractual rights or other types of choses in action are assignable and, if so, the way in which they can be assigned depends on rules of law which derive from the common law, equity, and statute law.

Before the passing of the Judicature (Ireland) Act 1877 all choses in action could be assigned in equity and equitable assignment is still possible. This does not include those which are not assignable at all such as the benefits of a contract involving personal skill or confidence or where an assignment is illegal or contrary to public policy.

A chose in action may be an "equitable" one if it is of a type, such as a legacy, that was only recognised by Courts of Chancery in the past. It is said to be a "legal" chose in action if it was recognised by the common law courts. A debt is an example of a legal chose in action.

Both types of choses in action can be assigned in equity. There is no particular formality required (*Northern Banking Co.* v. *Newman* H.C. 1927) but the person taking the property right, that is the assignee, has to give notice of the assignment to the person against whom the right operates, to the debtor, for example, in the case of a debt. If he does not give notice the assignment will still be valid as between the assignor and assignee but will not bind the debtor.

In the case of an equitable chose in action the assignee can sue in his own name following an absolute equitable assignment. If it involved a legal chose in action or a conditional assignment of an equitable chose in action, equity would only allow an action by the assignee where he could not enforce his right, by using the assignor's name in a common law action.

The assignee in any event takes the property right "subject to all the equities" existing between the assignor and the debtor at the time the assignment became binding. This means that the assignee merely steps into the assignor's shoes and any defects in the assignor's property right or any counterclaim or defence against it may be set up against the assignee also.

Statutory assignments

Certain types of choses in action may be assigned in the manner authorised by statute. These include shares, policies of life assurance and marine insurance, copyrights, patents, bills of lading, debts owed to moneylenders and negotiable instruments. Where the statutory requirements are not fully complied with there may still be a transfer of the chose in action in equity which gives a form of equitable ownership to the transferee.

The effect of the Judicature (Ireland) Act 1877

Under the provisions of the Judicature Act (s. 28 (6)) an

assignment in the manner specified will be regarded as a legal assignment which makes the assignee the legal owner of the chose in action, with legal rights to enforce and discharge the property right in question. To qualify under this provision the assignment must be in writing signed by the assignor; it must be an absolute assignment and written notice must be given to the party against whom the chose in action operates. It allows the legal assignment of choses in action which could previously be the subject of an equitable assignment only.

Instruments or documents of title

Choses in action are an intangible form of personal property and the owner of such property must usually have some document of title as evidence that he has such a valuable right and to facilitate the assignment of his interest to others. These documents of title are called instruments and they operate as a contract between the parties.

Instruments of title include share certificates, insurance policies, debentures, bills of lading, dock warrants, postal orders, bills of exchange, cheques, promissory notes, and share warrants.

Assignable and transferable instruments

Shares, debentures and life assurances can only be transferred by a proper assignment. Other types of chose in action, such as bills of lading, dock warrants and warehouse warrants, are said to be "transferable" because they can be transferred in a simple way by delivery with or without an indorsement of the instrument, without the need to give notice to the party liable on the chose in action. A bill of lading is a document in which a shipper acknowledges the receipt of goods and undertakes to deliver them to the specified person or to his order. The person to whom the goods are sent obtains possession by presenting a copy of the bill of lading to the shipper. A bill of lading is effective as a document of title. It became the practice to transfer bills of lading by indorsement and delivery so that property in the goods passed to the indorsee and this method was perfected by the Bills of Lading Act 1855 which gave the transferee of the bill of lading full rights to sue on it. In such cases, however, the transferee still takes the chose in action subject to the equities and his rights to the property are only as good as those of the original transferor.

Negotiable instruments

Banking and business activity long required an unrestricted

means of giving credit and of transferring and exchanging debts as a method of financing and paying for goods and services.

As a result, traders and merchants began to make common use of bills of exchange, including cheques, and promissory notes. By custom and usage these instruments which represented debts came to be regarded as freely transferable by delivery, or delivery and indorsement. But not only were these choses in action easily transferable they were also negotiable, which in essence means that the transferee who took the instrument in good faith and for value held it free from equities including defects in the transferor's title.

An instrument is said to be negotiable when it is capable of being transferred by indorsement or delivery so as to pass a legal title to the transferee who can sue on the instrument free from the equitable claims of others. An instrument which is otherwise negotiable may, however, cease to be fully negotiable unless it is acquired for valuable consideration, in good faith, and the instrument itself must be complete and regular and capable of being delivered to others free from equities.

The Bills of Exchange Act 1882

The law relating to negotiable instruments is mostly contained in the Bills of Exchange Act 1882 (the 1882 Act) and the Cheques Act 1959 (the 1959 Act). The common law rules still apply in so far as they are not inconsistent with the principal Act (1882 Act, s. 97 (2)). The 1882 Act deals with three types of negotiable instrument: bills of exchange, cheques and promissory notes. Where not otherwise indicated references below are to the 1882 Act.

Bills of exchange

A bill of exchange is defined as an "unconditional order in writing, addressed by one person to another, signed by the person giving it, requiring the person to whom it is addressed to pay on demand or at a fixed or determinable future time a sum certain in money to or to the order of a specified person, or to bearer" (s.30). A bill of exchange may involve three parties. These are the drawer who makes or draws the bill, the drawee on whom the bill is drawn who owes a debt or provides credit to the drawer and who is called the acceptor if and when the bill is accepted for payment, and the payee in whose favour the bill is drawn.

There are often, however, only two persons to a bill where a seller of goods draws a bill on the buyer for the price and the buyer accepts the bill in exchange for the goods or a bill of lading for the goods. If the bill is payable at a future date, the buyer is given credit and the seller may discount the bill for cash by negotiating it to a discount house so that the transaction becomes financed by a third party.

Cheques

A cheque is defined as a bill of exchange drawn on a banker payable on demand (1882 Act, s.73). The cheque is an order by a bank customer to his bank to pay the specified sum to the payee or to some other person indicated by the payee.

Promissory notes

A promissory note is "an unconditional promise in writing made by one person to another signed by the maker, engaging to pay, on demand or at a fixed or determinable future time, a sum certain in money, to, or to the order of, a specified person or to bearer" (1882 Act, s.83 (1)). Promissory notes are often given by borrowers as security for loans.

The note must contain an unconditional promise to pay "on demand or at a fixed or determinable future time." In *Creative Press* v. *Harman* (H.C. 1972) the issue arose as to whether a promise to pay a sum of money "on or before the 1st. day of November, 1970" complied with the definition. The court held that it did. Because of the fact that the promisors could not be made to pay prior to November 1, 1970, it constituted a promise to pay at a fixed future time although the promisors had an option of making an earlier payment.

Negotiation of negotiable instruments

An instrument is negotiable where it can be transferred by delivery or indorsement and delivery, without notice to the party liable, and the transferee can sue on the instrument, holds it free from equities, and takes it in good faith and for value without notice of defects in title. Bills of exchange, cheques and promissory notes can be negotiated by delivery or by delivery and indorsement (s.31). If the instrument is payable to bearer it can be negotiated by delivery. If it is payable to a specified person it may be negotiated by indorsement (signature) and delivery. An indorsement by a simple signature (in blank) makes the bill, cheque, or note payable to bearer. A special indorsement to a named person means that the signature of the specified person is required for the further negotiation of the instrument (s.32).

A negotiable instrument may cease to be negotiable, however, where it contains words prohibiting its transfer or which indicate an intention that it should not be transferable (s.8 (1)). An instrument which orders or promises payment "to P. Dwyer only" or "to P.

Dwyer not transferable" is valid as between the immediate parties but if the payee transfers it to another that other person can only sue the drawer or the party liable through Dwyer. A crossed cheque marked "not negotiable" is freely transferable but the transferee takes the cheque subject to any defects in the transferor's title (s.81).

Consideration

The drawer of a bill of exchange or a cheque and the maker of a promissory note undertake to pay a certain sum of money. This is a contractual obligation and as in all contracts a person is not usually bound by his promise unless he has been given consideration for it. Consideration for the giving of a negotiable instrument is primarily any "valuable consideration sufficient to support a simple contract" (s.27 (1)). Under ordinary contract rules "past consideration is no consideration." This does not apply to negotiable instruments because an "antecedent debt or liability" is sufficient (s.27 (1) (g)). A person will be bound, therefore, on his bill, cheque or note although the debt discharged thereby arose in the past.

If, however, there is no past or present consideration given for an instrument, the giver of the instrument is not liable on it. In *Industria Tessile Ambrosiana Marra C.S. P.A.* v. *Hydrotyte Ltd.* (H.C. 1974), Italian exporters shipped goods for the defendants to Irish shipping agents in Dublin. The defendants were unable to obtain the necessary documents due to a bank strike. Fresh documents were sent and given to the defendants who accepted a foreign bill of exchange for the price payable to the sellers 60 days after sight. No certificate of origin was sent with the goods so that the defendants could not obtain them from customs and had to purchase elsewhere. The court held that the plaintiff exporters failed to provide sufficient documents to enable the buyer to obtain possession of the goods and as the bill was accepted for no real consideration the defendants were not liable on it.

The antecedent debt or liability must be that of the person who gives the negotiable instrument.

Where an instrument is negotiated, however, there is an assignment of the chose in action and the assignee, called the holder, is entitled as owner of the obligation represented by the instrument to sue on it. If the assignee has received a cheque or other instrument as a valid gift he cannot sue the donor, who has received no consideration, but he has the donor's rights to sue all prior parties liable on it. A holder for value is one who has given consideration for it. Each time a person signs the instrument and negotiates it for value he becomes a party to the instrument and incurs a liability on it which is defined by law.

The liability of the parties

A person who signs a bill or cheque as a *drawer* undertakes that it will be accepted and paid on proper presentation and that if it is dishonoured by non-acceptance or non-payment that he will compensate the holder or indorser (s.55 (1)). The first indorser of a promissory note is deemed to correspond with the drawer of an accepted bill payable to the drawer's order (s.89 (2)). The person to whom a promissory note is given makes himself liable by his indorsement to pay the note if the maker does not do so, in the same way as the drawer of an accepted bill or cheque is liable if the acceptor does not pay. The drawer becomes surety for the acceptor; the first indorsee of a note becomes surety for the maker.

The *acceptor* of a bill of exchange or a cheque undertakes to pay on the instrument in accordance with the manner of his acceptance. He cannot refuse payment to a holder in due course on the grounds that the drawer does not exist, that the drawer's signature is a forgery or because of the drawer's lack of capacity or authority to issue the bill or cheque (s.54). The maker of a promissory note is in a similar position to an acceptor of a bill (s.89 (2)).

A *holder in due course* is a holder who has taken a bill or cheque in good faith and for value, complete and regular on the face of it, and who became the holder of it before it was overdue and without notice of previous dishonour or of any defect in the title of the person who negotiated it (s.29). It has been fully and properly negotiated to him and he has a good title to it. If the transferor's title was defective, in that he acquired the instrument through duress, fraud, or for an illegal consideration, a holder in due course would still get a good title. This is another exception to the rule that a person cannot give a better title than he himself has (*nemo dat quod non habet*).

The *indorser* of a negotiable instrument undertakes that it shall be accepted and paid on proper presentment for payment and that if it is dishonoured he will compensate the holder or a subsequent indorser who is compelled to pay it (s.55 (2)).

Actions on a negotiable instrument

A bill or cheque is an unconditional order which the recipient can negotiate for cash. A promissory note is similarly an unconditional promise to pay money. These instruments are therefore regarded as an equivalent of cash and can be sued upon when due. A seller of goods who has accepted a negotiable instrument by way of payment has two courses of action in the event of dishonour. He can sue for breach of contract or he can sue on the instrument. He will normally sue on the negotiable instrument as he can get a ready judgment for payment of the amount due with interest. Because of their nature the court will normally not allow the party liable to plead any cross-claims or defences other than those based on fraud, invalidity, or failure of consideration. Although the court has a discretion to allow a stay of execution it will only do so in exceptional circumstances (*Nova (Jersey) Knit Ltd.* v. *Kammgarn Spinneri GmBH* H.L. 1977; *Walek & Co. K.G.* v. *Seafield Gentex* S.C. 1978).

Forgery

As a general rule no title can be obtained through the forgery of the drawer's signature or of an essential indorsement required to negotiate the instrument (s.24). There are exceptions.

The holder in due course of a bill of exchange on which the drawer's signature has been forged can demand payment from the acceptor as he is deemed to have guaranteed that the drawer's signature is genuine (s.54). The indorser likewise guarantees the validity of the drawer's signature and all previous indorsements to a subsequent holder in due course (s.55).

Paying bankers are also protected. Where a bill or cheque is payable to order on demand, the banker on whom it is drawn is not liable although the instrument contains a forged indorsement, provided he pays in good faith and in the ordinary course of business (s.60).

There are special rules relating to crossed cheques. A cheque may be crossed generally which means that the drawee should pay it to a banker. It may also contain a special crossing by naming a particular bank. A cheque specially crossed should be paid by the drawee to the banker to whom it is crossed (the collecting bank). If the drawee or paying bank pays a crossed cheque in good faith and without negligence in accordance with the crossing it will be protected in that the payment will be deemed to be a payment to the true owner. If such a cheque has come into the hands of the payee, the drawer is likewise discharged (s.80).

Under the Cheques Act 1959 a bank will not incur any liability on the grounds only of there being an irregular or no indorsement on a cheque where it acts in good faith and in the ordinary course of business (s.1). Where a collecting bank receives payment on a cheque for a customer it does not incur any liability to the true owner provided it acted in good faith and without negligence (s.4).

6 Legal Problems of Marketing

A businessman is required to act in a responsible manner towards the consumers of his products and his fellow businessmen.

The laws regulating business activity in the market place can conveniently be divided into three groups. These consist of:

1. Protective legislation: to check abuses and dangers by imposing penalties on those responsible for them;
2. Product liability: under which a businessman may be liable for the loss or damage caused by the defective products he manufactures or markets; and
3. Competition law: which creates the ground rules of free and fair competition in the market place.

1. Protective Legislation

A large part of the law which protects the consumer operates indirectly by imposing obligations on businessmen which are enforced by criminal sanction.

Protection against inaccurate quantities. One of the oldest forms of protection ensures that weighing and measuring instruments are accurate. This protection is provided for by the Weights and Measures Acts 1878–1961. Measuring devices are approved, checked, and stamped by inspectors or specially trained Garda sergeants acting under the weights and measures section of the Department of Trade, Commerce and Tourism. The use or possession of an unstamped measuring device is a criminal offence. A new Bill is being prepared to implement EEC directives affecting measuring devices and to bring the legislation up-to-date.

Food quality and hygiene. The Sale of Food and Drugs Acts 1875–1936 afford protection to the public against impure or adulterated foods, drinks, and drugs provided for human consumption or use. It is an offence to sell adulterated food which is unsound or to provide food or drugs which are not of the "nature, substance, and quality" of those demanded.

Regulations concerning food and drink have been made under Part V of the Health Act 1947 as amended. This statute allows the Minister for Health to make regulations, such as the Food Hygiene Regulations, to prevent danger to the health of the public arising from the manufacture, importation, storage and distribution of food, and to deal with food which is diseased, contaminated or otherwise unfit for consumption. Standards in relation to content and quality of food and drink have also been stipulated under the Food Standards Act 1974.

Standard of goods

Standards have been developed for certain goods, such as toys and electrical appliances, by the Institute for Industrial Research and Standards. The manufacture or sale of products can be prohibited by the Minister for Trade, Commerce and Tourism if they do not comply with standards in force.

In recent years many of the standards adopted for both food and other goods have been developed by the EEC which has its own consumer protection policies. EEC directives which have been adopted in Ireland deal with food additives and packaging, the poultry and fresh meat trade, motor vehicle components, lifts, pesticides and household cleaning products

Dangerous substances

The law has long been concerned with the manufacture, handling and sale of dangerous substances such as poisons, pharmaceutical products, explosives, chemicals and petroleum. Various statutes deal with these problems including the Pharmacy Acts 1875–1962, the Poisons Act 1961, and the Misuse of Drugs Act 1977.

The Dangerous Substances Act 1972 was enacted to consolidate and amend previous statutes relating to explosives, petroleum and other dangerous substances. Under this Act it is forbidden to store petrol (except up to three gallons in suitable leak-proof containers) other than in a storage tank licensed by Local or Harbour Authorities. An amending Act in 1979 provided for the appointment of an advisory council to assist the Minister for Labour in regard to the Act.

False and misleading descriptions and advertising

The most important statute was, until recently, the Merchandise Marks Act 1887. This Act, however, gave very limited protection to the consumer. A new statute was introduced in Britain called the

Trade Descriptions Act 1968, which was amended in 1972, and similar provisions were adopted in Ireland in the Consumer Information Act 1978.

These statutes put an obligation on persons who are conducting a business or profession to ensure that statements made about their goods or services are true. The 1978 Act achieves this by amending the Merchandise Marks Act 1887, and by imposing new regulations on businessmen.

The Consumer Information Act 1978

Under the Merchandise Marks Act 1887, as amended by the Consumer Information Act 1978, every person who, in the course of any trade, business, or profession applies any false or misleading trade description to goods, or causes another to apply such a trade description, is guilty of an offence. In addition, every person who sells, or who exposes for sale, or who has in his possession for sale, in the course of any business, trade, or profession, any goods to which a false or misleading trade description is applied is likewise guilty of an offence.

"Trade Description" is given a very wide definition. It includes any description, statement, or other indication, direct or indirect, concerning almost every aspect of the goods such as attributes, quality, origin, fitness, composition, history, and other features. Almost any statement or indication of fact relating to the goods may be a trade description, including statements concerning the contents of books, films and recordings.

A "false trade description" is a trade description which is false to a material degree, but it also includes a trade description which is misleading to a material degree.

Advertisements

The Consumer Information Act 1978 applies to false or misleading trade descriptions made in advertisements as these are deemed to be applied or made in the course of business, trade or profession (s.2), and where a reference in an advertisement is made to a class of goods the description is deemed to apply to all goods of that class (s.5).

It is also an offence to publish or to cause to be published any advertisement relating to goods, services or facilities which is likely to mislead and thereby cause loss, damage or injury to members of the public to a material degree. The Director of Consumer Affairs can, following notice to the party responsible, seek a High Court injunction against such an advertisement (s.8).

Services

It is an offence under the Act for a person knowingly or recklessly to make a false statement as to any services, accommodation or facilities provided, where the statement is made, and the services, accommodation and facilities are provided, in connection with a trade, business or profession. A statement made regardless of whether it is true or false will be deemed to be made recklessly unless the person making it had adequate reasons for believing that it was true. A statement in this connection will be false when it is false to a material degree (s.6).

Prices

It is an offence for a person to give a false or misleading indication of the present or previous price of goods, services, or accommodation or the recommended price of goods, or of any charge for installation or servicing of goods, or the price of ancillary equipment. "Sale Prices" and "Reductions" are controlled indirectly only in so far as any indication as to a previous price or charge, unless the contrary is expressed, will be treated as an indication that they were so offered openly at the same place within the preceding three months for not less than 28 successive days.

Any indication as to a recommended price will be treated, unless the contrary is expressed, as the price recommended by the manufacturer, producer, or other supplier for retail supply in the area where the goods are offered.

The director of consumer affairs

The 1978 Act established the office and functions of the Director of Consumer Affairs, a civil service post with a five-year renewable tenure. The Director is appointed, and may be removed, by the Minister for Trade, Commerce and Tourism, but is otherwise independent in the performance of his functions.

The Director is required under the Sale of Goods and Supply of Services Act 1980 to review, examine and influence practices or proposed practices in respect of the obligations imposed on persons by any provision of that Act (1980 Act, s.55). He is also given authority (in addition to the Minister) to bring summary proceedings for any offence under the 1980 Act within 18 months from the date of the offence (1980 Act, s.7).

Other provisions

The 1978 Act also empowers the Minister concerned to make "marking orders" which require that specified information should accompany goods, and if the order is not complied with, he may prohibit or regulate their supply. An "advertisement order" may similarly be issued requiring the provision of specified information in certain classes of advertisements, and in either case it is an offence to fail to comply with these orders. The Minister may issue a "definition order" which defines words or expressions used in relation to goods, services, accommodation or, facilities (s.10).

Enforcement

Summary proceedings may be brought by either the Minister, the Director of Consumer Affairs, or by a local authority within 12 months of the date of the offence (1978 Act, s.18; 1980 Act, s.57). Proceedings on indictment are brought by the Director of Public Prosecutions. The onus of proving that a trade description or other indication is true lies with the person who made or gave it (s.20). A person found guilty of an offence under the Act is liable on summary conviction to a fine of up to £500, or six months' imprisonment, or both. If a person is found guilty on indictment he is liable to a fine of up to £10,000, or up to two years' imprisonment, or both (s.17): part of a fine may be used to compensate a prosecution witness who suffered loss because of the offence.

Defences available to a charge under the Act include mistake or reliance on information supplied to the person charged, the act or default of another, accident or some cause beyond one's control, provided all reasonable precautions and due diligence were taken to avoid the offence and provided, where applicable, assistance is given to the prosecutor in identifying a party allegedly at fault. These defences also apply to a charge of applying a false trade description under section 2 of the Merchandise Marks Act 1887.

It is a defence to a charge of selling, exposing or having in one's possession for sale, goods to which a false trade description applies, that the person charged did not know, and could not with reasonable, diligence have ascertained that the goods did not conform to the description, or that the description had been applied to the goods (s.22).

Packaging

The Packaged Goods (Quantity Control) Act 1980 has introduced the "average" system of quantity control on packaging. The new system allows an averaging of contents within specified limits. The actual contents must not be less on average than the marked quantity. The rules are specified in the Packaged Goods (Quantity Control) Regulations 1981 (S.I. 1981 No. 39) and a guidance manual for packers and importers has been issued in conjunction with the regulations. Provision is also made for "e" marking of packages to indicate that they comply with EEC requirements.

Unsolicited goods and directory entries

Under Part VI of the Sale of Goods and Supply of Services Act 1980 protection is given to persons receiving unsolicited goods and to persons billed for entries in directories. A person who is sent unsolicited goods who has neither agreed to acquire nor return them, may treat them as an unconditional gift, provided either (i) six months has expired since receiving the goods and the seller has not attempted to take possession of them or (ii) not less than 30 days before the expiration of that period the recipient gave notice to the sender in writing stating his name and address and that the goods are unsolicited, and the sender did not, during the following 30 days take possession of the goods, and the recipient did not unreasonably refuse to permit the sender to take them. It is also an offence for a sender of unsolicited goods to demand payment, threaten legal proceedings or to subject the recipient to various debt collection procedures (s.47).

There is no right to charge for a directory entry relating to a person, his trade or business unless he has signed an order or note in the manner specified. It is an offence to demand payment for unsolicited entries (s.48). Other statutes have been enacted to control undesirable business practices. These include the Occasional Trading Act 1979, the Casual Trading Act 1980, the Trading Stamps Act 1980, and the Pyramid Selling Act 1980. The advertising of tobacco products has also come under statutory control, and the hall-marking of precious metals regulations have been updated.

2. Product Liability

The protective legislation we have examined is of considerable indirect importance to the consumer. It is only in rare instances that these statutes give any remedy to the consumer personally as they operate by imposing criminal sanctions on offenders. The Merchandise Marks Acts 1887 (s.17) and 1970 (s.3) as amended, do provide that trade marks, trade descriptions, and indications as to quantity are warranted to be genuine in any contract for sale of the goods. A buyer, therefore, might be able to sue for breach of these contractual terms. The Consumer Information Act 1978 allows the court to award part of a fine to a person who suffers loss through a breach of the Act in certain cases.

The principal remedies, however, which are available to a person in relation to defective products are (a) an action for breach of contract and (b) a tort action for negligence.

(a) *Contract remedies*

A person who suffers loss as a result of a defective product may be able to recover damages for breach of an express or implied term of his contract. This remedy, however, is only available to a person who is a party to the contract under the privity of contract doctrine. Where a wife buys food which makes her husband ill, the husband cannot sue for breach of contract because he is not in a contractual relationship with the seller (*Kirby* v. *Burke and Holloway* H.C. 1944). Similarly a buyer who purchases goods from a retailer cannot sue the manufacturer of the goods for breach of contract because there is no contract between them. In such cases the buyer may have a case in tort. The only way round the privity rule is where it may be argued that the purchaser bought the goods as agent for the person who suffered the loss (*e.g. Lynch* v. *Phelan* H.C. 1962), or that there was a collateral contract in that the goods had been recommended to the person who suffered the loss and they had been purchased by another on the strength of that recommendation (*Shanklin Pier Ltd.* v. *Detel Products Ltd.* E.K.B. 1951).

Implied terms. Where there is a contractual relationship a person may recover damages for breach of the express or implied terms of the contract. Implied terms are particularly valuable where the person to whom the goods are supplied deals as a consumer. A person is deemed to deal as a consumer in relation to another party if he neither makes the contract in the course of a business nor holds himself out as doing so, and the other party does contract in the course of a business, and the goods or services are of a type supplied for private use or consumption (Sale of Goods and Supply of Services Act 1980, s.3).

Implied terms as to title. In a sale of goods contract there is an implied condition on the part of the seller that he has a right to sell the goods, or that he will have such a right when the property is to pass. There is an implied warranty that the goods are free from any charge or encumbrance not disclosed to the buyer before the contract is made, and an implied warranty that the buyer will have quiet possession of the goods except as regards any charge or encumbrance disclosed (1893 Act, s.12 (1)).

If there is a breach of these implied terms the buyer can recover damages for any loss suffered. In *United Dominions Trust (Ireland) Ltd.* v. *Shannon Caravans Ltd.* (S.C. 1976), the plaintiff hire-purchase company recovered £3,330 as the price given for the purchase of a caravan to which the defendant had no title. Similarly a customer recovered damages for breach of the implied condition as to title where a retailer sold him furniture which had already been sold to another customer (*O'Reilly* v. *Fineman*, C.C. 1942).

The amendments made by the 1980 Act introduced a new subsection 12 (2) to the 1893 Act which recognises the concept of a sale of a limited title. Where it is intended that the seller should transfer only such title as he or a third person may have, there are implied warranties that all charges or encumbrances known to the seller have been disclosed.

Similar terms are implied into hire-purchase contracts under section 26 of the 1980 Act as between the owner of the goods and the hirer. The implied condition relating to title, however, is confined to a right to sell at the time the property is to pass only.

Sales by description or by description and sample. Where there is a contract for the sale of goods by description there is an implied condition that the goods shall correspond with the description. If the goods are sold by sample as well as by description the goods must correspond with both the sample and the description (1893 Act, s.13 (1)). Provisions clarifying a sale by description were added by the 1980 Act. A sale of goods will not be prevented from being a sale by description by reason only that, being exposed for sale, the goods are selected by the buyer (s.13 (2)). A sale in a supermarket or other self-service store will, therefore, usually be a sale by description. It is also provided that a reference to goods on a label or other descriptive matter accompanying goods exposed for sale may constitute or form part of a description (s.13 (3)). In this way false trade descriptions may give rise to an action for breach of contract as well as constituting an offence under the Merchandise Marks Act 1887 as amended by the Consumer Information Act 1978.

Similar and equivalent terms are implied into hire-purchase or letting contracts where the goods are let by description (1980 Act, ss.27, 38). These terms cannot be excluded in contracts where the buyer or hirer deals as a consumer and can only be excluded in other contracts to the extent that such an exclusion is "fair and reasonable" (1893 Act, s.55 (4); 1980 Act, ss.22, 31 (3), 38). Most sales are sales by description as buyers rely to some extent on labels attached to goods (see, *e.g.* *O'Connor* v. *Donnelly* H.C. 1944). The implied term, however, only guarantees conformity with description and may not protect the buyer if the goods are not of good quality (*Wicklow Corn Co. Ltd.* v. *Edward Fitzgerald Ltd.*, C.C. 1942).

Implied condition as to merchantable quality Under section 14 (2) of the Sale of Goods Act 1893 as amended, there is an implied condition, where a seller sells goods in the course of a business, that the goods supplied are of merchantable quality. There are two exceptions to this rule. There will be no implied condition as to merchantable quality regarding defects drawn to the buyer's attention before the contract was made, or where the buyer examined the goods before contracting, as regards defects which that examination ought to have revealed. Where casks of defective glue were examined on the outside only, the buyer could not rely on this section (*Thornett* v. *Beers* E.K.B. 1919). This condition only applies to sales in the course of business. In the 1980 Act, which amended section 14 of the 1893 Act, "business" is defined to include profession and the activities of any state authority or local authority (s.2 (1)). "Merchantable quality" is defined as "fit for the purpose or purposes for which goods of that kind are commonly bought and as durable as it is reasonable to expect having regard to any description applied to them, the price (if relevant) and all the other relevant circumstances . . . " (1893 Act, s.14 (3)).

Where the owner of goods lets them under a hire-purchase or letting agreement, there is a similar implied condition as to merchantable quality, with the same exceptions as to defects disclosed and inspection by the hirer (1980 Act, ss.28 (2), 38).

Where the goods supplied in the course of business are not of merchantable quality the seller or owner is liable and this includes strict liability for injuries arising from this breach of condition. In *Egan* v. *McSweeney* (H.C. 1956) the plaintiff recovered damages, for the loss of an eye, from the defendant who sold him coal which was not of merchantable quality as it exploded when ignited, resulting in injury. Goods will not be of merchantable quality if they are not fit for their ordinary purpose (*O'Connor* v. *Donnelly*, H.C. 1944).

Implied condition of fitness for purpose Where the seller sells goods in the course of business and the buyer expressly or by implication makes known to the seller any particular purpose for which the goods are being bought, there is an implied condition that the goods supplied are reasonably fit for that purpose, whether or not that is a purpose for which such goods are commonly supplied. There is no such implied condition of fitness for purpose where the circumstances show that the buyer does not rely, or that it is unreasonable for him to rely, on the seller's skill and judgment (1893 Act, s.14 (4)).

An implied condition or warranty as to quality or fitness for purpose may be annexed to a contract by usage (s.14 (5)). There may be an implied condition as to fitness for purpose in a sale by a private seller acting through a business agent, unless the buyer knows that the seller is not selling in the course of a business, or reasonable steps are taken to bring this to the buyer's notice before the contract is made (s. 14 (6)).

Similar provisions apply where the goods are supplied under a hire-purchase or letting agreement with the addition that the goods hired must be fit for any purpose made known by the hirer to either the owner or the person "by whom any antecedent negotiations" are conducted (1980 Act, ss.28, 38). It is sufficient therefore to make the purpose known to either the finance house or the dealer. Where goods have only one normal use there will be an implied condition in a purchase from a seller in the course of his business, that the goods are fit for that purpose. Cooked crab, *e.g.* must be fit for human consumption *Wallis* v. *Russell* Ir.C.A. 1902); a motor cycle must not cause injury (*Sproule* v. *Triumph Cycle Co.*, C.A.N.I. 1926); a bicycle must be fit for normal cycling (*White Sewing Machine Co.* v. *Fitzgerald*, Ir.Q.B. 1894). Subject to the specified exceptions the goods must be fit for any special purpose specified to the seller. Alcohol must be fit, *e.g.* for creamery use (*Stokes* v. *Lixnaw Co-op. Creamery Ltd.*, H.C. 1937); cattle for human consumption (*Draper* v. *Rubenstein*, C.C. 1925).

Implied conditions in sales by sample. A sale of goods contract is a contract for sale by sample where there is an express or implied term in the contract to that effect. In a sale by sample there are implied conditions that the bulk corresponds with the sample in quality, that the buyer shall have a reasonable opportunity of comparing the bulk with the sample, and that the goods must be free from any defect rendering them unmerchantable which would not be apparent on reasonable examination of the sample (1893 Act, s.15). Similar terms are implied in letting and hire-purchase agreements where goods are hired by reference to a sample (1980 Act, ss.29, 38).

Fair and reasonable. Implied terms and liability for misrepresentation can only be excluded in many cases where the exclusion is fair and reasonable. A test as to what constitutes a fair and reasonable term is given in the Schedule to the 1980 Act and is based on a similar Schedule to the British Unfair Contract Terms Act 1977. A term is to be judged fair and reasonable "having regard to the circumstances which were, or ought reasonably to have been, known to or in the contemplation of the parties when the contract was made." In particular the court must consider, if relevant, the relative bargaining power of the parties, any inducement to the customer to agree to the term, his knowledge of the existence or extent of the term, the reasonableness of an exclusion which arises from failure of the customer to fulfil some condition, and whether any of the goods involved were manufactured, processed or adopted to the special order of the customer (1980 Act, s.2, Schedule).

Guarantees. For the purpose of the 1980 Act, a guarantee is "any document, notice or other written statement, howsoever described, supplied by a manufacturer or other supplier, other than a retailer, in connection with the supply of any goods and indicating that the manufacturer or other supplier will service, repair or otherwise deal with the goods following purchase" (s.15). It is an offence under the Act for a manufacturer or supplier who provides a guarantee to fail to make it clearly legible or to fail to state clearly the guarantor's name and address, the duration of the guarantee, the claims procedure (which must not be more difficult than "ordinary or normal commercial procedure"), what precisely is offered, and the charges to be met by the buyer (s.16).

A guarantee cannot exclude or limit the buyer's statutory or common law rights. Any provision which imposes additional obligations on the buyer, or which gives the guarantor or his agent the sole authority to decide whether goods are defective or whether his claim is valid, is likewise void (s.18).

The seller who delivers a guarantee to the buyer is liable for the observance of its terms as if he were the guarantor unless he expressly indicates the contrary to the buyer at the time he delivers it (s.17 (1)). If the seller, who is a retailer, gives his own guarantee to service, repair or otherwise deal with the goods following purchase, it is presumed, unless the contrary is proved, that he has not made himself liable on any other guarantee (s.17 (2)).

A manufacturer (or importer where the goods are imported) or a supplier are liable for failure to observe the terms of the guarantee as if the terms constituted a warranty and they had sold the goods to the buyer. Their liability extends to anyone who acquires title from the buyer during the guarantee period. The court may enforce the observance of the guarantee or award damages to the buyer (s.19).

These provisions relating to guarantees also apply to hire-purchase and the leasing of goods. The person conducting the "antecedent negotiations," usually the dealer, takes the place of the seller (1980 Act, ss.33, 38).

Supply of services. The Sale of Goods and Supply of Services Act 1980 introduced statutory implied terms for the first time into contracts for services. In every contract for the supply of a service where the supplier is acting in the course of a business there are implied terms

(a) That the supplier has the necessary skill to render the service,
(b) That he will supply the service with due skill, care and diligence,
(c) That, where materials are used, they will be sound and reasonably fit for the purpose for which they are required, and
(d) That, where goods are supplied under the contract of service, they will be of merchantable quality (s.39).

Where the recipient of the service deals as a consumer these implied terms can only be excluded by a term which is "fair and reasonable" and which has been specifically brought to his attention. An exclusion of the implied terms may be made in non-consumer contracts of service and they may be excluded in consumer contracts for an interruption, variation or defect in the supply of electricity (except when due to negligence), and to contracts for the international carriage of passengers or goods by land, sea, or air.

The implied terms do not apply at all to contracts for the carriage of passengers or goods within the state until such date and subject to such terms as the Minister, after consulting the Minister for Transport, thinks proper, and provides for by order (s.40).

(b) *Product liability in tort*

In many instances a person who suffers loss or injury as a result of a defective product cannot rely on a contract. The party at fault may be a manufacturer with whom the buyer has no contract; the defective goods may have been purchased by a person other than the party who suffers the loss. In such cases, the plaintiff may be able to recover in a tort action for losses suffered through the actionable negligence of another.

At one time it was generally accepted that the manufacturer did not owe a duty of care to the consumers of his products. There were some exceptions. A supplier was under a duty to disclose known dangers, he had a duty not to allow an article to fall into the hands of a person unable to use it with safety and was required to exercise a high standard of care in relation to goods which were inherently dangerous such as loaded guns, petrol, acids and poisons.

Donoghue v. Stevenson. This view of the manufacturer's duties changed rapidly following the decision of the House of Lords in *Donoghue* v. *Stevenson* (1935). In this case a lady suffered shock and illness after consuming some ginger beer bought by her friend in a café. There was alleged to be a decomposed snail in the bottle. It was held that the manufacturer owed a duty of care to the ultimate consumer of his products sold in such a form that they are unlikely to be subjected to intermediate examination.

The principle was approved in Ireland in the case of *Kirby* v. *Burke and Holloway* (H.C. 1944). A housewife bought a pot of rhubarb and ginger jam from a grocer. She did not eat any of the jam herself but her husband (the plaintiff) and some of her children did, and suffered food poisoning as a result. The action against the grocer was dismissed as the plaintiff had no contractual relationship with him. The manufacturer of the jam was held to have failed in his duty of care to the plaintiff and was liable in damages.

Duty of care. To succeed in an action based on negligence the plaintiff must establish the existence of a duty of care, breach of that duty by the manufacturer or other defendant and loss or damage suffered by him as a result of the breach.

Although the primary duty of care is owed to the consumer by the manufacturer, there is precedent to show that liability may be extended to any person marketing the goods who can be shown to be at fault. These may include assemblers, sub-contractors, packagers, bottlers, wholesalers, distributors, repairers and even retailers. In *Power* v. *Bedford Motor Co. Ltd.* (S.C. 1958), the negligent repairers of a car, and another garage which negligently failed to notice the defective repairs, were held liable for a subsequent accident which resulted from the defective repair. If a party can show that he was not under a duty of care, or had not breached the duty of care imposed on him, he will not be liable (see *e.g. Martin* v. *Pelling Stanley & Co. Ltd.*, C.C. 1942).

The standard of care. The plaintiff must establish that his loss was caused by some fault on the part of the manufacturer or other person dealing with the product. The law does not impose absolute or strict liability on the defendant but only such care as a reasonable person would exercise in the circumstances.

The burden of proof lies with the plaintiff but he can shift this burden where the defect in the product is so blatant that its mere existence presupposes negligence. In such cases it is said that the thing speaks for itself (*res ipsa loquitur*).

Where the manufacturer or other party can show that they took such precautions as could reasonably be expected of them in the circumstances, they will not be liable. A bakery was held not liable for glass in bread (*Butler* v. *Johnston, Mooney and O'Brien Ltd.* C.C. 1945) and a bacon factory was held not liable for bits of steel in black pudding (*Fleming* v. *Denny and Sons*, S.C. 1955) when it was shown that every reasonable precaution had been taken to prevent such occurrences. The manufacturers of pre-cast concrete beams which were inadequate to support the load for which they were intended were liable because they had not sought adequate information and had designed the beams on a mistaken assumption (*Lynch* v. *Beale* H.C. 1974).

Directions and warnings. A manufacturer or other party may also be liable for breach of his duty of care if he fails to provide adequate warnings or directions. He may even be liable for a misuse of the products which is reasonably foreseeable, such as the likelihood of its being ingested by a child. In such cases he may have to take steps by warnings or otherwise to prevent injury. The absence of warnings may not amount to negligence where the loss was not caused by dangers inherent in the product (*Bolands Ltd.* v. *Trouw Ireland Ltd.* H.C. 1978).

An action in contract is often more attractive to a person who suffer loss from a defective product as there is no need to prove fault. An action in negligence, however, may be the only remedy available to a person who has no contractual relationship with the defendant.

3. Competition Policy

We have seen how the marketing and provision of goods and services is regulated, mainly in the interests of the consumer, by protective legislation against fraudulent and unfair business practices, and by the availability of remedies for loss caused by defective products. The interests of the consumer are also indirectly protected by the regulation of the manner in which businesses are allowed to compete with one another. The purpose of these controls is partly to prevent unfair practices which frustrate free competition and so injure others including consumers, and partly to regulate the market in accordance with government policy.

Price control

The present system of price control is exercised under the Prices Act 1958 as amended in 1965 and 1972. These Acts give extensive powers to the Minister for Trade, Commerce and Tourism to make orders regulating the price of goods and services where he is of the opinion that excessive prices are being or may be charged.

The legislation provides for appointment of advisory committees to inquire into and report to the Minister on the pricing and marketing of goods and services. An additional body, the National

Prices Commission, was established in 1971 to keep under review the prices charged for commodities and services, and to advise the Minister on their findings (S.I. No. 285 of 1971).

The control of prices is achieved mainly by the imposition of maximum prices orders which are enforced by officials and inspectors from the Prices Division of the Department of Trade, Commerce and Tourism. These orders must not be arbitrary or unfair or they will be held to be *ultra vires* and void (*Cassidy* v. *Min. for Industry and Commerce*, S.C. 1978). Dissatisfaction has been expressed at the low level of fines imposed for offences under the Acts but the adverse publicity involved has often the desired effect. Retail price display orders are also made by the Minister requiring retailers to display in a specified manner the price charged by them for certain commodities.

Trade regulation – restrictive practices

Despite considerable opposition from vested interests, the Restrictive Practices Act 1953 was enacted and later amended in 1959. A Fair Trade Commission was established under the Act to promote fair trading rules relating to the supply and distribution of goods, and to investigate and report on the supply and distribution of any kind of goods, on its own initiative, on the instruction of the Minister, or following a request from members of the public. The powers of the Commission were limited in that it could only deal with the provision of services which affected the supply or distribution of goods.

The Restrictive Practices Acts 1953 and 1959 were repealed and replaced by the Restrictive Practices Act 1972. The Fair Trade Commission was renamed and became known as the Restrictive Practices Commission, and the Act provided for the appointment of an "Examiner of Restrictive Practices." The powers of the Commission were extended to cover services as well as goods, and the Examiner was empowered to investigate, at the Minister's request, any aspect of the supply or distribution of goods and services (including situations where these are provided by persons outside the state) and to investigate any aspect of the operation of an order under the Act. Both the Commission and the Examiner must consider the unfair practices listed in the Third Schedule to the Act when conducting their functions. These relate to such things as interference with free and fair competition, restraint of trade, profiteering, restrictions of supply, unfair conditions, excluding new entrants to any trade, industry or business, or any practice contrary to the common good or the principles of social justice. Two recent reports by the Commission concerned the distribution of motor spirit and an inquiry into retail sale of grocery goods below cost (below cost selling).

Mergers, take-overs and monopolies

The Restrictive Practices Acts were not intended to deal with abuses arising out of the dominance of the market by one or a few firms. In situations where the market for particular goods and services is dominated by a few suppliers there is said to be high industrial concentration which can lead to restrictive practices, price-fixing, collusion and market sharing among the small number of firms involved.

This problem was tackled by the Mergers, Take-Overs and Monopolies (Control) Act, 1978. This Act gives the Minister for Trade, Commerce and Tourism the power to control certain take-overs, mergers and monopolies in the interests of the common good.

A merger or take-over is deemed to exist for the purposes of this statute when two or more enterprises, at least one of which carries on business in the state, come under common control as defined by the Act. Proposed mergers or take-overs are controlled in that the Minister must be notified where the gross assets or turnover of the enterprises involved are in excess of specified amounts (currently £1,250,000 and £2,500,000, respectively), or where the proposed mergers are of a particular class, *e.g.* in the newspaper industry. The merger or take-over cannot commence until the Minister has indicated that he is not going to restrict it, or until he allows it to go ahead conditionally or, where he fails to act, three months elapses from the time that either the notification was made or from the time such additional information requested by the Minister was provided.

On receipt of a notification the Minister may allow the merger or take-over to go ahead or refer it to the Examiner of Restrictive Practices, who must make an investigation and then report on whether or not in his opinion it would operate against the common good on the basis of criteria set out in the Schedule to the Act. The Minister, having considered the report, may prohibit the proposed merger or take-over, or allow it provided specified conditions are fulfilled.

A "monopoly" for the purposes of the Act means an enterprise, or two or more enterprises under common control, which supply or provide, or to which is supplied or provided, not less than one-half of goods or services of a particular kind supplied or provided in the state in a particular year except where 90 per cent. of its output or more is directly or indirectly exported. The Minister or the

Examiner of Restrictive Practices may request the Restrictive Practices Commission to examine and report on any apparent monopoly. The Minister, having considered the report, may if he thinks that it is required for the common good, either prohibit the continuance of the monopoly, except on specified conditions, or require the division of the monopoly, by a sale of assets or otherwise, in a period specified.

EEC competition laws

In addition to domestic laws regulating competition, Irish businesses are also subject to the competition rules of the EEC. These rules, which are based on Articles 85 and 86 of the Treaty of Rome, are designed to ensure that competition is not distorted within the Common Market.

Article 85 (1) prohibits as incompatible with the Common Market all agreements between undertakings, all decisions by associations of undertakings, and all concerted practices which may affect trade between member states and which have as their object or effect the prevention, restriction or distortion of competition within the Common Market. Any agreement or decision prohibited by this article is automatically void.

Article 86 provides that any abuse by one or more undertakings of a dominant position within the Common Market or in a substantial part of it shall be prohibited as incompatible with the Common Market in so far as it may effect trade between Member States.

Regulations and directives have been made by the Council of Ministers to give affect to these principles. Under Council Regulation No. 17 (1962), detailed provisions were made for the practical implementation of Articles 85 and 86. The regulation also confirmed that all agreements, decisions, and concerted practices prohibited under Article 85 (1), and the abuse of dominant position under Article 86, were by their nature prohibited without a need for a prior decision to that effect. The detailed implementation of this competition policy is governed by a number of regulations made by the European Commission and Council of Ministers, as modified by the decisions of the Commission and the Court of Justice.

Patents, designs and trade marks

Not all market restraints imposed by law are intended as negative curbs on business activity. The law relating to patents, designs and trade marks has a significant influence on the marketing of goods and products but is designed to protect a right which a business may have.

A patent confers on the patentee the sole and exclusive right to make, use and sell a patented invention in the state for 16 years.

Patents and patent applications are governed by the Patents Act 1964 and the Patents Rules 1965 to 1979. An invention for which a patent may be granted is "any new and useful art, process, machine, manufacture or composition of matter . . . and any new method or process of testing applicable to the improvement or control of manufacture." An invention cannot be validly patented unless it is new. A patentee who requires foreign protection for his patent must register it in the country concerned. This is facilitated by the International Convention for the Protection of Industrial Property which allows an inventor to apply for a patent in a convention country within 12 months of his initial application, and thereby obtain the same priority abroad as for his Irish application.

Designs used for goods can also be registered and protected for a period of five years and may be extended for an additional period of five years thereafter. Design refers to the shape, pattern, configuration and ornament which is applied to any article by any industrial process or means. It is the outward appearance of a thing rather than the thing itself which is protected. Design registration and design copyright are governed by the Industrial and Commercial Property (Protection) Acts 1927–1957, and other types of copyright by the Copyright Act 1963.

Trade marks are protected under the tort of passing off at common law. They may also be registered under the Trade Marks Act 1963. A trade mark is a mark which a trader uses or proposes to use upon or in relation to his goods for the purpose of distinguishing them from the goods of other traders, and it may be registered in respect of particular goods or classes of goods. For the purposes of registration, goods are divided into 34 classes. The register is also divided into two parts – Part A and Part B. Registration in Part A is more strict as regards the distinctiveness of the trade mark but confers greater protection. There are trade marks which will not be protected under the tort of passing off but where registration will provide protection (see, *e.g. Addidas Sportschuhf Abriken Adi Dassler K.A.* v. *Charles O'Neill and Co. Ltd.*, H.C. 1978).

7 The Employer—Employee Relationship

THE ROLE OF LAW

Relations between workers and employers are primarily based on voluntary negotiation and agreement. Workers have a right to withdraw their labour to force concessions from their employers. It is generally accepted that the law must not interfere with this right or the extent to which it is used. The law can only insist that the right is pursued in a lawful manner. The use of legal remedies as opposed to negotiation may merely lead to more widespread industrial action or bad industrial relations within a business. Within the sphere allowed it, however, the law attempts to regulate the relationship between the individual employee and his employer and also, to a lesser extent, disputes between trade unions and employers.

EMPLOYEES AND INDEPENDENT CONTRACTORS

Persons can be engaged to do work in two ways. A person doing work for another may be self-employed and his provision of work or "services" will be governed by the ordinary principles of contract. He provides services at a contract price and the person who engages him has no detailed control over the way in which he does his work. A person employed in this way is called an independent contractor. The relationship between an independent contractor and the person who employs him is governed by the ordinary rules of contract relating to the provision of services, and the law of tort.

Alternatively a person may be employed, not to do a specified task at a contract price, but to simply provide his labour or his skill in whatever way his employer dictates in return for wages. This is an on-going relationship in which the employee hires out his labour or skill in return for remuneration. The relationship of the parties is regulated by a contract of employment or "service." In modern terminology the parties are called employer and employee. In more dated terminology they were referred to as master and servant. We are only concerned with the employment or service relationship in this chapter.

In most cases it is easy to recognise a contract of employment. It is characterised by the exchange of labour or skill for wages or other remuneration. The work is to be done subject to the employer's detailed control, and other provisions of the contract are consistent with this type of relationship (*Ready Mixed Concrete Ltd.* v. *Ministry of Pensions* E.Q.B. 1968). There are some situations, however, where the nature of the relationship is not clear. In such cases the court looks at the reality of the relationship as in the case of a semi-independent sales agent with responsibility for training new sales agents in *Kirwan* v. *The Tupperware Co. and May & Derry Leahy* (E.A.T. (Irl.) 1980). The court considers the control exercised over the worker, whether the worker was in business on his own account or was an integral part of his employer's business, whether the employer required the exclusive services of the employee and could dismiss or suspend him.

THE CONTRACT OF EMPLOYMENT

The relationship between employer and employee is based in the eyes of the law on a contract of employment. In some ways this contract is like other contracts and is governed by the ordinary principles of contract law. In essence it involves an agreement by the employee to do work of a certain type and under certain conditions in return for wages or remuneration. The contract is unusual, however, in that it is modified by statute and is an on-going and dynamic agreement to maintain a relationship on terms currently in force but which may be regularly changed by express or implied agreement of the parties.

Formation of the Employment Contract

A contract of employment may be created by a written or oral agreement or may be implied from the conduct of the parties. As a rule there is no formality required. A contract of employment which is not to be performed within one year is not enforceable unless it is evidenced by writing under the Irish Statute of Frauds 1695 (*Naughton* v. *Limestone Land Co., Ltd.* H.C., 1952). Certain contracts may also be invalid in so far as they conflict with the Merchant Shipping Acts. AnCo, The Industrial Training Board, may make rules specifying the form of a contract of apprenticeship to be used in specified industries (Industrial Training Act 1967, s.27).

In other situations a contract may arise from the conduct of the parties as where a person merely starts work on the instructions of an employer on the assumption that he will be paid. In such circumstances the terms of the contract are left to be implied by law or from the conduct of the parties. Where a nephew worked for his uncle for two years, for example, there was held to be an implied contract under the Agricultural Wages Act 1936 (*Mackey* v. *Jones* C.C. 1957). Where an employee is engaged subject to the sanction of another, such as a government minister, the contract is void if the sanction is refused (*O'Connell* v. *Listowel U.D.C.*, C.C. 1957).

Terms of the Contract

The terms of the employment contract may be expressed or implied. The express terms are those which are agreed orally or in writing between the employee and the employer or his agent. Typically the parties may agree on such issues as pay, commissions, bonuses, hours of work, holiday entitlement, the employees principal duties, overtime, sick pay, and pension, if any. Employment may also be offered on the terms set out in a job description which is brought to the employee's attention.

Terms may be implied into an employment contract on the same basis as terms are implied into other contracts. They will be implied where a term is necessary to give "business efficacy" to the contract. There are other terms which are inherent to the nature of the employment relationship and are equivalent to duties which will apply in practically all employment contracts. There may also be terms implied by custom or by statute.

Implied Duties of the Employee

To be available for work
The employee has an implied duty to attend and be available to do the work he has contracted to do, during the agreed working hours.

To obey lawful orders
He has a duty to obey all lawful orders which are within the terms of his contract. An employer was held to be justified in dismissing an accountant who was on holiday leave for failing to return to work during an emergency in the employer's business (*Hartery* v. *Welltrade*

Ltd. H.C. 1978). An employer has no right to order his employee to do something illegal or which endangers his health or safety.

To exercise care and skill

The employee has a duty to exercise reasonable care and skill in the performance of his work. A lorry driver, in a case in England, was held liable for damages which the employer had to pay to a third party who was injured because of the employee's carelessness (*Lister* v. *Romford Ice and Cold Storage Co. Ltd.* H.L. 1956).

There is also an obligation on the employee to act in good faith towards his employer. This means that he must act honestly and in the interests of the employer when dealing with the employer's property or in exercising any trust placed in him. The employee will be liable for any secret profit obtained out of the exercise of his duties. He will also be liable for injury caused by divulging confidential information or by exploitation of the employer's trade secrets or customer contacts. Any inventions made or registered designs prepared in the course of his work become the property of the employer.

The Implied Duties of the Employer

To pay wages or remuneration

The employer has a duty to pay the employee in accordance with the contract terms. A failure by the employer to pay wages, or a failure to pay wages within a reasonable time, may be treated as a breach of the contract which entitles the employee to treat the agreement as at an end.

An employer is not entitled to suspend or lay-off an employee, or to put him on short-time working with reduced pay, unless such an action is permitted by an express or implied term of the contract.

Under the Truck Acts 1831–1896 as modified by the Payment of Wages Act 1979, manual workers must be paid in legal tender which consists of coins and bank notes. Payment may be made by cheque, credit transfer, or other such method where the worker agrees to it, or where the worker is absent from his usual place of employment unless he objects to such a method of payment. All employees are entitled to receive a wage slip which clearly indicates the amounts of any deductions made from the gross wage and the reason for them.

The deductions which can be made by the employer are regulated by statute such as the Truck Act 1896, and by the employee's contract. Certain statutory deductions may be made relating to court orders for the payment of maintenance or debts, and to pay income tax and social welfare contributions. Deductions may be made and paid to other third parties such as the Voluntary Health Insurance Board or a trade union, with the employee's consent.

To provide work in some cases

As a general rule there is no obligation on an employer to provide work for an employee so long as he pays him his wages. If the employee is employed on a commission basis or to do piece work there may be an express or implied obligation on the employer to provide him with a reasonable amount of work. There may also be an obligation to provide a skilled worker with a reasonable amount of work to maintain and develop his skills, and a deprivation or change in work to force an employee to resign could be a constructive dismissal.

To provide for his employee's safety

The employer has a duty to take reasonable care for the safety of his employees in the course of their employment. This duty may arise in tort (see Chapter 7) or it may be regarded as an implied term in the contract of employment. The employer will be liable if he fails to take reasonable care to provide safe tools, a safe place of work, a safe system of work, and competent employees who are not a danger to their fellow-workers. The employer is obliged under the Factories Act 1955 to provide proper accommodation for clothing not worn during working hours.

Terms from Collective Agreements and House Rules

The most frequent method of establishing the rights and obligations of employees is by collective bargaining. Terms of employment are fixed as a result of negotiations between union and employer representatives. These may be nation-wide agreements such as national wage agreements or "national understandings"; they may cover a particular industrial sector such as the construction industry; or they may be house agreements negotiated between the representatives of the workers in a particular factory or work place and management.

Where a contract expressly states that it incorporates the terms of a particular collective agreement the agreement in question becomes an express term of the contract of employment. In other cases the situation is not so simple as issues may arise as to whether the collective agreement is binding on the unions and employers concerned and as to whether it binds employees as individuals who may or may not be members of a union involved.

Incorporation of Agreements into the Employment Contract

Under the principals of contract (see p. 75) a collective agreement will be an enforceable contract where the parties intend to
create legal relations. Because a collective agreement is of a
business nature the party asserting that it was not intended to be
binding must prove this (*Goulding Chemicals Ltd.* v. *Bolger* S.C. 1977).
But even where it is established that an agreement is binding as
between unions and employers this does not of itself incorporate the
agreement into the employment contract of individual employees
except in the rare cases where a union is acting as an agent and can
bind its members as principals under agency law. In other situations
a union member or a non-union worker will only be bound by the
provisions of a collective agreement when they are expressly or
impliedly incorporated into his employment contract. The provisions of a collective agreement may be incorporated into an
individual contract of employment where there is an express or
implied term that matters not specifically mentioned in the contract
shall be governed by any relevant collective agreement. It may also
be held to be a custom in that type of employment that certain
matters be regulated by collective agreement. Alternatively, an
employee who accepts increases in wages or changes in the
conditions of his employment as a result of a collective agreement
may be deemed to have accepted the agreement by his conduct.

House-rules

The legal status of house or work rules depends on whether they
constitute contractual terms or the employer's orders. In either case
the employee is obliged to obey these rules. He has a general duty to
obey his employer's lawful and reasonable orders. If the rules are
contractual terms the employee has the advantage that the rules
cannot be altered without his consent. If the rules are merely
employer's orders they may be altered unilaterally by the employer
and must, as far as the law is concerned, be obeyed if reasonable and
lawful. This is subject of course to the practical objection that any
alteration in the employee's conditions of employment which are to
his detriment are likely to be resisted on policy grounds and may
lead to an industrial dispute.

Statutory Regulation of the Contract Terms

A number of statutes have been enacted which directly or
indirectly establish minimum terms which are to prevail in some or
all contracts of employment.

Registered agreements

Under Part III of the Industrial Relations Act 1946 the parties to any agreement on pay or conditions of employment can apply to the Labour Court to have their agreement registered. The Labour Court examines the scope of the agreement and the extent to which the parties are representative of the class of workers and employers to which it applies. The agreement is published so that any objections may be heard. If the Labour Court is satisfied as to the suitability of the agreement it is registered. A registered agreement sets minimum wages and conditions for the category of workers concerned and these become binding on workers and employers to whom the agreement relates regardless of whether a particular person was or was not a party to the agreement. The registered agreements can be varied or cancelled on application of the parties. There are over 50 such agreements on the register but only a few, such as the employment agreement for the construction industry, have been amended on a regular basis.

Minimum wages and conditions

The 1946 Act also provides for the fixing of minimum wages and conditions in the lower paid and poorly unionised industries. These are based on proposals made by Joint Labour Committees which are established by the Labour Court and are representative of employers and workers in a particular industrial sector. The proposals are published for comment and the Labour Court may, at its discretion issue an Employment Regulation Order incorporating the proposals and which set the legal minimum wages and conditions of employment for all workers in the sector to which it applies. A similar system operates in relation to agricultural workers under the Industrial Relations Act 1976. There are over 20 joint labour committees which regulate the minimum wages and conditions of over 30,000 workers. The regulation orders are enforced by inspectors from the Department of Labour. An order will be invalid if a Joint Labour Committee acts in an unfair or unreasonable way (*Burke* v. *The Minister for Labour* S.C. 1978).

Other statutory regulations

There are other statutes which establish minimum terms which apply to specified categories of workers. The Holidays (Employees) Act 1973 gives workers the right to annual leave equivalent to three working weeks with normal pay and to paid leave or its equivalent on specified public holidays. An employee is to be treated as employed and entitled to normal pay while doing jury service (Juries Act 1976). Female employees are entitled to a minimum period of maternity leave of not less than 14 consecutive weeks and may also be eligible for four weeks of additional maternity leave and time off work in certain circumstances (Maternity Protection of Employees Act, 1981).

Conditions of employment. The maximum hours which many employees may work at a stretch and the rest periods they are entitled to are governed by statute. The relevant rules for industrial workers are contained in the Conditions of Employment Acts 1936 and 1944; employees working in retail shops, wholesale stores, warehouses and other service jobs are governed by the shops (Conditions of Employment) Acts 1938 and 1942; there are special provisions relating to work in bakeries (Night Work (Bakeries) Acts 1936 and 1981), mines (Mines and Quarries Act 1965), road transport workers (EEC Transport Regulations 543/69, 1463/70), and young workers including apprentices under 18 years of age (Protection of Young Persons (Employment) Act 1977). Special conditions applying to some industrial workers are contained in employment regulation orders where these are in operation.

Provision is also made by statute to protect the health, welfare and safety of clerical workers (Office Premises Act, 1958), factory workers (Safety in Industry Acts 1955 and 1980) and workers in mines and quarries (Mines and Quarries Act, 1965).

Minimum notice and terms of employment. An employee cannot be lawfully dismissed, except for serious misconduct, without being given the notice he is entitled to under his contract, or where no notice is specified, by being given reasonable notice. The amount of notice an employee is entitled to may be as long as he can negotiate with his employer but it may not be less than the minimum specified in the Minimum Notice and Terms of Employment Act 1973. This statute applies to most employees who have been employed continuously for 13 weeks or more with the same employer and who normally work at least 21 hours a week. If the employee has been in the continuous service of an employer for a period of 13 weeks or more he is entitled at least to a minimum statutory notice of one week. The amount of statutory notice increases with the length of service: two to five years, two weeks; five to ten years, four weeks; ten to fifteen years, six weeks; and eight weeks notice where the employee has been in continuous service for 15 years or over. An employee who has been in an employment for 13 weeks or more is required by the statute to give at least one weeks notice of his intention to leave his employment. This does not apply where the employee has a right to leave without notice because of a serious breach of contract by his employer.

The Minimum Notice and Terms of Employment Act 1973 also entitles most employees to a written statement of the following terms of his employment contract: the date employment commenced, details of pay or the method of its calculation, when payment is made, hours of work and overtime, the terms relating to holidays, holiday pay, sickness, sick pay and pension, the periods of notice required, and in the case of a fixed length contract, the date the contract expires. The statement may specify the required particulars or refer the employee to an easily accessible document which contains the information.

The employer is required to provide this statement to new employees within one month of their taking up employment. He must provide similar information to any employee who requests it within one month of that request. New employees must also be informed by notice of any agreed procedure to be used for dismissals, and employees must likewise be informed of any alterations in this procedure (Unfair Dismissals Act, 1977).

Whereas these statements are strong evidence of the principal terms of an employment contract they may not necessarily be accurate and, of course, they do not contain all the contract terms.

ENDING THE CONTRACT OF EMPLOYMENT

A contract of employment may be terminated in much the same way as other contracts by agreement, variation, frustration and breach.

By Agreement with Notice

The employer and employee may agree to end the contract by mutual consent. At common law the contract can be terminated by either party giving the notice required by the terms of the contract, or by giving reasonable notice where none is specified in the contract. The employer could alternatively pay wages in lieu of notice. This right is now subject to the protection given to employees under the Unfair Dismissals Act 1977 (see below).

Termination by notice or payment in lieu of notice is not sufficient where the employee is an office holder. An office holder at common law is usually a person of relatively high social status who occupies a relatively permanent position created by statute, charter, articles of association of a company, or statutory regulation. The principles of natural justice are required to be observed in the dismissal of an office holder who is entitled to be notified of the grounds of his dismissal and to be given an opportunity of defending himself (*The*

State (*Gleeson*) v. *Minister for Defence* S.C. 1976). Whereas it used to be the law that an office holder who held office at the will and pleasure of the grantor could dismiss the holder without observing the requirements of natural justice, this is no longer true. It has been held that the constitution guarantees basic fairness of procedure and that the implementation of this guarantee means that an office holder may not be removed without first according him natural justice, otherwise a dismissal will be invalid (*Garvey* v. *Ireland* S.C. 1979). The removal of a Director was likewise held to be invalid where he was dismissed without being given prior notice of the charges made against him contrary to natural justice (*Glover* v. *B.L.N. Ltd.* S.C. 1973). Although it has not been decided in practice there is reason to believe that a dismissal of an employee may likewise be invalid if there is such a contravention of natural justice as to deprive him of his constitutionally guaranteed protection.

Termination by Variation

An employment contract can be varied by agreement of the parties and where the changes are substantial it may amount to the creation of a new contract. This is not significant, however, where continuity of employment is preserved, where the employee works for the same employer, or for statutory purposes where a takeover of the business does not affect an employee's continuous service and rights based on the length of his service.

Frustration

An employment contract may be terminated by some frustrating event which is outside the control of the parties which renders impossible the continuance of the contract as envisaged by them. A serious injury which prevents the employee from doing his job any more (*Flynn* v. *Great Northern Railway Co.* 1955) or the death of one of the parties, or in the case of a merchant seaman, the wreck or loss of his ship (*Kearney* v. *Saorstat & Continental Shipping Co. Ltd.* H.C. 1943), are examples of frustrating events.

Termination by Breach

As in other contracts the employment agreement may also be ended by breach where the employee resigns without sufficient reason and without notice, or where the employer summarily dismisses the employee without justification. In other contracts a breach does not of itself end the agreement and no discharge of the contract occurs until the innocent party rescinds by exercising his right to treat the contract as at an end. To some extent, however, the contract of employment has unique features. The courts have tended to regard mere breach of the agreement as ending the contract because it would lead to a difficult situation if the aggrieved party insisted on the contract being fulfilled in circumstances where continuance of a satisfactory relationship was no longer possible. For this reason the court rarely reinstates a wrongly dismissed employee but grants damages instead.

EMPLOYER'S REMEDIES

Discipline, damages, injunction

Where the employee is in breach of some minor term of his contract, the employer may be entitled to take disciplinary action against him in accordance with the express or implied terms of the contract, and subject to the Truck Acts. Disciplinary action includes warnings, fines, suspension with or without pay or demotion.

The employer is also entitled to damages if he has suffered loss as a result of the employee's breach of contract or negligence. Damages are rarely sought, however, as it is often not worth the effort and may have an adverse effect on industrial relations.

An injunction to force an employee to fulfil his contract is never given in practice either, as it is not appropriate as a remedy. This does not apply where the employee is involved in working for a rival business or using his employer's confidential business secrets contrary to his contract. In such situations an injunction to restrain the employee will be granted readily.

Dismissal

Where an employee acts in gross breach of contract the employer is entitled to dismiss him without notice. This is referred to as summary dismissal and is the equivalent of rescinding the contract as a remedy for its breach. The conduct which justifies a summary dismissal varies to a great extent and depends on the circumstances of the case. Gross neglect or dishonesty on the part of the employee are usually sufficient. Summary dismissal (or "instant dismissal") will usually be justified where the employee's conduct prevents further satisfactory continuance of the employer-employee relationship. A history of misconduct on the part of the employee, as opposed to an isolated incident makes summary dismissal more likely to be justified. An employer is not entitled to rely on misconduct not known to him at the time of dismissal to justify his action unless the conduct constitutes a fundamental breach of contract. A company could not therefore rely on an incident involving a contract for the purchase of a carpet, in which an acting Manager Director had an interest, to justify his summary dismissal (*Carvill* v. *Irish Industrial Bank Ltd.* S.C. 1966). Where an express procedure for a summary dismissal is set out in the contract it must be followed. In applying such a procedure in the case of an office holder, and probably in all cases there is an implied term that the procedure will be applied fairly in accordance with natural and constitutional justice. Thus where a director was guilty of serious misconduct and neglect, his summary dismissal in breach of natural justice was held to entitle him to damages (*Glover* v. *B.L.N. Ltd.* S.C. 1972). If a summary dismissal is not justified, the employee can sue his employer for wrongful dismissal.

Dismissal with notice. As previously mentioned the employer at common law is entitled to dismiss his employee by giving him the notice required or by paying him wages in lieu of notice. If a termination of contract by notice is effected in accordance with the contract and natural justice there is no wrongful dismissal. If, however, the employee is covered by the Unfair Dismissals Act 1977 it may be a dismissal contrary to the Act and the employee may have a statutory remedy for "Unfair Dismissal" (see below).

EMPLOYEE'S REMEDIES

As a matter of practice rather than law the employee who is subjected to minor breaches of contract by the employer will normally report them to his union representative for redress. In theory an employee is entitled to sue his employer for damages for breach of contract where the employment contract remains in existence. Thus he may recover damages for the employer's failure to pay him his contractual wages or for loss suffered from an unjustified demotion. An employee may also by a declaratory action obtain an injunction to restrain an act by an employer which would be in breach of contract provided an injunction would be an appropriate remedy.

Damages for Wrongful Dismissal

An employer will be liable to pay damages for wrongful dismissal where he dismisses an employee without notice or payment in lieu of notice or with insufficient notice in circumstances that do not justify summary dismissal. This remedy is of limited usefulness as the employee is only entitled to lost notice pay less any money earned or which could reasonably have been earned during that period. In some cases where the employee is entitled to a long period of notice or where the contract is for a fixed term with a number of years to run the damages can be substantial. An employee can also recover damages for a dismissal resulting from his refusal to abandon a constitutional right such as his right to join or not to join a trade union (*Meskell* v. *C.I.E.* S.C. 1973).

Constructive Dismissal

Where the employer acts in serious breach of an express or implied term of the contract the employee is entitled to repudiate the contract. This amounts to a constructive dismissal by the employer which entitles the employee to leave his job without notice and to sue for wrongful dismissal. The employee who adopts such a course should ensure that his action is justified otherwise it may be held to be a voluntary resignation and his employer will not be obliged to give him back his job. Harassment and reducing the employee's wages are usually sufficient. In an English case there was held to be constructive dismissal where a dissatisfied employee who was demoted and had his wages reduced gave notice and resigned voluntarily (*Marriott* v. *Oxford Co-op Soc. Ltd.* E.C.A. 1970). For this purpose it may be implied that employers must not behave in any way which is intolerable or in a way which employees cannot be expected to put up with any longer (*B.A.C.* v. *Austin* E.A.T. (Eng.) 1978). In *O'Brien* v. *Murphy Plastics (Dublin) Ltd.* (E.A.T. (Irl.) 1980) a unilateral attempt by the employer to introduce continuous shift working led to the walk-out of the entire work-force. There was held to be a constructive dismissal following the rule in the English Court of Appeal case of *Western Excavating (ECC) Ltd.* v. *Sharp* (1978). As the continuance of their employment depended on the change the dismissal was held not to be unfair.

Unfair Dismissal

An employee may also, as an alternative, be entitled to a remedy for unfair dismissal. Whereas wrongful dismissal is a dismissal which is contrary to the employee's contractual rights, an unfair dismissal is a dismissal which is unfair under the provisions of the Unfair Dismissals Act 1977 as interpreted by the courts and the Employment Appeals Tribunal. An unfair dismissal is a statutory dismissal for which the 1977 Act provides remedies. It often happens that a dismissal is both a wrongful dismissal at common law and an unfair dismissal. Where this happens the employee must pursue his remedies at common law or under the Act. He is not entitled to both remedies (1977 Act s.15).

At common law the employer has the right to terminate the employment relationship in accordance with the contract by giving the employee the notice required by law. Where the Unfair Dismissals Act 1977 applies this right has been curtailed. The statute has given those employees to which it relates greater security in their jobs which is not based merely on their contractual rights. Their employment may still be ended, but if it is terminated for any cause other than their failure in their job, their bad conduct, or the lack of work, the employee can claim a remedy for unfair dismissal. Even where the dismissal arises from a lack of work the employee has certain rights under the Redundancy Payments Acts.

Employees Covered by the 1977 Act

Generally speaking the Act applies to all employees with more than one year's service except for the following: employees who have reached retiring age or who are employed by close relatives, members of the defence forces and Garda Siochana (Police), certain AnCo trainees and apprentices, state employees except specified industrial grades, certain officers of local authorities, vocational education committees, health boards and committees of agriculture.

It does not apply, with some exceptions, to fixed term employment contracts, to employees undergoing training or probation for not more than one year, to employees undertaking training for the purposes of obtaining qualifications or registration as a nurse, pharmacist, and other specified careers, or to dismissals of statutory apprentices within six months of beginning apprenticeship or within one month after completion of the apprenticeship.

Dismissals Deemed to be Unfair

A dismissal will be deemed to be unfair (unless there were substantial grounds justifying the dismissal) if it results wholly or mainly from any of the following:

(1) The employee's trade union membership, or his union activities carried on outside working hours or during working hours at times permitted by his employer.

A dismissal of this type is presumed to be unfair so that the onus of proving otherwise is on the employer. The protection in relation to trade union membership and activities extends to employees without a year's continuous service, to those at or over retiring age, and to persons on probation, training, or apprenticeship. In these cases, however, the onus is on the employee to prove that his dismissal was unfair.

The dismissal is deemed unfair if it results from

(2) The religious or political opinions of the employee;

(3) The race or colour of the employee;

(4) The participation by the employee in civil or criminal proceedings against his employer;

(5) An unfair selection for redundancy, where there are no grounds for a redundancy, or where an employee is selected for redundancy contrary to a fair or an agreed procedure;

(6) The pregnancy or matters concerned with the pregnancy of an employee, or a dismissal of an employee who takes maternity leave or time off work as allowed under the Maternity Protection of Employees Act, 1981.

There is no presumption of unfair dismissal (save as under the 1981 Act) where an employee because of her pregnancy is unable to do her work adequately or where her continuance in employment is unlawful by statute or statutory instrument. The employer, however, must first offer her any other suitable vacancy on similar employment terms, but if none is available, or if she refuses such an offer, her dismissal will not be deemed to be unfair.

Dismissals Not Deemed to be "Unfair"

A dismissal of an employee to whom the Act relates shall be deemed not to be an unfair dismissal if it results wholly or mainly from one of the following:

(1) The capability, competence, or qualifications of the employee for performing work of the kind which he was employed by the employer to do;

(2) The conduct of the employee;

(3) The redundancy of the employee (in accordance with fair or agreed procedures);

(4) Where continuation of employment would have resulted in contravention of a statutory restriction; and

(5) The dismissal of a civilian from the defence forces for the purposes of safeguarding national security.

The dismissal of an employee by way of a lock-out is deemed not to be unfair where the employee is re-employed from the date of resumption of work. The dismissal of an employee for taking part in a strike or other industrial action will be deemed to be unfair where the dismissal was selective in that one or more of the participating employees were not dismissed, or one or more who were dismissed were re-employed but the employee in question was not.

An employer is required by the Act to give a dismissed employee who requests it, a written statement of the reasons for his dismissal within 14 days.

Adjudication Procedures

An employee can refer his case in writing to a *Rights Commissioner* within six months of his dismissal. A copy of his application must be sent to his ex-employer. The case is heard in private and a recommendation is made. If the action is settled no further claim on the same issue is allowed (*Timmins* v. *Munster Simms Hardware Ltd.* E.A.T. (Irl.) 1980). If the recommendation is not acceptable either party can appeal within six weeks to the Employment Appeals Tribunal. The employee can refer his case to the tribunal in the first instance if he so wishes.

An unfair dismissals case can be brought directly to the *Employment Appeals Tribunal* (Formerly the Redundancy Appeals Tribunal) at the option of the employee, where the employer objects to the case being heard by a Rights Commissioner or where he fails to comply with the Commissioner's recommendation, or where either party appeals within the six weeks allowed from the Commissioner's recommendation. After the hearing of the case the tribunal is empowered to make a "determination" in relation to the claim.

The claim can be brought to the *Circuit Court* where either party appeals within six weeks against the determination of the Employment Appeals Tribunal, or if the Minister for Labour decides to proceed against an employer for failing to comply with a tribunal determination. The court has authority to grant a remedy (see below) to the employee.

Where the employee has also a case for wrongful dismissal he may instead bring an action at common law provided he has not brought a claim under the Act.

Remedies for unfair dismissal

An employee who is held to have been unfairly dismissed is entitled to redress consisting of whichever of the following remedies the Rights Commissioner, the Employment Appeals Tribunal or the Circuit Court considers appropriate in all the circumstances of the case:

    (1) The *Reinstatement* by the employer of the employee on the same terms and in the same position as he held before his

dismissal, together with a term that the reinstatement shall be deemed to have commenced on the date of dismissal. There is therefore no break in the employee's service.

(2) The *Re-engagement* by the employer of the employee either in the position which he held before his dismissal, or in a reasonably suitable alternative position, on such terms and conditions as are reasonable having regard to all the circumstances.

(3) Money *compensation* or damages, up to a maximum of 104 weeks pay, to be paid by the employer to the employee in respect of such financial loss, attributable to the dismissal, which is just and equitable having regard to all the circumstances.

In practice an unfairly dismissed employee is usually compensated where the break-down of the employer-employee relationship would make an award of reinstatement or re-engagement unworkable or inappropriate. The amount of damages awarded are not often close to the maximum as deductions are made for money received by the employee in mitigation of his loss and for any fault on the part of the employee himself in bringing on his own dismissal.

Redundancy and employment equality

Other statutes which give rights to employees relate to redundancy and employment equality. Redundancy arises where an employee is dismissed because the employer's requirement for employees has ceased or diminished. To alleviate the hardship to employees the Redundancy Payments Acts 1967 to 1979 provide for lump sum payments to be made to redundant workers based on their years of service. Most employees between 16 and the old age pension qualifying age, who have at least two years service, and who normally work 20 hours per week are entitled to redundancy payments. The amount payable depends on the employee's age, service, and wage. The employee may, if possible, negotiate a higher entitlement to severance pay but, where applicable, the employee must get the statutory minimum.

Under the Protection of Employment Act 1977 an employer must notify unions and the Minister for Labour of impending collective redundancies so that if possible they may be reduced or avoided.

Anti-discrimination measures

Two statutes have been enacted to combat discrimination in employment. These are the Anti-Discrimination Pay Act, 1974 which promotes equality between men and women as regards pay, and the Employment Equality Act 1977 which makes unlawful certain kinds of discrimination on the grounds of sex or marital status, and which established the Employment Equality Agency to promote equality of opportunity between men and women.

Under the 1974 Act a woman has a right to the same rate of pay as a man who is employed on like work by the same employer or by an associated employer, in a work place or work places located in the same city, town or locality. Men have likewise a right to the same rate of pay as women on like work.

Equal pay disputes may be referred to an Equality Officer (formerly called an Equal Pay Officer) attached to the Labour Court, by either the parties or the Employment Equality Agency. An appeal may be made to the Labour Court and a further appeal on a point of law may be made to the High Court.

Under the Employment Equality Act 1977 it is unlawful to discriminate on the grounds of sex or marriage in relation to access to employment, training, promotion, working conditions, or in other ways. Allegations of discrimination may be referred to the Labour Court which can attempt a settlement with the help of an Industrial Relations Officer or an Equality Officer. There is then an appeal to the Labour Court and a further appeal on a point of law to the high court.

THE LAW AND COLLECTIVE BARGAINING

Although collective bargaining is primarily based on free negotiation uncontrolled by law, the boundaries within which that negotiation takes place are to a great extent regulated by law.

At common law trade unions are unlawful, as constituting a conspiracy to commit the offence of interfering with the right of every person to freely dispose of his capital or labour. Any agreements to regulate conditions of employment were illegal as contrary to public policy as they were in restraint of trade. In these circumstances legal recognition of trade unions had to be given by statute. The Trade Union Act of 1871 made trade unions and trade union agreements lawful and provided for registration of unions. A limited right to picket was given to striking workers by the Conspiracy and Protection of Property Act 1875. This protection was swept away, however, by judicial decisions (*Quinn* v. *Leathem* H.L. 1901; *Taff Vale Railway Case* H.L. 1901) which made workers liable in tort for damage caused to employers by their actions and which made trade unions liable for the torts of their agents. As a result certain legal immunities were given to trade unions by the Trade Disputes Act 1906 which facilitate them in pursuing their task of improving the lot of the workers they represent.

Trade Union Structure

The Irish Constitution Guarantees the right of every citizen to form associations and unions subject to the right of the Oireachtas to regulate and control this right in the public interest. The Oireachtas cannot however deprive citizens of their constitutional right to join the association or union of their choice. Thus an attempt by means of Part III of the Trade Union Act of 1941 to give a tribunal the right to determine that a particular union would have the exclusive right to organise employees of a particular category was held to be unconstitutional (*National Union of Railwaymen* v. *Sullivan* S.C. 1947).

The rationalisation of the trade union movement could therefore be promoted by indirect methods only. Other provisions of the Trade Union Act 1941 restricted the right to negotiate wages and conditions of employment to "authorised unions" and "excepted bodies," as defined by the Act. Sections 2, 3 and 4 of the Trade Disputes Act 1906 which confer certain immunities on unions and their members and officials are restricted by the Trade Union Act 1941 to authorised trade unions which hold a negotiation licence.

The Trade Union Act 1971 made it more difficult for workers to form a new trade union and, with a view to reducing the number of unions, the Trade Union Act 1975 simplified the process of amalgamating unions.

The rationalisation of the trade union movement from within was also made more difficult by the constitution. A citizen has not only the right to join an association of his choice but has the right to refuse to join a union if he so wishes. Picketing to coerce workers to join associations has been held to be unlawful (*Educational Company of Ireland Ltd.* v. *Fitzpatrick* S.C. 1962). The dismissal of an employee for refusing to join a trade union is also unlawful (*Meskell* v. *C.I.E.*, S.C. 1972), although an employee may bind himself by a term of his employment agreement to join a particular union, and such a term is binding and not unconstitutional (*Becton Dickinson and Co. Ltd.* v. *Lee* S.C. 1972). The creation of a closed shop by agreement does not seem to be unconstitutional. A worker has a right to join the union of his choice but an employer is not obliged to negotiate with that union although he cannot deny the right of the worker to insist on being represented by such a union as regards his personal grievances (*Aboot and Whelan* w. *I.T.G.W.U.*, H.C. 1980).

A number of institutional arrangements have been made to help resolve industrial relations disputes. We have already mentioned the Industrial Relations Act 1946 in regard to joint labour committees and registered employment agreements. The Act also provided for Joint Industrial Councils representative of a particular class of workers or employers which can negotiate on wages or conditions of employment without the need for a negotiation licence. The Labour Court was also established by the 1946 Act and its size and functions were extended by later Acts. Its principal functions are to investigate and make recommendations in relation to trade disputes and to provide a conciliation service to assist parties to resolve a dispute when direct negotiations have failed.

The Industrial Relations Act 1969 enlarged the Labour Court and authorised the appointment of rights commissioners who can investigate certain types of disputes referred to them affecting individuals, such as dismissals or suspensions. The Industrial Relations Act 1976 replaced the Agricultural Wages Board by a new joint labour committee for agricultural workers.

Immunity for Industrial Action

The Trade Disputes Act 1906 grants certain immunities under sections 1 to 3 for certain acts done by persons in contemplation or furtherance of a trade dispute. Under section 1 an Act which is not unlawful if done by an individual will not be unlawful if done by two or more persons by agreement or in combination. Section 2 authorises picketing "for the purpose of peacefully obtaining or communicating information, or of peacefully persuading any person to work or abstain from working." Section 3 gives immunity to persons acting in contemplation or furtherance of a trade dispute from legal actions for inducing a breach of a contract of employment or for interference with another's trade, business, or employment, or with his right to dispose of his capital or labour. Section 4 prohibits any legal action arising out of the acts of a trade union.

The immunities in sections 1 to 3 only arise where there is a trade dispute which must involve a dispute between employers and workmen or workmen and workmen (s.5). Since "workmen" are defined as persons employed in trade or industry the courts have held that disputes involving persons not engaged in trade or industry are not protected. Civil servants, nurses, teachers and such persons are not protected.

It has also been held that section 3 which gives immunity for tort actions arising from loss due to inducing a breach of employment contracts does not apply to loss resulting from breaches of commercial contracts. An injunction was therefore granted prohibiting an embargo imposed on a motor car importer because it interfered with commercial contracts existing with dealers and its parent company (*Talbot (Ireland) Ltd.* v. *I.C.T.U.*, S.C. 1981). Since any all-out picket is likely to cause loss by interfering with commercial contracts the strikers would be liable for such loss. In effect the basic immunity granted by the 1906 Act has been seriously undermined. Legislation has, however, been promised to give legal protection to all-out strike pickets and to extend legal immunity to workers in the non-trade or industry sectors.

8 Employer's Liability

Legal Liability

Business people like other classes of citizens are liable at law for the civil and criminal wrongs which they commit.

Although there is considerable over-lap between civil and criminal wrongs they are treated separately and independently. Even the terminology used is different. The person bringing a civil action is called a plaintiff, and the person from whom he claims a legal remedy is called the defendant. The plaintiff is said to "sue" the defendant, and the process is referred to as "litigation" or a "civil action." Although one citizen can initiate a criminal action against another citizen, criminal cases are almost invariably brought on behalf of the state by the Garda or the Director of Public Prosecutions. The party bringing the criminal action is called a prosecutor, and the person against whom he brings the case is referred to as the accused, where the crime is serious, or the defendant, where the offence is a minor one.

Civil and criminal actions are brought in separate courts and the purpose of the action is different in each case. A crime is a wrong against the state or the people in their collective capacity. The essential purpose of the criminal law is to maintain public order and to compel obedience to the state's mandates. In a criminal action the accused is found innocent or guilty, and if he is found guilty he is usually punished by fine or imprisonment.

The purpose of a civil action is to decide the liability or non-liability of the defendant for some private wrong alleged to have been committed against the plaintiff. The purpose of the action is not to punish the wrongdoer but to compensate the injured party by some appropriate remedy, usually by an award of money compensation by way of damages.

Criminal Liability

Business operations by their nature facilitate the commission of particular criminal acts such as fraud, embezzlement, false accounting and larceny.

As a rule a person is not guilty of committing a serious crime where he has done a prohibited act only, as where an employee takes company property. There must be a criminal intent as well as a criminal act. An employee who takes company property believing it to be his own does not commit a crime as he took the company's property without intending to deprive the company of it. These two elements, the prohibited act and the guilty intent, are referred to as the *actus reus* and the *mens rea*. As a rule an act does not make a person guilty unless the mind is guilty (*actua non facit reum nisi mens sit rea*).

This principle does not apply, however, to many of the minor offences created by statute such as those designed to protect the consumer (see Chapter 6). These may be strict liability offences where the mere fact that they were committed is sufficient to establish liability. In some instances specified defences only are permitted as in the Consumer Information Act 1978.

Civil Liability

A person may be held civilly liable for loss caused to another because that person committed a tort or a breach of contract or trust. In this chapter we are mainly concerned with liability in tort. The most important tort is one based on negligence. We have already examined one type of negligence action relating to liability for defective products (Chapter 6). There are other torts, including other types of negligence action, which give rise to legal liability, some of which are particularly relevant to the conduct of a business.

The Nature of a Tort

Whereas liability for breach of contract or trust depends to a great extent on the creation of a contract or trust, liability in tort arises from the infringement of rights recognised by the law. Different torts protect an individual's right to the integrity of his person, his property interests, his right to his good name and certain economic interests. If another infringes these rights he commits a tort and may be held liable to compensate the injured party for the damage caused.

Trespass

An individual's person and property are protected by the actions involving trespass to the person and trespass to property. A trespass to the person may be either an assault, battery or false imprisonment. An assault is the tort of putting another, either directly or negligently, in an immediate fear of violence. An apparently real threat to harm another is an assault. To negligently or intentionally apply force to another is a battery, and any total restraint on a person's freedom, even for a brief period, is false imprisonment if there is no justification for such an action.

There may also be a trespass to land or to a person's goods. Trespass to land will occur where a person enters, or dumps rubbish or other matter on the land or premises of another without authority. The owner has the right to use reasonable force to eject a trespasser who refuses to voluntarily leave his property. Trespass to goods usually involves some wrongful interference with, dealing in (conversion), or withholding of (detinue) another's goods.

As a rule trespass actions do not arise too frequently out of the conduct of business but there are exceptions. Actions for assault and battery or false imprisonment may arise from picket line scuffles, attempts to remove sit-in workers, or unjustified action taken against alleged shoplifters or pilfering employees. Tort actions in detinue and conversion have been used, as we have seen, by hire-purchase companies to recover goods from third parties who have wrongly acquired them from hirers. A landlord who trespasses on premises let to a tenant in flagrant breach of the tenant's rights may be liable for aggravated damages (*Whelan* v. *Madigan* H.C. 1978). A farmer was held liable for brucellosis infection caused by his cattle trespassing on his neighbour's land (*Neenan* v. *Kelleher* H.C. 1979).

Nuisance

A nuisance is an unlawful annoyance caused to others. A private nuisance is an unreasonable interference with another's enjoyment of his land or premises. An injunction or damages may be awarded against a business responsible for a nuisance. Damages were awarded, *e.g.* because of dust, noise, vibrations and blasting caused by quarrying and lime processing (*Malone* v. *Clogrennane Lime Co.* H.C. 1978), (*Patterson* v. *Murphy* H.C. 1978), and for damage to dwellings caused by vibrations from mining activities (*Halpin* v. *Tara Mines Ltd.* H.C. 1976). Interference caused by other factors such as noise, fumes, smells and smoke may also constitute a private nuisance.

A public nuisance is some unlawful act or failure to perform a legal duty which causes a public obstruction or which endangers the lives, health, safety or comfort of the public or a section of the public. It is primarily a crime, but where a public nuisance causes particular damage to a person he may sue in tort. The commonest form of tort action for public nuisance arises from creating obstructions or dangers on or close to a public road. The owners of a factory were liable for public nuisance where their lorries damaged the road at the entrance to their premises and this contributed to the death of a motor cyclist who skidded on the ice covered pot-holes which they left unrepaired (*Wade* v. *Connolly and South of Ireland Asphalt Co.* S.C. 1977).

Liability for fire and other dangerous things

The common law rule is that a person is strictly liable for damage caused to another's property by fire which he ignites or which accidentally occurs on his land or premises. This rule was modified by an Irish Statute of 1715 (2 Geo.I c.5) which exempted a person from liability where the fire originated accidentally in a house, chamber, or out-house. But the statute did not apply to a fire which began accidentally in a factory (*Richardson* v. *Athlone Woollen Mills* S.C. 1942) and the law was changed to take this into account. Under the Accidental Fires Act 1943 a person is not liable for any fire which accidentally occurs in or on his buildings or land. A person who kindles a fire which negligently spreads or who negligently allows an accidental fire to spread remains liable for the damage caused. He will be also liable when an accidental fire occurs because of his negligence as when he carelessly stores inflammable materials.

The law imposes strict liability on persons who collect or store non-natural things on their property which are likely to do harm if they leave the property. A defendant is liable for the loss they cause regardless of whether it happened through his fault or not. This is known as the rule in *Rylands* v. *Fletcher*, from a case in which a defendant who authorised the construction of a reservoir on his own land was held strictly liable for damage caused to neighbouring mines by the water which escaped through a disused mine shaft. The rule has been applied to the escape of many kinds of non-natural things such as water, gas, vibrations, sewage, explosives and even poisonous yew trees projecting over the boundary of the defendant's property.

Defamation

The law of torts also protects a person's good name and reputation by allowing him to take an action for defamation. Two types of action are recognised by the law. These are libel, which

involves defamatory matter in some permanent form such as writing
or print, and slander, which consists of an attack on a person's
character in a transient form, such as the spoken word.

   To succeed in an action for defamation the plaintiff must show
that the matter complained of would lower his reputation in the eyes
of right-thinking people. Anyone who publishes the defamatory
matter, *i.e.* who repeats it, is as liable as the originator. A
businessman or his employee who wrongly accuses a customer of
stealing or shoplifting may be liable for slander (*Coleman* v. *Keanes
Ltd.*, H.C. 1946). If he physically detains the customer without
justification he may be liable in addition for trespass to the person.

Negligence

   The most important and widely used tort is that of negligence.
There are different categories of negligence action and those which
are particularly relevant to business are treated separately. There
are some general principles common to all negligence cases which
must first be considered.

   A defendant is liable in negligence when he causes loss to the
plaintiff by a breach of a legal duty of care owed to the plaintiff. The
situations in which a person owes a legal duty of care to others are
numerous. There is no definitive list and it is possible for the courts
to "discover" new duties. The existence of a duty of care is therefore
a question of law. Some duty situations are well known. Persons who
use a public road owe a duty of care to other road users. If they
cause loss to others by a breach of that duty of care, such as by
dangerous driving, they will be liable in negligence. Doctors,
dentists, solicitors, bankers, and professional advisers owe a duty of
care to their clients. The manufacturers and distributors of goods
may be liable for defective products. Duties are imposed also by the
law on employers in relation to their workmen, and on the occupiers
of premises in relation to persons who enter their premises.

The essentials of negligence

   In order to succeed in a negligence action the defendant must owe
a duty of care to the plaintiff, he must have breached that duty of
care, and the plaintiff's loss must have resulted from the breach.

   Problems arise not only in relation to whether the defendant owed
a duty of care but in relation to whom he owes the duty. An estate
agent or valuer may give wrong advice to a client and will be liable if
the client suffers loss as a result. The client might also have passed
the bad advice on to his brother, and the question arises as to
whether the estate agent owed a duty of care to his client's brother so
as to be also liable for his loss. The law tries to resolve this problem

by applying what is called the "neighbour principle." The defendant has a duty not to injure his "neighbour," *i.e.* anyone so closely and directly affected by his act or omission that he should reasonably have had them in mind.

The plaintiff must establish not only that a duty was owed to him by the defendant but that the duty was not fulfilled. This raises the problem of the extent of the defendant's duty. The law does not impose impossible standards or demand perfection. The defendant must act with the care that an ordinary reasonable man would exercise in the circumstances. If the defendant was acting in a professional or skilled capacity then he must exercise the knowledge, skill, and care which could be reasonably expected from the ordinary doctor, surgeon, accountant, electrician as the case may be. A duty to take reasonable care to avoid a particular risk may vary with the gravity of the risk; the extent to which it is foreseeable, and the ease or difficulty of guarding against the risk involved.

The plaintiff must also prove that his loss resulted from the defendant's breach of a legal duty. The burden of proof rests with the plaintiff except where the *res ipsa loquitur* (the thing speaks for itself) rule applies. Under this rule the facts of a particular case may be such as to raise a presumption of negligence where there is no other apparent cause of the incident.

Where part of the damage suffered by the plaintiff arises from his own contributory negligence the damages recoverable are reduced under the Civil Liability Act 1961 by the amount which the court thinks is just and equitable having regard to the degrees of fault of the plaintiff and defendant. In addition the damage suffered by the plaintiff may be too remote a consequence of the defendant's breach of duty, or the real cause of his loss may be some intervening act of a third party or of the plaintiff himself. A defendant is not liable for damage caused by his breach of duty, which he could not reasonably have foreseen (*The Wagon Mound* P.C. 1961).

Occupiers' Liability

Persons who are in control of premises whether they are occupiers or not, may be liable for damage caused by their dangerous state, to persons who enter their premises. This is known as "occupiers' liability" and is in effect a form of negligence in relation to premises. In this context a premises includes not only land, private dwellings, shops, offices and factories but also structures such as platforms, pylons and scaffolding, as well as motor cars, ships, and planes.

As in other types of negligence the plaintiff must prove that the defendant as occupier owed him a duty of care, that he breached that duty and that the plaintiff suffered damage as a result. The defendant may also owe a duty of care to the plaintiff under a contract which exists between them and which entitles the plaintiff to be on the premises. The occupier's duties may be extended or restricted by the express terms of the contract. Where there is no express term there is an implied term that the occupier has taken reasonable care to make the premises safe for the purposes covered by the contract (*Coleman* v. *Kelly* S.C. 1951). An occupier will not therefore be liable to paying customers at a cinema, theatre or sports event where he has taken reasonable care to provide for the safety of his customers. At a sports event, such as horse racing, it will also be assumed that the spectators accepted the risk involved and the occupier may not be liable. This is referred to as the doctrine of *volenti non fit iniuria* (*Callaghan* v. *Killarney Race Co. Ltd.* S.C. 1958).

Occupier's tortious liability

The law of torts imposes a duty on occupiers to exercise care towards persons who enter their premises regardless of any contractual relationship between them. Occupiers' liability is concerned with the occupier's duties and liability for damage caused by the static state or condition of the premises. His liability for activities or operations being conducted on the premises is governed by the ordinary principles of negligence. In relation to business activities, therefore, the occupier owes all visitors, of whatever class, a duty to take reasonable care in the circumstances for their safety.

As regards the static condition of the premises, the occupier's duty varies with his relationship to the visitor. For this purpose the law recognises three types of visitor:

(1) The *invitee* who enters the premises for some purpose or business in which the occupier has some interest or concern;
(2) The *licencee* who is permitted on to the premises for his own purposes or benefit; and
(3) The *trespasser* who enters the premises without permission and who has no right to be there.

The occupier's duty of care depends on the category to which the visitor belongs. As regards the state or condition of the premises the occupier generally owes a duty to the invitee to take reasonable care to prevent damage from unusual dangers of which he knows or ought to know. He owes a duty to the licencee to warn him of concealed dangers of which he knows. He has a duty not to leave the premises in such a state as to intentionally or recklessly injure a trespasser. The defendant must be an occupier in the sense of having some control over the premises or otherwise he will not be liable for its condition. Thus nuns were held not to be liable as occupiers of a field lent to them for the purposes of a carnival which was run by a special committee (*Keegan* v. *Owens* S.C. 1951).

Liability to invitees. An invitee is a person who enters a premises with the express or implied invitation of the occupier so as to confer a material benefit on him. Invitees include customers in a shop, workmen at their place of work, delivery men, parents attending a school play and paying patrons at a dance or similar function.

The occupier owes a duty of care to the invitee to prevent injury to him from any unusual danger of which he knows or ought to know (*Indermaur* v. *Dames* 1866). This duty of the occupier only applies while the invitee is on that part of the premises where it may reasonably be said he is entitled to be (*Reaney* v. *Thomas Lydon & Sons Ltd.* H.C. 1956).

Whether a particular danger is unusual or not depends on the nature of the danger and the circumstances of the case. The nature of the premises, the training and skill of the invitee, any disability suffered by the invitee are relevant in establishing whether the danger is an unusual one for which the occupier may be liable. A defective flagpole which fell and struck the plaintiff was held to be an unusual danger (*Boylan* v. *Dublin Corporation* S.C. 1948). So also was torn lineoleum on a dance floor (*Kelly* v. *Woolworth* Ir.C.A. 1921) and a darkened staircase without a handrail which led to a toilet in a public house (*O'Donoghue* v. *Greene* S.C. 1967). A heap of rubbish in a timber yard over which the plaintiff consciously drove his cart was held not to be an unusual danger (*Cooney* v. *Dockrell & Sons Ltd.* S.C. 1963).

An occupier will not be liable to an invitee for damage suffered from an unusual danger where he takes reasonable care to prevent such damage. In some cases a warning of the danger will be sufficient, but this is so only when such a warning enables the invitee to carry out his tasks without danger.

Liability to licencees. A licencee is a person who enters premises with the express or implied consent of the occupier but he confers no material benefit on him. Licencees include social guests, visitors to parks, playgrounds and churches open to the public, school-children at school and children using waste ground as a playground without objection (*Boughton* v. *Bray U.D.C.* S.C. 1964).

The occupier owes a lower duty of care to the licencee than he does to the invitee. The licencee must generally take the premises as he finds them. The occupier will only be liable if he fails to warn of or prevent damage from concealed dangers which are known to him.

What may be an obvious danger to an adult, such as an open fire (Boughton case) or a defective railing on steps (*Macken* v. *Devine* 1946), may be a concealed danger to a child.

Liability to trespassers. A trespasser is a person who enters another's premises without the express or implied consent of the occupier. It may also include a person who goes into a part of a premises to which his invitation does not extend, or a person who stays on premises after his invitation is spent. A plaintiff who was conducted out of a hotel in the early morning and who was injured when he went to the back of the premises was held to be a trespasser when the accident happened and had no case against the proprietor (*O'Keeffe* v. *Irish Motor Inns. Ltd.* S.C. 1978).

An occupier has a duty not to leave his premises in a state or condition which is intended to injure a trespasser, or is so reckless that it is likely to injure any trespasser whose presence is known or ought to be known to him. The occupier is entitled to use deterrent dangers, such as a barbed wire fence or a guard dog, to keep out trespassers but he is not entitled to set "traps" to injure them in a vengeful or retributive way while they are on the premises.

Trespassers who are known to come regularly on to premises and are not prevented from doing so may be treated as licencees especially if they are children. Similarly a premises or something on a premises may constitute an allurement to children in that it is so attractive to them that it compels them to play with it, and at the same time is a concealed danger. In such cases the child is treated as a licencee to whom the occupier owes a greater duty of care. The more recent approach is to impose a duty on an occupier to take reasonable care in the circumstances to prevent reasonably foreseeable injury to trespassers, particularly infant trespassers. The E.S.B. as occupier's of an electricity transformer station were held liable for negligence in not adequately preventing access by children (*McNamara* v. *Electricity Supply Board* S.C. 1974) but were not liable where they had taken reasonable steps to prevent access and injury (*Keane* v. *Electricity Supply Board* S.C. 1980).

Employer's Duty to his Employees

An employer has a duty in law to take reasonable care for the safety of his employees when they are acting in the course of their employment. Where he breaches this duty of care he will be liable in negligence for the damage which his employee suffers as a result.

An employer will also be liable to his employee as an invitee, but workmen who suffer injuries in the course of their employment normally prefer to sue as employees because of the higher duty of care owed to them in that capacity. An injured workman may also be entitled to injury benefit or disablement benefit following an accident arising out of and in the course of employment. These entitlements arise under the Occupational Injuries Code which replaced the Workman's Compensation Acts, and which is presently regulated by Chapter 5 of the Social Welfare (Consolidation) Act 1981. A workman who is in receipt of benefit may still sue his employer for negligence but the benefits received will be taken into account in assessing damages.

Plant and equipment

An employer's duty of care involves the provision and maintenance of safe equipment and plant. The employer may be liable where an employee is injured when using a dangerous machine. An employer was negligent, *e.g.* where a machine operator's hand was severely injured when caught between the rollers of a chopping machine (*Burns* v. *Irish Fibres Ltd.* S.C. 1967), where the unfenced gears of a cement-mixer near a greasing point crushed the hand of a builder's labourer (*Crowe* v. *Brennan* S.C. 1967), and where an employee was provided with steel masonry nails which tended to disintegrate when struck by a hammer (*Deegan* v. *Langan* S.C. 1966).

The duty of care to provide safe plant and equipment is a duty which is owed to each individual employee. A greater duty of care must therefore be exercised in protecting an employee who is disabled, incompetent or inattentive. An employee may recover for injury caused by the strain of defective equipment (*Burke* v. *John Paul & Co. Ltd.* S.C. 1967).

Safety in the work place

An employer will also be liable in negligence for injuries to employees which are caused by hazards and dangers in the work place or in the access to it. In *Kielthy* v. *Ascon Ltd.* (S.C. 1970) an employer was held liable for the death of a workman who had fallen from the top of a wall used as an access route to a site office.

Safe system of work

There is an obligation on an employer to provide a safe and suitable system of work for his employees. A workman can recover damages provided he proves that the system was unsafe, that something could be done to make it safe, and proves that the employer's failure to do so was the cause of the accident (*Caulfield* v. *Bell & Co. Ltd.* H.C. 1958). An employer who failed to supply a screen on a grinding machine or to provide goggles was held liable for the loss of sight in the plaintiff's eye caused by a particle of steel (*Quinn* v. *Avery Ltd*. S.C. 1967).

Competent employees

There is a duty on an employer to employ competent employees and independent contractors. The employer will be liable for damage caused to an employee arising out of the incompetence, lack of skill, or misbehaviour of a fellow-worker, unless he has exercised reasonable care in hiring the worker or independent contractor in question.

Breach of statutory duty

A workman or other person who is injured as the result of an employer's breach of a duty imposed by statute may recover damages in tort. To succeed in an action for breach of statutory duty, the plaintiff must show that the statute gives him a right to sue, that the statute was broken by the defendant, and that the breach caused his injury. An employer may be liable, *e.g.* for breach of statutory duty where the plaintiff's injury resulted from his failure to fence dangerous machinery under the Factories Act 1955, or under the Mines and Quarries Act 1965 (*e.g. Gallagher* v. *Mogul of Ireland* S.C. 1975).

Vicarious liability

In certain situations an employer may be liable for the torts of his agents and employees on the grounds of vicarious liability. A principal is jointly and severally liable with his agent for torts committed by the agent acting within the scope of his authority. An employer is similarly liable for the torts of his employees committed in the course of their employment.

Where the agent or employee have acted negligently or have committed some other tort, they will themselves be liable. If the agent was acting within the scope of his authority, or if the employee was acting in the course of his employment, the principal or employer is also vicariously liable to the injured party who will usually prefer to sue the principal or employer who is more likely to have the means to satisfy the claim. In *E.S.B.* v. *Hastings & Co. Ltd.* (H.C. 1965) the employers of the driver of a mechanical shovel were held liable for damage to the plaintiff's cable caused by the opening of a trench.

If the employee was not acting in the course of his employment when he committed the tort his employer will not be liable (*Doyle* v. *Fleming's Coal Mines Ltd*. S.C. 1953). An employer was held not liable for damage caused by his taxi which had been stolen from outside his employee's house because the employee had taken the taxi home without permission. The employee's negligence did not occur within the scope of his employment and his employer was not liable (*Quilligan* v. *Long* C.C. 1952). An employee is acting in the course of his employment whenever he is doing authorised work for his employer. This includes carrying out authorised duties in an unauthorised manner.

An employer is not usually liable for the torts of his independent contractor. He may be liable however where injury was caused to the plaintiff because he hired an incompetent contractor without due care, or where he authorises the contractor to commit a tort, or where he adopts or ratifies his tort.

Insurance

The usual way in which a business provides for its liabilities and unexpected losses is by taking out insurance by means of which loss is absorbed easily by many rather than falling heavily on the few. The co-ordinating role of spreading the burden of risk is taken on by profit seeking insurance companies. These companies are partly regulated by the Insurance Acts 1909–1978 which require them, among other things, to hold a licence, to maintain deposits with the High Court and to make annual returns. These requirements are designed to ensure that the insurance companies remain solvent to meet claims.

The insurance contract

Insurance is provided under a contract or policy of insurance in which the insurer (the insurance company), in return for payments called premiums, agrees to pay a sum of money or its equivalent to the assured on the happening of a specified event or contingency.

The insurance contract is formed in the same way as other contracts by agreement, consideration and intention to create legal relations. The person seeking insurance usually fills out a proposal form by which he offers to take insurance and this offer is accepted by the insurer when he signifies acceptance, or issues a policy, or when he retains the premium. A new contract is made every time the insurance is renewed.

Insurable interest

An insurance contract is similar to a betting agreement in that the payment of money depends on the occurrence of an uncertain event such as a fire or death. To prevent gambling by means of insurance any insurance contract is illegal and void unless the assured has an insurable interest.

A person will have an insurable interest in the subject-matter of the insurance or the *life insured* if his relationship to it is such that he will suffer loss if the event insured against occurs. It is permissible to take out life assurance on one's own life or the life of another, but in the latter case it is essential to have an insurable interest in the life of the other person. A wife has an insurable interest in her husband and a creditor has an insurable interest in the life of his debtor. The assured may insure his life for the benefit of someone without an insurable interest by becoming a trustee of the policy for him or by assigning it to him.

As regards *property insurances* the insured need only have an interest in merchandise covered by marine insurance at the time of the loss. An insured must have an interest in property covered by a fire policy both when the insurance is taken out and at the time of the loss. The insured's interest may be that of a mortgagee such as a bank, a tenant or joint tenant, or any interest which gives him a relationship to the insured property so that he benefits by its safety and is prejudiced by its loss or damage.

Insurances of liability protect the insured person from legal liabilities which might arise from the conduct of his business including his liability for defective premises, products, or bad professional advice. These policies are variously described as public liability, employers' liability or product liability insurances.

These insurances indemnify the insured in respect of his legal liability to pay damages arising from his negligence, nuisance or even contract. The insured must be subject to some liability which will cause him loss if it arises in order to have an insurable interest.

Insurance Principles

Indemnity

All contracts of insurance except insurances of the person are contracts of indemnity. In the event of loss the insured cannot recover more than the amount lost. He is not allowed to profit from his policy as this would be against public policy as a temptation to actively cause the loss against which the person is insured.

Life and personal accident insurances are exceptions to this rule. These types of policy are not based on indemnity but are ordinary contracts. A life assurance policy is a contract to pay a certain sum of money on the insured's death or on his reaching a specified age in return for the payment of a fixed annuity or premium based on his life expectancy. A personal accident policy involves the payment of a specified sum to the insured if and when an accident occurs.

Subrogation

The insurer is said to have a right of subrogation after paying out on a policy of indemnity. If the insured has any right to recover all or part of his loss from a third party, his right must be exercised for the benefit of the insurer who has paid his claim. This ensures that the policy holder obtains no more than a full indemnity.

The insurer has the right of subrogation even if the right is not specifically mentioned in the policy. The policy may also allow the insurer to exercise his right of subrogation before he makes any payment so that the insurance company often makes claims or defends actions on the insured's behalf.

Contribution

The principle of contribution arises where the same interest is covered against the same risk by more than one insurer. It applies to indemnity insurances only and it prevents the insured from recovering more than his full loss.

Where there is more than one insurer the policy holder can claim the whole of his loss from one insurer only if allowed by the policy, or he may claim against all. If he claims against one insurer only that insurer can claim contribution from fellow insurers if he had to pay out more than his share.

The insurance policy may contain a contribution condition which obliges the insured to proceed against all the joint insurers for a pro rata payment of his claim.

Contract Uberrima Fidei

Insurance contracts are referred to as contracts *uberrima fidei* (of the utmost good faith) and contain special rules relating to disclosure and misrepresentation which do not apply to ordinary contracts. Special duties are put upon the insured to disclose all relevant facts because he knows all about the risk whereas the insurer must provide him with cover with nothing to depend on but the proposer's answers.

The proposer may be in breach of his duty to act with the utmost good faith where he fails to disclose or conceals a relevant fact or where he prevails upon the insurer to provide him with insurance by means of a misrepresentation.

The non-disclosure of a material fact makes the contract voidable unless it would be unreasonable to expect the proposer to recognise that the fact was material. The contract is void where the proposer conceals a material fact concerning the risk to be insured.

If an insurance proposal is accepted on the basis of an innocent or fraudulent misrepresentation the contract is voidable. An employer's liability insurance policy was held to be void, *e.g.* where the insured misstated the annual amount of wages paid which was the basis on which the premiums were calculated (*McMillan* v. *Carey* H.C. 1978). Similar principles concerning disclosure apply to the renewal of insurance policies.

Index

222

Index